The Financial Crisis

Ted Azarmi • Wolfgang Amann
Editors

The Financial Crisis

Implications for Research and Teaching

Springer

Editors
Ted Azarmi
Heilbronn University and the University of Tuebingen
Heilbronn and Tuebingen, Germany

Wolfgang Amann
SBUM/EMBA
HEC Paris School of Management in Qatar
Doha, Qatar

ISBN 978-3-319-20587-8 ISBN 978-3-319-20588-5 (eBook)
DOI 10.1007/978-3-319-20588-5

Library of Congress Control Number: 2016942537

Printed on acid-free paper

This Springer imprint is published by Springer Nature
The registered company is Springer International Publishing AG Switzerland

Preface

This book is partially based on the proceedings of a finance conference titled "Teaching Finance in Turbulent Times," which Mathias Moersch and I organized at Heilbronn University in Germany in September 2013. Included here are a number of academic papers accepted for publication based on the subject matter of that conference.

Wolfgang Amann and I believed writing several additional chapters in this book would help students learn about financial crisis. These chapters allowed us to retrace the goals of the conference in written form.

Our first goal is to prepare students to deal with financial crisis in their future careers. At the conference, we arranged presentations from a high ranking financial regulator, the dean of a pioneering German MBA school, and the director of one of the best German financial executive education programs.

Our second goal is to highlight financial perspectives outside the standard neoclassical framework of commonplace ideas, such as sustainable finance and behavioral finance.

Our third goal is to present a holistic approach to financial education, which includes new research frontiers from both senior and assistant professors. In the conference, we asked presenters to discuss how they would use their research in their teaching in order to ensure their discussions were focused on the pedagogical implications of that research.

Our fourth objective is to focus on international perspectives in finance, not the perspective of international finance in academics, because international finance is an established field of study that focuses on market structure, trading, and arbitrage in foreign exchange markets, parity conditions, hedging transaction, translation and operating risk, cross-border valuations, international corporate governance, swaps, and a few related topics. By a focus in perspectives in international finance, we mean finance as practiced and taught in Germany, Japan, Russia, Ukraine, Israel, the Arab World, EU, etc., in contrast to the standard, US-based body of financial knowledge and practice.

Finally, we are interested in introducing finance as a field of study to business students about to choose a major. In particular, Chap. 2 of this book focuses on the major achievements and tools of this field, its failures, and shortcomings. In this way, we hope to motivate students considering finance as a field of study to actually pursue it.

One of the challenges to achieving our goals during the Heilbronn finance conference was to facilitate the active participation of undergraduate and graduate students, in addition to the usual participation of Professors and PhD students. To do this, we encouraged students to participate in the conference in every finance class and particularly in the introductory financial management course. In order to translate the high level of awareness about the Heilbronn conference into actual student attendance and participation, we relied on a conference blog site where students work and essays related to the conference could be posted. To read the blog, visit: http://www.azarmi.org/forum/index.php/board,355.0.html.

One factor attracting student attention was that the blog was made public allowing for a wide readership, including one student blog on finance that received 4181 views.

After working for hours and answering several questions by students, one prominent senior finance professor volunteered to spend time with undergraduates to chat informally about finance. Some 12 students took him up on the offer, and their impromptu meeting was still in progress over an hour after the day's conference ended. In effect, we captured an audience passionate about finance as a field of study, all at a time when the field suffered a figurative black eye from the many recent financial scandals and the crisis. Indeed, it was a turbulent time for finance!

Our business program at Heilbronn strongly emphasizes eastern European studies, intercultural studies, and the Arab world. This includes advanced language and business culture courses in Arabic, Russian, Spanish, and French. Students may choose to take all their required business courses either in English or in German for the entire period of their bachelor studies. Within a single semester, they have the opportunity to participate in two sessions of the same introductory finance course, one in German and the other in American English. Our average finance student is fluent in three languages. So in addition to course work in English and German, a typical finance graduate is required to take several language and culture courses in Arabic, Spanish, or French.

The finance program has begun to standardize and assimilate content from our English finance courses with their sister courses taught in German. Despite this effort, we realize that German finance differs in certain significant aspects from US finance, requiring a chapter or two of additional course discussion elucidating those differences. For example, the accounting information provided by German HGB and the European accounting differs from US GAAP. There are also fundamental differences in how German firms are financed in practice.

We also experienced setbacks in achieving some of the Heilbronn finance conference's goals. In particular, we only partially covered the implications of the financial crisis. However, we are optimistic that with sufficient effort and persistence, our goals can be achieved. We hope that building upon our modest success, this book—let's call it volume I—will enable us to convince our stakeholders to participate in the production of a second volume that will elaborate the various issues that this volume cannot encompass.

Heilbronn, Germany Ted Azarmi

Contents

About the Editors

Prof. Ted Azarmi, PhD, trains doctoral students in finance at the University of Tuebingen. He is also a finance professor at Heilbronn University. He has 25 years of experience as a business professor in USA, Japan, and Germany. Ted Azarmi has several teaching excellence awards from USA for which he received newspaper coverage in Los Angeles area.

Prof. Dr. Wolfgang Amann has been designing and delivering executive education seminars for more than 17 years. He now serves as academic director and professor of strategy and leadership at HEC Paris in Qatar. Next to his doctorate in international strategic management from the University of St. Gallen, he also graduated from the major faculty development programs worldwide, such as Harvard University's MLE, IMD's ITP, IESE's IFP, and EFMD IDP. He published 15 books for executives and compiled more than 100 case studies for his executive education seminars. He won several global and pan-European prizes for his research as well as teaching efforts and was awarded several honorary professorships.

Introduction: Finance and the Financial Crisis

Ted Azarmi

Consider that you are about to undertake a *long-term project*, such as building a house, providing piano lessons as an ongoing business, growing apples, or manufacturing a new medicine. Within the academic field of finance, the goal of this project is to maximize the value of what you produce. The best way to put a measurable value on your project's output is to wait until it is produced and see how much it sells in the marketplace. That is, *the future market value* of your output measured in monetary terms can be used to arrive at an accurate indication of your project's current value.

As an owner, you need to pay suppliers of raw materials, to manage and control the production process, and help to market and advertise your output. Your business activity may affect others who may make claims against you. For example, the society at large is affected when your production causes environmental harm; the government demands taxes from you for infrastructure, law and order, and the general market environment it provides, and your customers may make future warranty and product safety claims against you. That is, there are various *stakeholders* who you must convince to cooperate with you and there are numerous claims to your assets now and in the future. In effect, you need to secure the cooperation of a number of individuals to pull up their sleeves and work toward the production of your project's future output.

To make the analysis a bit more general, consider your position as owner as another stakeholder's claim to the production undertaken by a firm. Numerous stakeholders, including equity holders, debtholders, managers, employees, suppliers, the government, customers, and society at large, are affected by a firm's

T. Azarmi (✉)
Heilbronn University and University of Tuebingen, Max-Planck-Str. 39, Heilbronn 74081, Germany

Tuebingen University, Tuebingen, Germany
e-mail: ted.azarmi@hs-heilbronn.de

T. Azarmi, W. Amann (eds.), *The Financial Crisis*,
DOI 10.1007/978-3-319-20588-5_1

production and may have claims on the firm's assets and demand compensation from it.

The central question of finance is how to provide such compensation. The above discussion lays a foundational context, providing greater insight into the field of finance than the following familiar definition: finance is about the financial decisions a firm makes for how to raise money to pay for long-term assets and about investment decisions related to the production activities it undertakes.

This elementary definition fails to highlight several crucial points needed to understand finance. The first point relates to the words "long-term project" and "future output." By long term we mean more than a year. Financial information, communicated through accounting methods and statements, measures a firm's long-term financial performance and reports it annually to the tax authority, the owners, and the other stakeholders. By convention, quarterly and interim reports of less than 1 year are considered short term. Thus, as you already know or suspect, accounting is central to finance. A strong focus on real-world accounting data is one of the factors that sets finance professionals apart from economists.

The long-term nature of a firm's projects implies risk and uncertainty regarding output. For example, farmers may work rigorously now and still have a poor harvest in the future due to a drought or a natural calamity beyond their control. Overproduction of apples by competing farmers may cause a drastic reduction in the market price of apples and leave little value at harvest time. So it is more precise to calculate the current value of a project by considering the "expected future market value of output." That is, we need to use measures of variability, central tendency, simulation, and other academic methods of probability and statistics to arrive at the current value for our future uncertain output. So it is safe to say that probability and statistics are at the core of finance.

However, using probability and statistical tools to arrive at independent production risk, based on assessed fluctuations in past data, is inadequate for accurate financial analysis. In finance, we are concerned with *the future market values*. That future value is best measured by considering how sensitive the fluctuation of our project value is to the fluctuation of market value of all assets as a whole. This market sensitivity is termed "beta" and is introduced within "portfolio theory," in particular the "CAPM or the Capital Asset Pricing model." Three finance professors set the foundation for this theory: Harry Markowitz with his PhD dissertation at the University of Chicago, William Sharp at Stanford University, and John Linter from Harvard University. They won the 1990 Nobel Memorial Prize for their contribution to finance. Of course, within finance there are also elaborations and criticisms of their model as well as competing models.

The second point necessary to understanding finance is that valuation tools are central to this field of study. In effect, a financial professional works like an engineer. So in practice, finance calculators or spreadsheet software and finance tools are required to assess the value of assets, businesses, projects, and firms. These tools use data derived from a firm's current and Pro Forma (or projected future) financial statements in order to estimate its expected future cash flows. These cash flows are then discounted at an appropriate risk-adjusted cost of capital to arrive at the present value of a project. Discounting reduces future cash flows so as to arrive at a current value that accounts for paying the cost of capital, another costly input required for production.

The appropriate cost of capital is called WACC (or weighted average cost of capital) and is estimated most accurately when current bond and common and preferred stock prices of a firm are used as input variables. That is, a firm's underlying riskiness may be best estimated when market prices of its primary securities are used as inputs in calculation of its WACC. This calculation, together with real-world accounting data for future cash flow estimation (using spreadsheet analysis, which allows for simulation), is termed financial modeling. For a reference for a working understanding of these methods, see the text "Investment Valuation: Tools and Techniques for Determining the Value of Any Asset, Wiley, 2012," by Aswath Damodaran.

The third point we need to examine in finance is the source of financing. In a general economic sense, financing comes from individuals' savings. Those individuals who have a surplus of capital may enter the financial markets and provide financing to firms and individuals who need funds. Therefore, a central, practical question in finance is how to funnel the savings of those with surplus funds to those who need capital for their projects.

One source of financing is the owner's equity. The owner's assets, or the funds a business generates as a going concern, may be used to finance the firm's investments. Alternatively, external funds may be used.

One external source of financing is the institutions engaged in financial intermediation. The most common example is a bank that pools depositors' surplus funds and makes them available as capital through bank loans. Of course, there are exotic sources of financing too. For example, a business owner may partially finance a project through prepayments and deposits by customers or capital provided by the suppliers and other stakeholders, such as the government.

A complete understanding of finance requires consideration of other financing vehicles, such as real estate, insurance, pensions, personal finance, private equity, venture capital, fund management, etc. For the moment, let us omit those alternatives and focus on a general definition of corporate finance as follows: the academic field of finance studies the practice of finance, which involves issuing financial instruments as sharing rules that bring stakeholders to a nexus of contracts in order to produce an uncertain output that maximizes owner's wealth.

Let us now move to the implications of a financial crisis, considering the above discussions as a context for the field of finance. Financial crisis can be best understood by considering its consequences and its symptoms. A number of these consequences will be discussed later in this book.

One consequence of financial crisis is that businesses shrink in size. They cut costs, divest, and sell off assets and divisions. Divestitures are a major sign of turbulent economic times and have adverse consequences for corporate stakeholders.

A classic example of a divestiture with severe financial consequences for stakeholders is when Siemens sold its mobile devices division, forming a subsidiary called BenQ-Siemens. In the Siemens' mobile device trade sale, the German workers of that division of Siemens became the employees of a Taiwanese corporation and therefore lost their employment safeguards provided under the German corporate governance system. Siemens promised 700 Million Euros to get the Taiwanese firm to take that subsidiary off its hands in June 2005. Following this negative sale-price deal, in September 2006, BenQ discontinued funding its German mobile phone subsidiary. Subsequently, 3000 German BenQ-Mobile (former Siemens) workers lost their jobs.

David Marutschke and I discuss this and other related cases in a research paper titled "Two-Stage Spin-off Asset Impairment Theory"[1] in which we argue that separation of control and asset claims leads to asset impairment ex post of a contractual obligation. Particularly during times of financial crisis, a firm may expropriate assets of a class of its stakeholders through spin-offs.

The paper continues by developing a corporate governance tool that advocates maximizing shareholder wealth, while considering another stakeholder's claim when management is in the position to impair the stakeholders' assets without being observed.

Chapter 2 of this book contains a research contribution by Professors Dmitri Boreiko and Maurizio Murgia from the Free University of Bolzano-Bozen School of Economics and Management who study the financial and corporate governance aspects of restructuring transactions and spin-offs. They document that spin-off decisions in Europe are often triggered through a crisis. These include the appointment of a new CEO or the threat of a takeover. They show that in Europe, break-up decisions are often due to the monitoring activity of outside investors and capital markets at a time of financial crisis. Boreiko and Murgia find abnormal returns associated with spin-off announcements, which may be strongly tied to reversing earlier value-decreasing mergers.

A second consequence of financial crisis is that banks experience financial stress and insolvency and generally slow down the supply of capital available as loans. This book contains three research papers that focus on the role of the banks.

The first research paper is on the alternative specifications of bank lending in France and Germany: "Theory, Evidence and Policy Implications" by Professor Robert E. Krainer of the University of Wisconsin-Madison. In this paper, the supply of bank loans as capital to businesses is analyzed using a model based on the tools and theories of the academic field of finance as opposed to the usual models used by economists. This "finance" model argues that bank investments in the form of loans to businesses, just like any other capital budgeting decision, must meet a cost-of-capital hurdle.

The capital budgeting model of bank lending assumes that equity share valuations reflect the relevant information about future returns of borrowers. This specification of bank lending is tested against the traditional supply and demand analysis of bank loans in economics.

[1] http://papers.ssrn.com/sol3/papers.cfm?abstract_id=1553988

Professor Krainer's empirical tests show that in France the traditional economic model of bank loans, based on the demand for loans from borrowers, is not supported. However, the capital budgeting specification hypothesis, based on stock market valuations for banks and nonfinancial enterprises, cannot be rejected. In Professor Krainer's paper, the mixed results are similar but weaker for German banks.

The second paper on banking in this book addresses banking unions in Europe—an interim assessment by Christian Schmidt from the financial market authority in Liechtenstein. This paper analyzes the implications of the financial crisis and the exposed shortcomings of financial regulation in Europe. In particular, Christian Schmidt argues that financial regulation remains decentralized in Europe.

Dr. Schmidt also analyzes another implication of the financial crisis in Europe, namely that European policymakers did not have the tools to effectively deal with the crisis caused by international banking operations. He then focuses on the European Commission's proposal in 2012 to create a single supervisory mechanism as a first step toward an integrated "banking union," which includes a single rulebook, common deposit protection, and a single resolution mechanism.

Christian Schmidt discusses the difficulties associated with a European banking union. He also discusses the costs of a failure to agree on a strong banking union when an emphasis is placed on regulatory crisis prevention.

Revolutionary regime change ideas tend to receive attention at times of financial crisis. The third banking paper included in this book is one example of such an idea, articulated by Professor Ottmar Schneck from Reutlingen University of Applied Sciences. The paper is titled a "World without money needs no banks and no rating."

Financial fraud and misbehavior are often connected to a financial crisis and sometimes are the significant factors causing that crisis. Paul Borochin and I propose a regulatory tool to allow the detection of financial irregularity in options and stock markets, in a paper titled, "Put–call parity violations under limited arbitrage: a case study and a simulation tool for detecting financial irregularity."

In addition, this book contains papers that focus on various aspects of financial education, including "enabling holistic finance education in turbulent times" by Wolfgang Amann, "Actual problems of finance teaching in Ukraine in the postcrisis period" by Serhiy Lyeonov and Olga Liuta, and "measuring the success of executive education—comprehensively depicting holistic finance education" by Wolfgang Amann.

Lastly, managerial compensation and its excesses are a focal point during times of financial crisis. A paper titled "Executive compensation and risk taking: the impact of systemic crises" by Alon Raviv and Elif Sisli-Ciamarra focuses on this issue.

Corporate Governance and Restructuring Through Spin-Offs: European Evidence

Dmitri Boreiko and Maurizio Murgia

1 Introduction

Adapting a firm's size to the current business conditions is a prevailing feature of any industry. A lot of research has been conducted on firms' mergers and acquisitions (M&A) that take place mostly in times of economic booms. Virtually every course in advanced corporate finance devotes a lecture or two to M&A activity, buyers and target returns, their patterns, and differences. However, in times of economic and financial crises the firms usually shrink in size, trying to optimize their structure, divesting the unprofitable divisions to cut costs or get cash. Thus, divestitures, although being a reciprocal activity of M&A, play a major role in turbulent times but are relatively under-researched and usually ignored by the finance lecturers. With this contribution, we try to fill the gap by studying various financial and corporate governance aspects of particular restructuring transactions and spin-offs, arguing that this study might serve as a useful source of topics for teaching corporate finance in turbulent times.

A spin-off is one of several tools for asset redeployment and a firm's restructuring. Some spin-offs are the reverse of previous mergers, but more frequently an internally grown business unit is spun off as a separate publicly traded firm. From a legal point of view, a spin-off is a pro rata distribution of subsidiary shares to a parent firm's existing shareholders, and often it is a nontaxable transaction for the parent corporation. What distinguishes a spin-off from other types of asset redeployment (e.g., equity carve-outs, asset sales) is that they do not provide a cash inflow to either the parent firm or the subsidiary firm. The absence of external financing and taxes makes spin-offs an interesting corporate transaction to analyze

D. Boreiko (✉) • M. Murgia
School of Economics and Management, Free University of Bolzano-Bozen, piazza Università 1, Bolzano 39100, Italy
e-mail: dmitri.boreiko@unibz.it; mauirzio.murgia@unibz.it

T. Azarmi, W. Amann (eds.), *The Financial Crisis*,
DOI 10.1007/978-3-319-20588-5_2

the determinants and the economic effects of decisions that alter the scope of the firm.

There is a great deal of empirical literature on spin-offs, primarily based on US data. Many studies document the parent-firm positive stock price effect associated with the announcement of spin-offs.[1] More controversial is the issue of whether spin-offs produce ex post performance improvement and the channels through which long-term value is created. Cusatis et al. (1993) present evidence of abnormal stock returns for parents and subsidiaries that are merged or acquired after the spin-off. Some studies fail to find post-spin-off improvement in operating performance (e.g., Michaely and Shaw 1995). Daley et al. (1997) and Desai and Jain (1999) show that only when parent firms and subsidiary firms operate in different industries (focus-increasing spin-offs), there is evidence of post-spin-off efficiency measured by improvements in both abnormal stock returns and operating performance. Moreover, their results indicate that improvement in post-spin-off performance is mainly associated with parent firms, while non-focusing spin-offs are typically associated with the underperformance of subsidiaries. Chemmanur and Nandy (2006) use plant level data to analyze change in productivity after spin-offs. They find that productivity increases only in parent-firm plants, mainly through cost cuts. In contrast to existing empirical studies, Chemmanur and Nandy show that productivity improvements after the transaction are found in both acquired and non-acquired business units, regardless of whether the spin-off is focus-increasing or non-focus-increasing. Furthermore, their results indicate that subsidiary firms do not perform worse than parent firms before a spin-off.

In this chapter, we attempt to shed light on the conflicting results of published research by examining a sample of European firms that completed spin-offs between the years 1989 and 2005 and provide evidence related to two questions. First, what factors motivate European firms to undertake spin-offs? Second, do spin-offs result in performance improvements?

There are several reasons why a study on European spin-offs may reveal alternative determinants and long-term effects. First, differences in firms' ownership structure and corporate governance among the EU countries (or compared to the USA) suggest that these factors may contribute differently to firms' spin-off decisions. It is well known that concentrated ownership structures prevail in Europe (e.g., Faccio and Lang 2002), and these are associated with larger benefits of control. Thus, given the larger private benefits of control typically observed in firms with concentrated ownership structure, it is interesting to examine why a controlling shareholder would voluntarily reduce firm size and control rights in a (relatively) costly spin-off that does not raise capital. Second, differences in laws

[1] For examples that use US data, see Hite and Owers (1983), Miles and Rosenfeld (1983), Schipper and Smith (1983), Allen et al. (1995), Michaely and Shaw (1995), Slovin et al. (1995), Daley et al. (1997), Desai and Jain (1999), Krishanaswami and Subramaniam (1999), Mulherin and Boone (2000), Chemmanur and Paeglis (2001), Gertner et al. (2002), Wruck and Wruck (2002), Maxwell and Rao (2003) and Ahn and Denis (2004). Veld and Veld-Merkoulova (2004) analyze a sample of European spin-offs, while Choi and Han (2006) study a sample of Japanese spin-offs.

and enforcement are known to explain the intensity and pattern of mergers and acquisitions around the world (e.g., Rossi and Volpin 2004). Consequently, we conjecture that decisions to reverse mergers by spinning off subsidiaries to facilitate takeovers should also be influenced by differences in national regulations. Third, corporate spin-offs in Continental Europe are a relatively recent phenomenon. In 1982, the EU issued the Sixth Directive (82/891, December 17, 1982) with the goal to harmonize EU countries' national laws and to make spin-offs a viable and economically efficient restructuring transaction. Since then tax-free spin-offs have become more common in EU countries.

In this study, we document that spin-off decisions in Europe are often triggered by a firm's governance earthquakes, such as an appointment of a new CEO or a takeover threat. We obtain this result by comparing sample firms with control firms that did not undertake spin-offs during the entire period of study. We use univariate analysis and logistic regressions to provide evidence on the determinants of the likelihood of spin-offs. These findings indicate that even in less active markets for mergers and corporate control, break-up decisions are enforced by the monitoring activity of outside investors and capital markets.

Second, we provide new evidence on the factors explaining the well-known spin-off announcement effects. We show that a significant component of stock price reaction is related to spin-offs that originated from past acquisitions, and this effect supersedes the much-reported effect of focus-increasing spin-offs. This result suggests that spin-off research should pay attention when identifying a subsidiary's origin, a characteristic that appears to be more relevant than classifying spun-off units as focus-increasing or non-focus-increasing.

We next analyze the long-run efficiency improvements of spin-offs. Looking at abnormal stock returns and operating performance, we find that only internally developed subsidiaries and parent-related units (non-focusing) are the spin-offs that create significant market value and operating efficiency improvements. These findings contrast the US evidence where focus-increasing spin-offs and spin-offs involved in a subsequent merger are those showing significant value creation and efficiency improvements. Further, our evidence highlights that much of increased efficiency is generated by spun-off units and not by parent firms.

The remainder of the chapter is structured as follows. Section 2 briefly reviews the spin-off theory and summarizes empirical findings on spin-off value creation and post-transaction efficiency improvements. Section 3 describes the data, variables, and control measures and provides descriptive statistics for the sample. Section 4 reports empirical results. Section 5 brings the chapter to its logical conclusion.

2 Literature Review and Hypotheses

Finance and economics literatures suggest several motives for value-maximizing spin-offs. Among them, four are prominent: (1) the managerial incentives hypothesis, (2) the focus (or efficiency)-increasing hypothesis, (3) the asymmetric information hypothesis, and (4) the corporate control hypothesis.[2] Theoretical models also derive specific predictions on three relevant moments of a typical corporate spin-off: (a) before the decision is announced (predicting the likelihood of a spin-off); (b) when the spin-off is announced to capital markets (explaining the short-term change in parent-firm shareholders' wealth); and (c) after the spin-off is completed (explaining the long-term operating performance and stock returns of separated business units). These theories are not mutually exclusive, and thus we expect to find some support for each. Moreover, it is interesting to analyze whether some of these theories describe the data better than others.

Managerial incentives: Aron's (1991) theoretical model proposes that spin-off efficiency improvements will be obtained by designing new incentive contracts for divisional managers. Schipper and Smith (1983) were the first to suggest that spin-offs may enable shareholders to better monitor managers and reduce agency costs. Consistent with this hypothesis, Seward and Walsh (1996) document a significant increase of incentive contracts for CEOs of spun-off subsidiaries, although they show there is no association between incentive contracts and stock market announcement effects. Pyo (2006) more directly tests the prediction of the managerial incentives hypothesis and shows that new compensation packages are significant motives for spin-offs and may lead to improved post-spin-off operating efficiency.

The managerial incentives hypothesis predicts that new compensation plans for managers are an important determinant of spin-off decisions and will be closely related to shareholder's value creation and efficiency improvement after the transaction.

Focus (or efficiency) increasing: The corporate focus literature (see, e.g., Comment and Jarrell 1995; John and Ofek 1995) suggests that spin-offs that increase corporate focus (i.e., eliminate negative synergies among different firm's divisions)

---

[2] Other explanations for spin-off gains include tax and regulatory benefits (Schipper and Smith (1983), the transfer of wealth from bondholders to stockholders (Galai and Masulis (1976), Parrino (1997) and Maxwell and Rao (2003), and the optimal allocation of debt between the two firms resulting from the spin-off (John (1993). We do not investigate the validity of these hypotheses in our study as we analyze only tax-free and voluntary spin-offs. Moreover, the predictions of the bondholder–stockholder wealth redistribution hypothesis and of the debt allocation hypothesis are difficult to verify in the European context, as European firms tend to carry much less market debt than US firms and the vast majority of debt finance is provided by bank loans, which are typically senior to public debt and carry greater guarantees than a bond or debenture. Therefore, differences in bargaining power between lenders and bondholders could exert a better creditor protection and result in lower or insignificant wealth or debt transfer among security holders when a corporate restructuring is undertaken.

should create value and improve efficiency.[3] There is significant support for the efficiency hypothesis. Daley et al. (1997) and Desai and Jain (1999) show that announcement returns for focus-increasing spin-offs are significantly higher than non-focus-increasing ones. Furthermore, they document that, after the transaction, significant increases in accounting profitability and stock returns are concentrated in focusing spin-offs only.

The focus-increasing hypothesis makes specific predictions about spin-off announcement returns and post-transaction performance measures. It predicts that spin-offs in which the subsidiary operates in a different industry should have greater value creation and ex post larger efficiency improvements.

Asymmetric information: The asymmetric information hypothesis is built on the idea that multidivisional firms are less transparent and typically undervalued. Breaking up the conglomerate firm could reduce the information asymmetry in the market and improve the quality of information on each division's cash flows, which could then be inferred by both incumbent managers and outside investors. Theoretical models by Habib et al. (1997) and Nanda and Narayanan (1999) predict that a spin-off will help remove parent undervaluation, augment market attention on firms' securities, and allow firms to obtain better conditions in security issue transactions. Krishnaswami and Subramaniam (1999) report evidence that there are changes in the information environment of firms following spin-offs. They document increased earnings, forecast accuracy, and lower dispersion in analysts' earnings forecasts after spin-offs. Moreover, firms that undertake spin-offs raise more capital following the breakup than before, and relative to comparable firms. Gilson et al. (2001) find that after a breakup there is an increase in analyst coverage leading to more accurate earnings forecasts.

The asymmetric information hypothesis has specific implications for the likelihood of spin-offs and for the parent firm's announcement price effects, but it has no predictions for post-transaction performance. This theory implies that parent-firm undervaluation will be an important determinant of spin-off decisions and that the two separated units will be more active in raising funds in capital markets after the transaction.

Corporate control: The corporate control hypothesis is proposed by Chemmanur and Yan (2004), who posit that spin-offs discipline management by increasing a firm's exposure to the possibility of a takeover. The empirical implications are basically four: (1) a more active market for corporate control will influence spin-off decisions as activist investors and takeover threats can put pressure on a parent firm's decision to restructure through a break-up, (2) spin-off announcement price effects will be correlated with the degree of takeover activity in the parent-firm industry, (3) after the transaction, improvements in long-term operating performance will be observed for spun-off subsidiaries because of higher managerial

[3] Focus-increasing spin-offs are usually defined when the parent firm and subsidiary firm operate in different industries. In Sect. 4.5, we provide details about the focus/non-focus spin-off classification we adopted in this paper.

discipline and efficiency, and (4) post-spin-off, long-term, positive, abnormal stock returns will be observed only with parents and subsidiaries involved in mergers and acquisitions.

3 Sample Selection and Descriptive Statistics

3.1 Data Sources and Sample Construction

This research focuses on pure, voluntary, tax-free, completed spin-offs by European, nonfinancial firms.[4] It is crucial to the objective of this study to correctly identify pure spin-offs and separate them from other types of restructuring and divestiture transactions with which they are frequently confused.

The study constructs a unique dataset compiled from many different databases.[5] We start assembling the sample by searching the Thomson Financial ONE Banker Mergers and Acquisitions database in order to identify all spin-offs announced by listed Western European companies. The initial sample covers the period from January 1985 to June 2005, and it includes 338 transactions. We next verify the accuracy of the ONE Banker M&A data by comparing it to news articles found in Lexis/Nexis, including related news reported in local languages in each country's major national newspapers. Stock market and accounting data were retrieved from Thomson Financial DataStream International and Worldscope databases. We also used the Research Insight Compustat Global and the Amadeus Top 250,000 databases to perform further checks of accounting data and transactions' characteristics.[6] We believe this level of scrutiny makes our sample of European spin-offs unique and clean of confounding events frequently described as corporate spin-offs in available databases.

From the initial list, we drop 193 transactions for the following reasons: 142 entries were incorrectly recorded as spin-offs (30 carve-outs and right issues, 38 split-ups, and 74 internal restructuring programs); 5 cases of duplicate data entry; 7 cases where the subsidiary was already listed prior to the spin-off; and 39 cases where a clear announcement date and news article were not found. From the remaining list of 145 announced spin-offs, we then eliminated 15 pending/ withdrawn transactions as of June 2005 and 6 cases in which parent-firm stock price

[4] In a tax-free spin-off, shareholders of the parent firm receive a distribution of stock in the subsidiary representing all or a majority of the parent's shares in the subsidiary. Upon distribution, the parent does not have to pay tax on any gain, and shareholder tax is deferred until the shares are sold. We check the tax status of each spin-off in the sample by examining the tax code of the parent firm's country and announcement statements. Also see European Tax Handbook (various years since 1990).

[5] Detailed variable definitions and data sources are reported in Appendix 1.

[6] Research Insight Compustat Global is a trademark of Standard & Poor's, and Amadeus Top 250,000 is a trademark of Bureau Van Dijk.

data were unavailable. We finally exclude 27 spin-offs completed by firms with operations in regulated industries [utilities (2 cases, SIC code 4911) and financial services (25 cases, SIC codes between 6000 and 6999)], as regulation may confound comparisons. Thus, our final sample consists of 92 listed, nonfinancial corporations headquartered in 12 Western European countries that announced and completed the spin-off of 97 subsidiaries between January 1989 and June 2005.[7]

3.2 Control Sample of Non-spin-off Firms

Our empirical methodology requires comparing characteristics and performance of firms involved in spin-offs with that of similar firms that do not undertake spin-offs. Accordingly, we construct a matching sample for each parent and subsidiary by selecting firms that did not undertake a spin-off in the 5 years centered on the spin-off completion year (−2,. . .0,. . .+2), that are headquartered in the same geographic area [(1) UK and Ireland; (2) Nordic Countries (Denmark, Finland, Norway, and Sweden); and (3) Continental Europe (Belgium, Germany, Italy, Netherlands, Spain, and Switzerland)], that have the same three-digit SIC code, and that are closest in market value of equity (±30 %) and book-to-market ratio. If we do not find a matching firm in the same geographic area and/or with same three-digit SIC code, we rely on the whole European dataset to identify the closest firm by two-digit SIC code, market value of equity, and book-to-market ratio.

3.3 Sample Characteristics

Table 1 shows the sample country distribution, where it emerges that spin-offs are more frequent transactions in Great Britain and Sweden than in Continental Europe. The average spin-off relative size reveals that spin-offs in Europe are large transactions; on average, larger than similar transactions sampled in recent US studies (see, e.g., Desai and Jain 1999; Krishnaswami and Subramaniam 1999). The median time required to complete (from announcement date to ex date) the European spin-off is 4 months, but it can be worked out in just 40 days in countries such as Spain, or require about 1 year as in Germany. Consistent with past studies, Table 1 shows that the majority of spin-offs are represented by focus-increasing transactions (61 or about 63 % of final sample). In panel A, we also document that 73 spin-offs (75 % of final sample) are internally developed subsidiaries. The rest of the sample (25 %) consists of spin-offs that unwind earlier acquisitions. To distinguish and identify which spin-offs were internally developed and which spin-offs originated from a previous acquisition, we construct a complete "corporate history"

[7] Five parent firms complete two spin-offs each separated by several years.

Table 1 Distribution of the Sample

	Belgium	Denmark	Finland	Germany	Ireland	Italy	Netherlands	Norway	Spain	Sweden	Switzerland	UK	Total
Total number	5	2	1	3	4	5	2	3	1	15	4	52	97
Median rel. size (%)	17	27	82	6	58	64	52	27	5	19	29	33	31
Days to completion	112	291	253	339	117	132	225	129	46	111	167	110	125
Non-focus/focus	3/2	2/0	0/1	2/1	1/3	2/3	0/2	3/0	0/1	3/12	2/2	18/34	36/61
Internal growth/prev. acquired	5/0	2/0	0/1	2/1	4/0	5/0	2/0	3/0	1/0	11/4	4/0	34/18	73/24

of parent firms and subsidiary firms through press articles (LexisNexis and major national European newspaper databases), information available on Thomson ONE Banker database and by reviewing a parent firm's public files, and corporate websites. The distinction between internally developed and previously acquired spin-offs is important, as it may reflect different corporate strategies. We conjecture that a spin-off decision can either signal that the breakup will be through a potential winner or by correcting a past mistake. This aspect is often neglected in the spin-off literature.[8] One notable exception is the study by Allen et al. (1995), providing evidence that shareholder gains associated with spin-off announcements are in some cases the undoing of earlier unwise acquisition. They label this as the "correction-of-a-mistake" hypothesis, which predicts a larger rebound in parent-firm stock price when the spin-off of previously acquired subsidiaries is announced.

Our sample of parent and subsidiary firms represents about 35 different industries, with the largest concentration in the Chemicals and Allied Products Industry, Business Services, and Electronic and Other Electric Equipment. Moreover, the sample includes primarily European domestic spin-offs, where both parent firm and subsidiary firm operate and are listed in the same country. We find only two cases of cross-border spin-offs, each involving the assets of a subsidiary operating in a different country.

In Table 2, we present selected statistics on parent firms and control firms at the end of month before the spin-off announcement date or, in case of accounting figures as of fiscal year end, prior to the spin-off announcement year (Year 1). The median size of the European parent firms that undertake a spin-off is relatively large, as measured by market value of equity (1.08 billion euros), total assets (1.26 billion euros), or total sales (1.65 billion euros). Matched control firms show similar characteristics, with mean and median market value, profitability, investment, leverage ratios, and residual standard deviation not statistically different from those measured for parent firms. Table 2 also shows summary statistics on subsidiary firms and their control firms at the end of spin-off completion month or, in case of accounting figures, as of fiscal year end following spin-off completion year. The subsidiary and their matched firms have similar values for all the variables reported; we detect no significant mean or median differences with respect to size, profitability, investment, and leverage ratios.

Table 3 presents descriptive statistics for multi-segment parents and their respective control firms for the 2 years surrounding the spin-off completion (year 1 and year 0). Of the 97 sample spin-offs, we were able to gather segmental data for 82 parent firms; 63 (65 %) were undertaken by parents with two or more business segments as reported in Worldscope database and single-segment parents were 19 or 20 % of the whole sample. Table 3 shows that multi-segment parents have

---

[8] However, it is worth noting that some authors have argued that although spin-offs and divestitures frequently reverse past mergers, these transactions are not always past failures, as parent firms may separate business segments because of evolving corporate strategies and changes in product markets. See, for example, Weston (1989) and Kaplan and Weisbach (1992).

Table 2 Summary statistics of parents, spin-offs, and control firms

	Parent firms			Control firms		
	Mean	Median	*N*	Mean	Median	*N*
Market value of equity (million euros)	7260.7	1078.1	97	6930.4	793.3	97
Total assets (million euros)	6414.2	1256.7	95	7490.1	1175.5	95
Total sales (million euros)	4732.0	1649.7	95	5639.1	1191.2	95
B/M ratio	0.72	0.42	90	0.60	0.49	89
Operating income ratio	0.06	0.07	95	0.07	0.08	94
Investment ratio	0.26	0.05	94	0.21	0.03	86
R&D to sales ratio, %	1.61	0.00	95	1.43	0.00	95
Leverage	0.25	0.24	94	0.22	0.22	94
Residual standard deviation	0.02	0.02	97	0.02	0.02	97
	Spin-off firms			Control firms		
	Mean	Median	*N*	Mean	Median	*N*
Market value of equity (million euros)	1251.2	235.9	89	1047.9	214.7	89
Total assets (million euros)	2060.6	344.0	80	2116.2	369.3	78
Total sales (million euros)	1334.0	386.4	79	1837.2	247.7	76
B/M ratio	0.78	0.52	76	0.69	0.54	75
Operating income ratio	0.06	0.07	78	0.04	0.07	77
Investment ratio	0.22	0.05	75	0.21	0.05	71
R&D to sales ratio, %	0.69	0.00	78	1.18	0.00	72
Leverage	0.25	0.22	80	0.21	0.20	76

on average more than three business segments in the year before the spin-off is completed. By contrast, similar firms have on average two business segments, and both the mean and median differences are statistically significant at the 5 % level. As expected, parents have a statistically significant decline in the number of segments in the spin-off completion year, while the reduction in the number of segments is not observed for control firms. To analyze the degree of diversification, we also compute the sales-based Herfindahl index. Parent firms exhibit a significant increase in both the mean and median Herfindahl index from the year before the spin-off to the year the spin-off is completed. By contrast, no change in the Herfindahl index is observed for matched control firms in the same time period. Based on evidence, on the number of segments and the Herfindahl index, we find that parents undertaking spin-offs are more diversified than control firms. This result is, however, consistent with past studies of US spin-offs. Next, we look at Tobin's Q for parent and control firms to ascertain differential performances. We compute Tobin's Q as the ratio of market value of equity plus book value of total assets minus the book value of equity, over book value of total assets. Parents' Tobin's Q declines after the spin-off is completed, but the change is not statistically significant. Perhaps more interesting, matched firms show a similar Tobin's Q in the same time period and no significant change across the 2 years. Finally, Table 3 presents the diversification value for the year preceding the spin-off and the

Table 3 Multi-segment parent-firms and control-firms' statistics

			Parent-firms		Control firms	
	Year	Statistics	Obs.	Value	Obs.	Value
Number of segments	*t*−1	Mean	63	3.19	55	2.42
		Median	63	3.00	55	2.00
	*t*0	Mean	58	2.57	49	2.24
		Median	58	2.00	49	2.00
		Diff. in means [medians], *p*-value		0.006 [0.001]		0.456 [0.423]
Herfindahl index	*t*−1	Mean	63	0.30	55	0.52
		Median	63	0.20	55	0.51
	*t*0	Mean	58	0.50	49	0.57
		Median	58	0.43	49	0.54
		Diff. in means [medians], *p*-value		0.001 [0.002]		0.479 [0.553]
Tobin's Q	*t*−1	Mean	63	1.69	63	1.70
		Median	63	1.34	63	1.31
	*t*0	Mean	58	1.50	58	1.75
		Median	58	1.23	58	1.38
		Diff. in means [medians], *p*-value		0.281 [0.211]		0.800 [0.749]
Diversification discount (−) premium (+) (%)	*t*−1	Mean	50	−40.2	38	−4.1
		Median	50	−22.1	38	0.2
	*t*0	Mean	48	−28.5	31	−0.1
		Median	48	−30.0	31	2.3
		Diff. in means [medians], *p*-value		0.522 [0.779]		0.366 [0.645]

This table is a description of the sample of 97 spin-offs announced and completed from January 1989 until June 2005 in 12 European countries. Spin-offs were first identified from Thomson ONE Banker Mergers and Acquisition Database and confirmed by searching Lexis-Nexis and national newspapers' databases. The sample excludes spin-offs undertaken by parent firms in regulated and financial industries. Market value and accounting data is obtained from DataStream. Table 1 reports each spin-off parent firm's country of incorporation and selected statistics. Median rel. size is the median of the ratio of spin-off and parent-firm market values at the end of the month following completion date. Days to completion is the median number of days elapsing from spin-off announcement to ex-date. Non-Focus/Focus classification shows the number of spin-offs with the same/different two-digit primary SIC code of the parent firm. Internal Growth/Prev. Acquired split shows the number of spin-off subsidiaries that originated from the parent itself/were acquired by the parent firm before the spin-off announcement. Median MV refers to parent-firm market value and is taken at the end of the month preceding the spin-off announcement date. Table 2 presents descriptive statistics of selected financial variables for parent firms and spin-offs and their control firms matched by geographic area, industry (two-digit SIC Code), size (within 70–130 % of parent's firm market value), and book-to-market that didn't undertake a spin-off in the 5-year period centered on the spin-off completion year. We define three geographic areas across Europe: (1) UK and Ireland; (2) Nordic Countries (Denmark, Finland, Norway, and Sweden); and (3) Continental Europe (Belgium, Germany, Italy, Spain, Switzerland, and The Netherlands). Market value is taken at the end of the month preceding the spin-off announcement date. B/M is the book-to-market ratio and is computed as the ratio of net tangible assets over market value. Operating income is total sales minus cost of goods sold and other expenses, before depreciation and

(continued)

amortization, and is measured as a ratio relative to the total assets. Investment ratio equals the ratio of firm capital investment to total sales. Leverage is measured as the ratio of all debts to total assets. Residual standard deviation is the dispersion of the market-adjusted, daily stock returns in the spin-off pre-announcement period (days −220, ..., −21, where day 0 is the announcement day). Table 3 reports summary statistics of the number of segments, Herfindahl index, Tobin's Q, and the value of diversification discount for a sample of multi-segment parent firms and matched control firms. Year $t-1$ is the year before the spin-off announcement, whereas year $t0$ refers to the spin-off completion year. Diversification discount/premium is computed as in Berger and Ofek (1995) by estimating the difference between the market value of the diversified firm and the sum of the imputed value of all the firm's segments, based on the sales-multiplier valuation method of the stand-alone firms. Significance of differences across groups is measured using a t-statistic for means and Wilcoxon signed-ranks test for medians (p-values reported in brackets). All value figures are millions of 2005 euros, using the EU-15 CPI index from DataStream

completion year. To compute the diversification value, we closely follow Berger and Ofek's (1995) methodology.

Their algorithm computes the difference between the market value of the diversified firm and the sum of the imputed value of all the firm's segments, based on the sales multiplier valuation method of the stand-alone firms. Furthermore, we require that the sum of segment sales, as reported by Worldscope, must be within 1 % of total sales from annual profit and loss accounts. This requirement results in a drop of 13 parent firms for which total sales exceed those reported in consolidated statements. Thus, the final sample is of 50 parent firms.[9] Consistent with the diversification and the spin-off literature, we find that multi-segment parent firms in the year prior to the spin-off trade at substantial discount (mean −40 % and median −22 %) relative to comparable single-segment firms. Both mean and median are significantly different from zero at the 1 % level. Matched firms, by contrast, exhibit relative value similar to comparable single-segment firms. They show slightly negative (−0.4 %) diversification discount, on average, while median

[9] We believe that most of the validity of the value loss from diversification of parent firms presented in Table 3 depends on management disclosure policies and is, therefore, subject to the well-known self-reported bias (e.g., Villalonga 2004). In fact, contrary to US regulation (FASB 14 and SEC S-K), which requires US firms to report segment information since fiscal years ending December 1977, European firms started to release voluntarily segmental data gradually from the end of 1980s. European Union (EU) regulation on corporate financial statements is under the Seventh European Directive (86/635/EEC), which was adopted by the EU Council of Ministers on June 13, 1983, and implemented by Member States on January 1, 1988. The directive, art. 34, par. 8, requires segmental reporting of consolidated net turnover by activity and geographical markets. The directive, art. 45, par. 2, allows omission of segmental reporting if its nature would be prejudicial to any undertakings affected by that disclosure. Omission must be disclosed in the statement notes. France, Germany, and Greece implemented the Directive before January 1, 1988. Luxembourg, the Netherlands, and the United Kingdom enacted legislation to be effective during the financial year 1990. Belgium, Denmark, and Portugal adopted the Directive by the financial year 1991. Ireland and Spain follow in the financial year 1992, and Italy adopted it by financial year 1994. Starting in the 2005 financial year, European listed companies had to have consolidated group account statements according to IAS (International Accounting Standards). IAS 14 concerns segmental reporting.

is slightly positive (0.2 %), and both are not significantly different from zero. Furthermore, the mean and median differences in diversification discount between parents and controls are statistically significant at the 1 % level in both years.

The level of diversification discount of European parent firms undertaking spin-offs seems high when compared to studies such as Lang and Stulz (1994) and Berger and Ofek (1995), who find that discount averages 10 % across large samples of US multi-segment firms, and Lins and Servaes (1999), who find no diversification discount for German conglomerates and 15 % discount in the UK. However, more recently Ahn and Denis (2004) found that the mean (median) diversification discount for a sample of US parent firms undertaking spin-offs is 31 % (18 %), a finding much closer to our figures for European parents.[10] In the spin-off completion year, parent firms' mean discount is lower (−28 %), but the median is higher (−30 %). However, while mean and median are still significantly different from zero at the 5 % level, we find no significant change between values in the 2 years. These results show that (1) multi-segment parents continue to be traded at discount relative to stand-alone firms even after the spin-off transaction is completed and (2) multi-segment parents have significantly larger discount than similar multi-segment firms that do not undertake a spin-off.

4 Empirical Results

4.1 Motives for Corporate Spin-Offs Decisions

We first turn our attention to analysis of spin-off announcement statements made by parent-firm managers and financial analysts reported in the financial press to assess the spin-off motives. We find it interesting to investigate the consistency between the reported motives for spin-offs and the theoretical predictions outlined in Sect. 2. The reasons most commonly reported at spin-off announcement time are strengthening of corporate focus strategy (57 %), restructuring operations and underperforming assets (42 %), a part of a merger/acquisition plan (22 %), improvement of information flows, and gaining a better access to capital markets (20 %).[11] This preliminary evidence supports the predictions of refocusing, asymmetric information, and corporate control hypotheses on the factors affecting spin-off decision.

[10] Ahn and Denis (2004) compute the excess value following the methodology proposed by Rajan et al. (2000). However, our diversification discount calculation is very much similar. Our findings are also consistent with empirical results presented in Berger and Ofek (1999) and Dittmar and Shivdasani (2003). These papers show that refusing firms experience a mean value destruction of about 30 % at time of divestiture-related announcements, which include asset sales and spin-offs.

[11] The total percentage of motivations is greater than 100 % because several announcements reported more than one reason for undertaking the spin-off.

4.2 Corporate Control Events Before Spin-Off Decision

In this section, we investigate whether market discipline affects spin-off decision in Europe. Past research on the restructuring of US firms (see, e.g., Denis et al. 1997; Berger and Ofek 1999; Dittmar and Shivdasani 2003) has found that corporate control changes are common before these events. Moreover, some studies of US spin-offs highlight the role of corporate governance in increasing the probability of undertaking a spin-off (see, e.g., Wruck and Wruck 2002; Ahn and Walker 2007).

Table 4 reports the frequency of several corporate control and capital structure events observed during the time period from 12 months before to 1 month after the spin-off announcement, both for parents and their control firms. A CEO change

Table 4 Corporate control and capital structure events of parent firms

	Parent firms		Control firms		Mean-diff.
	Obs.	in %	Obs.	in %	*p*-value
Management/Board turnover					
Turnover of CEO	32	33.33	10	10.42	0.01
Turnover of Board Chairman & President	19	19.79	19	19.79	1.00
Outside shareholder pressure					
Merger and/or controlling acquisition attempt	18	18.75	3	3.13	0.00
Activism by outside investors	13	13.54	6	6.25	0.09
New block holder	12	12.50	10	10.42	0.65
Management compensation					
New compensation plan	5	5.21	1	1.04	0.09
Financial distress					
Dividend cut	17	17.71	10	10.42	0.15
Debt restructuring and/or refinancing	6	6.25	2	2.08	0.15
Liquidation	1	1.04	0	0.00	0.32
Restructuring and/or divestment activity					
Restructuring or divesting a division	57	59.38	23	23.96	0.00
Capital structure changes					
New debt issue	12	12.50	16	16.67	0.42
New equity issue	11	11.46	14	14.58	0.52
Summary					
At least on external control event	81	84.38	58	60.42	0.00

This table shows the total number and frequency of corporate control and capital structure events reported by the parent firms announcing and completing spin-offs from January 1989 until June 2005 in 12 European countries and by matched control firms. The period extends from the 12 months before the spin-off announcement month until 1 month after that announcement and the news search uses data from Lexis-Nexis and national newspapers databases. Control firms are matched by geographic area, industry, size, and book-to-market within firms that either didn't undertake a spin-off or originated from a spin-off in the 5-year period centered at the spin-off completion year. We define three geographic areas across Europe: (1) UK and Ireland; (2) Nordic Countries (Denmark, Finland, Norway, and Sweden); (3) Continental Europe (Belgium, Germany, Italy, Spain, Switzerland, and The Netherlands). Significance of mean-differences across groups is measured using a *t*-statistic occurred in 32 parent firms (33 %) prior to the spin-off, whereas it is observed in only 10 control firms (10 %) in the same time period, with difference being statistically significant at the 1 % level. We also found that parents received a merger proposal or were a target of a takeover attempt before the spin-off in 18 % of cases, while only 3 % of control firms experienced such pressure. The two rates are significantly different at the 1 % level. Other types of events where we detect a statistically significant difference between parents and their controls are observed for outside investors (defined as pension funds, hedge funds, and individual blockholders) activism and the establishment of new compensation plans for top managers.

Events related to financial distress decisions and capital structure changes are also observed during the spin-off announcement time period, but their frequency is not statistically different from that of matched firms. Overall, 81 parent firms (84 %) undertaking a spin-off experience at least one corporate control event in the 13 months surrounding the spin-off decision. However, what is remarkable is that spin-off announcement statements almost never mention external pressures, take-over threats, or other facts we uncover in our search. Taken all together, these results confirm the intuitions of both the managerial incentives and corporate control hypotheses on the economic factors affecting spin-off decisions.

4.3 The Determinants of Corporate Spin-Off Decision

The results of univariate analysis of the previous section show that CEO turnover and discipline imposed by the market for corporate control are important events around the time the spin-off decision is publicly announced. In this section, we directly tackle the issue of the determinants of spin-off decision by estimating several logit regression models to determine whether univariate results hold after controlling for other variables associated with spin-off decision. The dependent variable of logit models is an indicator equal to 1 for parent firms and 0 for control firms matched on industry, size, country, and book-to-market ratio and that did not undertake spin-offs during all period of study.

We employ specific variables to test predictions of the theoretical literature on spin-offs. The CEO CHANGE and COMPENSATION PLANS are dummy variables, which take the value of 1 when a CEO change and a new top management compensation plan have been announced and/or realized in the year before the spin-off announcement date. Both variables are predicted by the managerial incentives hypothesis to exert a positive influence on the likelihood of a spin-off. The TAKEOVER THREAT variable is linked directly to the predictions of Chemmanur and Yan's (2004) corporate control theory. The variable is constructed as a dummy that takes the value of 1 whether either a merger or a controlling acquisition were announced/attempted in the 12 months before the spin-off announcement date. Also linked to the corporate control theory are the variables DIVESTITURES and ACQUISITIONS. They measure, respectively, the number of asset sales and acquisitions completed by the firm in the 12 months before spin-off announcement date. The two variables are also proxies for the intensity of the market for corporate control and it is predicted that they will be positively associated with the spin-off decision. The variable ANALYSTS FORECAST is the forecast error of mean analyst estimate of firm earnings per share (source: I/B/E/S) in the year preceding the spin-off announcement date. The variable is directly linked to the predictions of asymmetric information theory of spin-offs (Habib et al. 1997) and has been used in prior empirical research (e.g., Krishnaswami and Subramaniam 1999). It predicts that higher analyst forecast error will be associated with higher information asymmetries and it will positively affect the spin-off decision. DIVERSIFICATION VALUE is computed as in Berger and Ofek (1995) by estimating the difference between the market value of the firm and the sum of the imputed value of all the firm's segments, based on the sales-multiplier valuation method of the stand-alone firms.

Table 3 shows that multi-segment parent firms typically suffer from a large and significant value loss from diversification in the year before the spin-off announcement date. The diversification value variable is also related to the asymmetric information theory, as undervalued firms wish to undertake a spin-off to be correctly valued by capital markets and reduce adverse selection costs (Nanda and Narayanan 1999). We predict an inverse relationship between the firm's diversification value and the likelihood of spin-off decision, since the lower is the diversification value (the discount), the higher will be the probability a firm will undertake the spin-off.

The logit regression models include a fixed set of three independent variables to control for a firm's performance, degree of diversification, and growth rate, all measured before the spin-off public announcement date. Similar variables have been used in prior empirical research (e.g.,Krishnaswami and Subramaniam 1999). Furthermore, as the sample of parents and matched firms included in the logit regressions are of the same industry, similar size, and book-to-market ratio, we need not control for these specific factors, which could be correlated with spin-off decision.[12]

The logit regression (1) in Table 5 shows that the CEO CHANGE variable is significantly positively related to the spin-off decision, consistent with the managerial incentives hypothesis. Next logit regression (2) indicates that the variable COMPENSATION PLAN is positively associated with the spin-off decision, but it is not significant at conventional level. Comparing the first two regressions Pseudo-R^2, we observe the much higher effect of CEO CHANGE on the spin-off decision.

[12] Our control variables are (1) operating performance ratio (ROA), (2) sales-based Herfindahl index (HERFINDAHL), and (3) the average sales growth over past 3 years (SALES GROWTH). We also run logit regressions using alternative control measures. We use previous-year, parent's stock return to replace ROA, the number of segments at the three-digit SIC code level (SEGMENTS) to replace HERFINDAHL, and the average R&D expenses from the past 3 years (R&D RATIO) to replace SALES GROWTH. When we use a different set of control variables, we obtain similar results.

Table 5 Dependent variable: spin-off indicator

Regression	(1)	(2)	(3)	(4)	(5)	(6)	(7)
CONSTANT	0.319 [0.345]	0.619** [0.325]	0.553* [0.331]	0.211 [0.449]	0.060 [0.600]	0.530 [0.346]	0.586 [0.328]
ROA	−2.045 [1.290]	−2.162* [1.245]	−2.180* [1.304]	−0.469 [2.143]	−0.382 [2.776]	−2.031* [1.228]	−2.031* [1.228]
HERFINDAHL	−0.718* [0.442]	−0.802* [0.445]	−0.941** [0.456]	−0.623 [0.496]	0.251 [0.919]	−0.714 [0.448]	−0.746* [0.443]
SALES GROWTH	0.909 [1.245]	0.997 [1.234]	0.784 [1.250]	1.503 [1.487]	2.298 [2.319]	1.053 [1.246]	0.802 [1.225]
CEO CHANGE	1.416*** [0.449]						
COMPENSATION PLAN		1.504 [1.217]					
TAKEOVER THREAT			2.250*** [0.769]				
ANALYSTS FORECAST				2.712 [1.978]			
DIVERSIFICATION VALUE					−0.486* [0.281]		
DIVESTITURES						0.119 [0.130]	
ACQUISITIONS							0.227 [0.226]
Number of observations	154	154	154	135	85	154	154

(continued)

Table 5 (continued)

Regression	(1)	(2)	(3)	(4)	(5)	(6)	(7)
Pseudo-R^2	0.077	0.034	0.082	0.029	0.035	0.029	0.029
LR-test (χ^2) p-value	0.002	0.124	0.001	0.241	0.398	0.191	0.180

Logit regressions for the determinants of the spin-off decision: This table provides the results of Logit regressions with the spin-off indicator (taking value of one for parent firms and zero for the control firms) as the dependent variable. The sample consists of 97 parent firms and 97 control firms. Parent firms announced and completed a spin-off between January 1989 and June 2005 in 12 European countries. Spin-offs were first identified from Thomson ONE Banker Mergers and Acquisition Database and confirmed by searching Lexis-Nexis and national newspapers databases. The sample excludes spin-offs undertaken by parent firms in regulated and financial industries. Control firms are identified by matching firms by geographic area, industry, market value, and book-to-market ratio ROA (Return on Assets) is measured as the ratio of operating income (total sales minus cost of goods sold and other expenses, before depreciation and amortization) over total assets in the year before the spin-off announcement date. HERFINDAHL index in the year before the announcement of the spin-off is computed as the sum of squares of each segment's sales revenue as a proportion of total sales revenue. SALES GROWTH is the average of the 3-year period before the spin-off announcement date of the annual change in total sales. R&D is the average of 3-year period before the spin-off announcement date of the ratio of R&D expenses over total sales. CEO CHANGE is a dummy that takes the value 1 if the firm experienced a CEO turnover in the year before the spin-off announcement date and zero otherwise. COMPENSATION PLAN is a dummy that takes the value 1 if the firm experienced a change in management and board compensation plans in the year before the spin-off announcement date and zero otherwise. TAKEOVER THREAT is a dummy that takes the value 1 if the firm experienced a merger and/or controlling acquisition attempt in the year before the spin-off announcement date and zero otherwise. ANALYSTS FORECAST is the forecast error of mean analyst estimate of firm earnings per share (source: I/B/E/S/) in the year preceding the spin-off announcement date. DIVERSIFICATION VALUE is computed as in Berger and Ofek (1995) by estimating the difference between the market value of the firm and the sum of the imputed value of all the firm's segments, based on the sales multiplier valuation method of the stand-alone firms. DIVESTITURES is the number of asset sales completed in the year preceding the spin-off announcement date. ACQUISITIONS is the number of acquisitions completed in the year preceding the spin-off announcement date. The χ^2 statistics (log-likelihood ratio) tests the null hypothesis that all the coefficients of the independent variables (except the constant) are equal to zero. Heteroscedasticity-consistent (White 1980) standard errors are in parentheses under the parameter estimates

*, **, *** denote significance level, respectively, at the 10 %, 5 %, and 1 %

Logit model (3) shows that TAKEOVER THREAT is a highly significant determinant of spin-off decision: the estimated coefficient is significant at the 1 % level and the regression is highly significant.

This result is consistent with disciplining effects of market for corporate control, as predicted by the corporate control theory of spin-offs. Logit model (4) directly tests one implication of the asymmetric information hypothesis. Model (4) uses the financial analyst mean forecast error-on-earnings per share, and the estimated coefficient is positive as predicted by theory, but it is not significant at conventional level. Logit regression (5) uses the diversification discount as an alternative proxy of the asymmetric information hypothesis. Although the sample size is reduced due to missing segmental data, the estimated coefficient is of predicted sign and significant at the 10 % level. Regressions (6) and (7) use the DIVESTITURES and ACQUISITIONS variables as alternative proxies to test the corporate control hypothesis. In all the cases, estimated coefficients are positive as expected, yet not significant at conventional levels.

Overall, logit regression results confirm predictions of both the managerial incentives and corporate control hypotheses. We find only weak support for the asymmetric information theory, based on variables related to financial analysts' forecast error and parent-firm relative valuation. The empirical results on the determinants of European spin-offs are novel, and to a certain extent surprising given the prevailing ownership structure, corporate governance, and market mechanisms.

4.4 *Parent Firms Announcement Returns*

In this section, we report evidence of spin-off announcement returns for European parents. We estimate a market model event-study methodology as described in Brown and Warner (1985).[13] We focus on the 3 days announcement window (−1,0, +1), where day 0 is the announcement day retrieved either from Thomson ONE Banker database or an earlier announcement date found in Lexis/Nexis or national press databases. The cumulative abnormal returns (CARs) to parent firms in sample are summarized in Table 6, where, consistent with existing literature, we

[13] We assume that a domestic one-factor model represents the returns generating process: $R_{it} = \alpha_i + \beta_i R_{mt} + \varepsilon_{it}$, where R_{it} is the return of security i on day t, R_{mt} is the return of the DataStream General market index of the parent-firm country on day t, and ε_{it} is a random error term. For each security, the market model is computed over days −220 and −21 relative to the announcement date of the spin-off (day 0). To take into consideration possible problems of nonsynchronous trading, each regression was run using the Scholes and Williams (1977) procedure, and OLS coefficients were adjusted accordingly. Finally, to test for significance of abnormal returns, we follow the Dodd and Warner (1983) method of aggregating standardized abnormal returns.

Table 6 Spin-off announcement-period cumulative abnormal stock returns

Spin-off classification	*N*	Mean	Median	Diff. in means	Diff. in medians	%, positive
Whole sample	97	0.048***	0.027***			64.9***
Focus	61	0.057***	0.022***	0.024*	0.022	62.3**
Non-focus	36	0.033*	0.044***			69.4**
Internally developed	73	0.037***	0.022***	−0.042**	−0.024	64.4***
Previously acquired	24	0.079***	0.046***			66.7**
Internally developed only						
Focus	43	0.036***	0.013**	−0.005	−0.031	58.1
Non-focus	30	0.041***	0.044***			73.3***
Previously acquired only						
Focus	18	0.107***	0.050***	0.112**	0.027	72.0***
Non-focus	6	−0.005	0.023			50.0
Parent M&A within 3-year	13	0.036	0.023	−0.014	−0.005	61.5
No parent M&A	84	0.050***	0.028***			65.5***
Subsidiary M&A within 3-year	15	0.060**	0.041**	0.014	0.016	66.7
No subsidiary M&A	82	0.046***	0.025***			64.6***
Announcement value-added creation (2005 million euros)	97	26.8	8.3			

This table shows cumulative abnormal stock returns over a 3-day interval (−1,0,+1) around the day of spin-off announcement for a sample of 97 spin-offs announced and completed from January 1989 to June 2005 in 12 European countries. The spin-off announcement date was first identified from Thomson ONE Banker Mergers and Acquisition Database and confirmed by searching Lexis-Nexis and national newspapers databases. The sample excludes spin-offs undertaken by parent firms in regulated and financial industries. Abnormal stock returns are computed based on one-factor market model residuals as in Brown and Warner (1985), estimated from day −220 to −21. Market model estimated parameters are adjusted using the Scholes and Williams (1977) procedure to take into account nonsynchronous trading. Focus/Non-Focus classification shows the number of spin-offs with the different/same two-digit primary SIC code of the parent firm. Internally developed/previously acquired classification shows the number of spin-offs that originated from the parent firm's internal growth/past acquisition. Parent (or subsidiary) M&A/no M&A within 3-year classification shows the number of parent firms (or subsidiary firms) that either merged or were involved in a full control acquisition/neither merged nor were acquired within the 3-year period following the spin-off completion month. Tests of significance (Z-statistic) of abnormal returns are done using the Dodd and Warner (1983) method of aggregating standardized abnormal returns. The significance of the difference in means and medians is assessed using the *t*-test, adjusted for difference in sample variances, and a nonparametric median test, respectively. The percentage of positive values is tested for significance using a binomial test. Announcement value-added creation is estimated by multiplying the total market value of equity of the parent firm at the end of month before the announcement date, times the respective 3-day cumulative abnormal stock returns. The results are similar over (−1,0), (−2,+2), and (−5,+5) windows

*, **, *** denote significance level at the 10 %, 5 %, and 1 %, respectively

find an average CAR of 4.8 % (median 2.7 %) for the whole sample of European spin-offs. Both mean and median are significant at the 1 % level, and about 65 % of the sample exhibits positive announcement returns.[14] Moreover, the increase in parent-firm shareholders' wealth averages 26 million euros (median 8 million euros), and it translates into about 10 % of the end-of-ex-month market value of the spun-off unit.

We then turn our attention to differences in abnormal returns between spin-off subgroups. First, we document the difference between focus and non-focus spin-offs. Earlier studies of US spin-offs found that announcement effects of focus-increasing spin-offs are larger than non-focusing spin-offs,[15] which is consistent with predictions of the focus theory. In this study, we define a focus-increasing spin-off when the parent firm and subsidiary firm operate in different two-digit Standard Industry Classification (SIC) codes.[16] Our results show that the average CARs of focus-increasing spin-offs is 5.7 %, significantly greater (at the 10 % level) than the 3.3 % we detected for non-focusing spin-offs. However, there is no significant difference in the two groups' median CARs. Second, when we split the sample between internally developed and previously acquired subsidiaries, we find that previously acquired spin-offs exhibit much larger announcement effects. The difference of average CARs, between the internally developed and previously acquired subgroups, is significant at the 5 % level, but median CARs are not statistically different from each other. This result is consistent with the "correction-of-a-mistake" hypothesis of Allen et al. (1995). Third, we divide the subsample of internally developed spin-offs between focus and non-focus and compute their respective CARs. Our findings show that there is no significant difference between mean and median announcement effects of focus and non-focus spin-offs when we condition on spin-off's origin. This result may also imply that the generally observed higher announcement effect of unconditional focusing spin-offs is probably affected by the higher announcement effect of previously acquired subsidiaries. In order to shed light on our conjecture, we split the sample of previously acquired spin-offs between focus and non-focus.

Focus-increasing spin-offs of previously acquired subsidiaries show a much higher announcement effect (+10.7 %) than non-focusing spin-offs of prior acquired units (−0.5 %). The mean CARs difference is statistically significant and confirms that the

---

[14] Results computed over windows of (−1,0), (−2,+2), and (−5,+5) are similar to those for the (−1,+1) event window.

[15] See, for example, Daley et al. (1997) and Desai and Jain (1999). However, more recently, Gertner et al. (2002) find insignificant differences in the announcement effects of a US sample of focusing versus non-focusing spin-offs.

[16] To verify consistency of the focus/non-focus spin-off classification, we also use the Herfindahl index. Using Worldscope segment data on sales revenue on individual segments, we compute the index as the sum of squares of each segment's sales revenue as a proportion of total sales revenue. Focus-increasing spin-offs are those with an increase in the Herfindahl index of the parent firm from the year before the announcement to the spin-off completion year. With both approaches we obtain the same classification between focus-increasing and non-focus-increasing spin-offs.

higher announcement effect of focusing spin-offs is mostly driven by the "correction-of-a-mistake" hypothesis. Fourth, we directly examine one implication of the corporate control theory, which posits that announcement effects are increasing in the extent of takeover activity and that stock markets are able to anticipate that some spin-offs are undertaken to pursue a merger and acquisition strategy. In order to do this, we split our sample between successively and non-successively merged or acquired parents in the 3 years following the spin-off completion year. Next, we classified spin-offs that were or were not successively merged in the 3 years following the spin-off completion year.[17] Table 6 shows that although all these subgroups exhibit statistically significant announcement mean and median CARs; all estimated differences are insignificant. Finally, we investigated whether there were differences across countries in sample on market reaction to spin-off announcements (results not reported). Although estimated CARs for each country in sample differ, we do not find any statistically significant difference.

The evidence on parent-firm announcement returns shows that the focus/non-focus distinction fails to explain the market reaction on European spin-offs. Instead, our results indicate that a significant component of the focus-increasing explanation of announcement effects is driven by the much higher announcement gain generated by the spin-off of a previously acquired subsidiary, as predicted by the correction-of-a-mistake hypothesis. We also find some evidence of the impact of proxies for information asymmetries on stock price changes. Taken together, we believe our results are consistent with the views proposed by the correction-of-a-mistake hypothesis and asymmetric information theory. There is no evidence that spin-offs announcement returns are somehow related to predictions of managerial incentives and corporate control theories.[18]

[17] Table 6 shows that 13 parents (14 % of the whole sample) and 15 subsidiaries (15 % of the whole sample) were merged or taken over in the 3 years following the spin-off. These figures could be compared to Cusatis et al. (1993) who report that 14 % of both parents and their subsidiaries were taken over or merged in the same time period following the spin-off. Similar figures are reported by Desai and Jain (1999) for 15 % of parents and McConnell et al. (2001) for 13 % of parents and 16 % of subsidiaries. However, a control sample of European firms not involved in a spin-off in the 5 years surrounding (−2,. . .0,. . .+2) the spin-off announcement year (year 0) shows in the same time period that 33 % of parent control firms and 10 % of subsidiary control firms are merged or taken over. It follows that parents in sample are less likely, and subsidiaries in sample are more likely to merge after the spin-off when compared to similar firms. Furthermore, it is worth noting that our sample period is characterized by an increase of both domestic and cross-border mergers across European markets.

[18] A different approach to testing the focus-increasing hypothesis is to document the stock price effects for other firms in the same industry. The information conveyed by spin-off announcements may be relevant for rivals in at least two ways. First, the information may reflect economic conditions facing the industry as a whole. Second, the information may reflect change in the competitive balance within the industry. Thus, in principle, spin-off announcements can have positive, negative, or insignificant price effects on rivals. We implement this test by constructing a sample of parent rivals based on four-digit (or three-digit if four-digit is not available) SIC codes, searching through the whole European databases of DataStream International, Global Vantage, and Amadeus. We then run the event study and compute abnormal returns following the same methodology applied to parents in sample. We obtain the following results: (a) rival firms show no significant price reaction when spin-

4.5 Multivariate Analysis of Spin-Off Announcement Returns

In this section, we use multivariate regression models to test various theories explaining price effects associated with spin-off announcements. We select explanatory variables by following previous studies and inserting new control variables that are not yet tested in the spin-off literature.

The spin-off size is measured as the ratio of subsidiary market value at the end of spin-off completion month to the total firm value before the announcement (RELSIZE). Previous studies have shown that this variable is a significant factor in explaining parent's announcement effects, and it is often associated with evidence-of-efficiency improvements from spin-offs. The focus (FOCUS) indicator is a dummy that is set to 1 if the parent and subsidiary have different two-digit SIC codes and is used to test the main prediction of focus-increasing theory. Univariate evidence of shareholders' wealth creation in Table 6 has shown that share price changes associated with focus-increasing spin-offs are mostly influenced by the spin-off announcement of previously acquired subsidiaries operating in unrelated business. We control for this factor by adding an interaction dummy (FOCUS PASTACQ), which takes the value of 1 if the parent and subsidiary have different two-digit SIC codes and the subsidiary originated from a prior acquisition. In addition, we insert further control variables: a dummy that takes the value of 1 if the subsidiary was created from the parent's past acquisition (PREVIOUSLY ACQUIRED SPIN-OFF), the median industry (defined at the two-digit SIC code level) Tobin's Q of both the parent firm (Q-PARENT INDUSTRY) and the subsidiary firm (Q-SPINOFF INDUSTRY) at the end-of-month prior to the spin-off announcement date.

Furthermore, we use a sales-based Herfindahl index (HERFINDAHL) to control for the claim that that parent firm's announcement share price changes are related to the degree of firm diversification. We expect to find a negative relation between parent-firm announcement excess returns and the Herfindahl index, since the lower the index, the higher the firm extent of diversification. Parents announcing a spin-off are typically refocusing and decreasing the degree of diversification, which

offs are classified as either focus-increasing or non-focus-increasing; (b) rival share prices are negatively and significantly affected when the announcement is related to internally developed subsidiaries; and (c) a positive—although statistically insignificant—price impact is observed for rival firms at the announcement of the spin-off of a previously acquired subsidiary. Furthermore, tests of mean and median differences between the subgroups are all statistically significant at the 5 % level. These results contradict the predictions of the focus-increasing hypothesis and show some evidence that internally developed spin-offs are expected to generate efficiency improvements, maybe at the expense of competitors. The rival firms' weakly positive reaction to previously acquired spin-offs suggests that competitors may gain from the listing of these units, perhaps because of the future availability of potential target firms; a result that would be consistent with predictions of corporate control hypothesis. Rival firms' announcement returns are not tabulated; however, they are available from authors upon request.

should capture some of the further efficiency improvement expected at the time of the spin-off announcement.

The asymmetric information hypothesis predicts that value creation at the spin-off announcement date should be larger when information asymmetries are larger before the breakup and when the firm is more undervalued. We use the residual standard deviation of the market-model-adjusted daily stock returns (RESIDUAL STD) in the event study estimation period (−220, −21) as the first proxy for the level of asymmetric information prior to the spin-off announcement. Following Krishnaswami and Subramaniam (1999), we use another measure of information asymmetry, namely, the standard deviation of financial analysts' earnings forecasts made in the month preceding the spin-off announcement date (ANALYST STD FORECAST), as reported on the Institutional Brokers Estimate System (IBES) database.

The corporate control hypothesis predicts that announcement effects are related to the extent of takeover activity in the parent-firm and subsidiary-firm industries. We construct two types of variables to test the predicted positive relation between takeover activity and spin-off announcement effects. The first type is a dummy that takes 1 for either parents (PARENT MERGER DUMMY) or spin-offs (SPINOFF MERGER DUMMY) that were involved in a merger or were taken over in the 3-year period following the spin-off completion month. The second variable is the ratio of corporate control transactions (million euros) in the 12 months prior to the spin-off announcement for European firms within the same industry (two-digit SIC codes) to the grand total of all European corporate control transactions over the same time period as reported in the Thomson One Banker Mergers and Acquisitions database. Our definition of corporate control transactions includes mergers, acquisitions, and buyouts.

Two independent variables related to corporate governance effects are also inserted in the abnormal return regression models. The first variable is the La Porta et al. (1998) shareholder rights protection, which is a proxy for good governance (ANTIDIRECTOR RIGHTS). It predicts that the higher the country index, the higher should be the market reaction to the spin-off announcement. The second variable is a dummy that takes the value of 1 if the parent firm experiences top management turnover, board changes, outside shareholder pressures, and changes in management compensation plans in the 12-month period prior to the spin-off announcement date (GOVERNANCE CHANGES). We expect a positive relation between recent governance changes and spin-off shareholder wealth effects. Finally, to control for possible country effects in our geographically dispersed sample, we insert country dummies for parents incorporated in Nordic countries (Denmark, Finland, Norway, or Sweden) (COUNTRY DUMMY-Nordic) and UK and Ireland (COUNTRY DUMMY-UK & Ireland).

Table 7 reports the results of the multivariate analysis of determinants of spin-off announcement excess stock returns. The results show a positive relation between the cumulative abnormal returns and the spin-off relative size and alternative proxies for the asymmetric information hypothesis. In the latter case, either the standard deviation of financial analysts' forecasts or the residual market model

Table 7 Multivariate tests of spin-off announcement-period excess returns

	Predicted sign	(1)	(2)	(3)	(4)	(5)
INTERCEPT		−0.006 [−0.41]	0.049 [0.82]	−0.053 [−1.57]	−0.054** [−1.93]	−0.028 [−0.52]
RELSIZE	+	0.072** [1.97]		0.103** [2.48]	0.097*** [2.40]	0.094*** [2.59]
FOCUS	+	0.015 [0.78]	−0.000 [−0.15]	0.023 [1.27]		
FOCUS PASTACQU	+				0.063* [1.73]	0.066** [2.21]
PREVIOUSLY ACQUIRED	+	0.009 [0.37]	0.001 [0.53]			
Q-PARENT INDUSTRY	+		−0.041 [−1.18]			−0.022 [−0.76]
Q-SPINOFF INDUSTRY	+		0.022 [0.92]			−0.012 [−0.57]
HERFINDAHL	−				−0.018 [−0.70]	
RESIDUAL STD	+			1.083 [0.83]	2.457** [2.02]	3.189*** [2.77]
ANALYSTS STD FORECAST	+	0.001*** [4.45]	−0.001 [−0.22]			
PARENT MERGER DUMMY	+	−0.032 [1.61]		−0.008 [−0.33]		
SPINOFF MERGER DUMMY	+	0.028* [1.76]		0.006 [0.30]		
PARENT MERGRESTR	+		−0.003* [−1.85]			
SPINOFF MERGRESTR	+		0.002 [0.81]			
ANTIDIRECTOR RIGHTS	+		0.002 [0.49]	0.008 [1.58]	0.005 [1.06]	0.005 [0.97]
GOVERNANCE CHANGES	+	−0.008 [−0.49]				−0.008 [−0.44]
COUNTRY DUMMY-NORDIC		−0.005 [−0.30]				
COUNTRY DUMMY-UK		−0.002 [−0.11]				
Number of observations		73	67	97	82	88
Adjusted R^2 (%)		7.1	−2.6	7.9	17.6	20.9

(continued)

Table 7 (continued)

	Predicted sign	(1)	(2)	(3)	(4)	(5)
F-test p-value		0.13	0.61	0.04	0.001	<0.001

This table presents OLS regressions to explain parent firms' excess returns around the announcement date of a spin-off for a sample of 97 parent firms that completed a spin-off from January 1989 to June 2005 in 12 European countries. Spin-offs and their announcement dates were first identified from the Thomson ONE Banker Mergers and Acquisition Database and confirmed by searching Lexis-Nexis and national newspaper databases. The sample excludes spin-offs undertaken by parent firms in regulated and financial industries. The dependent variable is the cumulative abnormal stock returns over a 3-day interval (−1,0,+1) around the day of spin-off announcement. Abnormal stock returns are computed based on one-factor market model residuals as in Brown and Warner (1985) estimated from day −220 to −21. Market model estimated parameters are adjusted using the Scholes and Williams (1977) procedure to take into account nonsynchronous trading. The independent variables are as follows: RELSIZE is the ratio of the subsidiary-firm market value to parent-firm market value; FOCUS is a dummy that takes the value 1 if the spun-off subsidiary two-digit primary SIC code is different from the parent firm's main SIC code and zero otherwise; FOCUS PASTACQU is a dummy that takes the value 1 if the spun-off subsidiary has a different two-digit primary SIC code of the parent firm and it originated from the parent firm's past acquisition and zero otherwise; PREVIOUSLY ACQUIRED is a dummy that takes the value 1 if the spun-off subsidiary originated from the parent firm's past acquisition and zero otherwise; Q-PARENT INDUSTRY is median Tobin's Q of all Western Europe firms with equal two-digit SIC codes to parent firms and the end-of-month date before announcement, and it is defined as the ratio of market value of equity, plus book value of total assets minus book value of equity, over book value of total assets; Q-SPINOFF INDUSTRY is median Tobin's Q of all Western Europe firms with equal two-digit SIC codes to subsidiary firms and the end-of-month date before announcement, and it is defined as the ratio of market value of equity, plus the book value of total assets, minus the book value of equity, over book value of total assets; HERFINDAHL is the Herfindahl index before the announcement date and is computed as the sum of squares of each segment's sales revenue as a proportion of total sales revenue; RESIDUAL STD is the residual standard deviation of the market-model-adjusted daily stock returns in the spin-off estimation period (−220 to −21); ANALYST STD FORECAST is the standard deviation of all parent-firm earnings forecasts (from IBES) in the month preceding the spin-off announcement date; PARENT MERGER DUMMY is a dummy that takes the value 1 if the parent firm merged or has been involved in a full control acquisition within the 3-year period following the spin-off completion month and zero otherwise; SPINOFF MERGER DUMMY is a dummy that takes the value 1 if the subsidiary firm merged or has been involved in a full control acquisition within the 3-year period following the spin-off completion month and zero otherwise; PARENT MERGRESTR is the ratio of corporate control transactions (mergers, acquisitions, and buyouts) reported in the Thomson One Banker Mergers and Acquisitions database for all Western Europe firms with same two-digit SIC codes of parent firms over the grand total of European corporate control transaction in the 12 months before the spin-off announcement date; SPINOFF MERGRESTR is the ratio of corporate control transactions (mergers, acquisitions, and buyouts) reported in the Thomson One Banker Mergers and Acquisitions database for all Western Europe firms with same two-digit SIC codes of subsidiary firms over the grand total of European corporate control transaction in the 12 months before the spin-off announcement date; ANTIDIRECTOR RIGHTS is an index aggregating shareholders rights in the parent firm's country and is computed following La Porta et al. (1998); GOVERNANCE CHANGES is a dummy that takes the value 1 if the parent firm experienced either a Management/Board Turnover, an Outside shareholder pressure, or a change in management compensation plans as reported in Table 4 in the 13-month period around the spin-off announcement date and zero otherwise; COUNTRY DUMMY-Nordic is a dummy that takes the value 1 if the parent-firm country of incorporation is either Denmark, Finland, Norway, or Sweden and zero otherwise; COUNTRY DUMMY-UK & Ireland is a dummy that takes the value 1 if the parent-firm country of incorporation is either the United Kingdom or Ireland and zero otherwise. The t-statistics for the regression coefficients are reported in brackets and use the heteroscedasticity-consistent standard errors of White's (1980)

*, **, *** denote significance level, respectively, at 10 %, 5 %, and 1 %

volatility enters the regression model with the expected sign and significant at conventional levels. On the contrary, we find no significant relation between announcement effect and the refocusing dummy. Moreover, when we condition the refocusing dummy on previously acquired subsidiary, the variable becomes statistically significant at 5 % level, confirming the univariate results of Table 6 that most of shareholder wealth effects on refocusing strategy are driven by larger share price changes following the announcement of previously acquired spin-offs. These results support predictions of the efficiency gain, the asymmetric information, and the correction-of-a-mistake hypotheses. In contrast, no support is found for the corporate control hypothesis.

4.6 Spin-Off Firms' Long-Term Stock Returns

Our main measure of spin-off efficiency improvements is based on abnormal stock returns observed up to 3 years after the transaction is completed. Furthermore, we examine ex post operating performance for the separated units in order to provide a different perspective on spin-off efficiency improvements. In this section, we focus on long-term, abnormal stock returns following the monthly calendar-time portfolio approach proposed by Fama (1998) and used by Mitchell and Stafford (2000) and McConnell et al. (2001). In the next section, we present robustness tests that look at an alternative approach to measure long-run abnormal stock returns.

We create equally weighted (EW) and value-weighted (VW) portfolios of parent firms and subsidiary firms each month, from January 1993 to October 2006, that were involved in the spin-off transaction within the previous 3 years, and sample firms are included in each portfolio starting from the spin-off completion-month (ex-month).[19] We follow the Fama and French (1993) approach to construct the three-risk-factor regression model, as in Eq. (1):

$$R_{p,t} - r_{f,t} = a_p + b_p\left(R_{\mathrm{M},t} - r_{f,t}\right) + s_p\,\mathrm{SMB} + h_p\,\mathrm{HML} + \varepsilon_{p,t} \tag{1}$$

The market excess return $\left(R_{\mathrm{M},t} - r_{f,t}\right)$ is constructed as the difference between the value-weighted Morgan Stanley International Europe index and the 1-month Euro interest rate (the corresponding German 1-month interest rate is used as risk-free rate proxy from January 1993 to December 1998). The small-minus-big, zero-investment portfolio (SMB) is computed as the difference between the value-weighted Morgan Stanley International Europe Small Cap index and the value-weighted Morgan Stanley International Europe index. The high BE/ME stocks minus the low BE/ME stocks zero-investment portfolio (HML) is computed as the difference between the value-weighted Morgan Stanley International Europe

[19] We exclude parent and subsidiary firms' stock returns from 1989 to 1992 from our calendar-time portfolio tests because of the small number of observations in those first 4 years.

Value Stocks index and the value-weighted Morgan Stanley International Europe Growth Stocks index. Monthly returns are converted to Euro using DataStream exchange rate series.[20] Within the Fama and French's (1993) framework, the intercept a_p measures the portfolio-average monthly abnormal return, and it is zero under the null hypothesis of no abnormal performance.

Table 8 reports the regression coefficient estimates for parent firms. The results for the whole sample are presented in panel A and show that the intercept is a monthly 0.5 %, statistically significant for both EW and VW portfolios. This implies that investing in a portfolio of parent firms undertaking a spin-off would have earned an average risk-adjusted return of over 19 % over the 3-year holding period from the spin-off completion month. Panel B1 of Table 8 reports the results for the focus-increasing parents. Although intercept estimates are positive for both EW and VW portfolios, their *t*-statistics are not significant at 5 % level. In the panel B2, we report the estimates for the non-focus-increasing parents. The results show a statistically significant 0.8 % for the EW and an insignificant 0.6 % for the VW portfolio.

Panel C1 of Table 8 shows the estimates for the internally developed spin-offs. In this sample too, we uncover a statistically significant intercept in the case of the EW portfolio, but a positive (although insignificant) estimate for the VW portfolio. Panel C2 of Table 8 shows the estimates for the previously acquired spin-offs, and none of the intercepts are significant at conventional levels. Panel D of Table 8 reports results when conditioning on parents involved/not involved in merger and acquisition activity after the spin-off completion. There are very few cases of parents being acquired or merged subsequently to the spin-off, and we are not able to provide meaningful regression results for that subsample of parent firms. However, panel D reports that parent firms, not involved in merger and acquisition transactions in the years following a spin-off, generate positive long-term excess returns. The estimates are statistically significant for the EW portfolio and also positive, although of lower significance level (10 %) for the VW portfolio. Table 8 results of parent-firm, long-term stock returns are novel in the spin-off literature, but can be compared to earlier studies of spin-off, long-term returns using different empirical methods. Our findings neither confirm that parents involved in takeover activity are creating value in the long term (e.g., Cusatis et al. 1993) nor confirm that parents that increased their focus exhibit a positive and significant stock market performance following spin-offs (e.g., Desai and Jain 1999). The results suggest instead that the parents that engage in a spin-off, of either an internally developed subsidiary or a close business segment (nonfocusing), and avoid being involved in a

[20] It is interesting to note that the European version of the Fama and French (1993), three-factor model is statistically similar to the US version available on Kenneth French's website. In the calendar-time portfolio regression sample period, the risk factors' Spearman correlation coefficients are 0.78, 0.21, and 0.22, respectively, for market excess return, SMB, and HML. All correlation coefficients are significant at the 1 % level. Moreover, mean and median monthly returns of European risk factors are not significantly different from the US Fama–French risk factors.

Table 8 Calendar-time portfolio regressions for parent-firms

	OBS	Average no. of firms in portfolio	Regression model	Constant $\hat{a}_i$	Europe market excess return $\hat{b}_i$	Europe small-minus-big return $\hat{s}_i$	Europe high-minus-low return $\hat{h}_i$	Adjusted $\overline{R}^2$ (%)
Panel A: All parent-firms	166	34.4	Model 1—Equally weighted portfolio $R_{p(\text{EW})} - r_f$	**0.005** [2.473]	0.936 [18.064]	0.534 [7.034]	−0.220 [−2.535]	71.7
			Model 2—Value-weighted portfolio $R_{p(\text{VW})} - r_f$	**0.005** [2.028]	0.836 [12.003]	0.205 [2.132]	−0.029 [−0.280]	58.9
Panel B1: Focus-increasing parent-firms	166	23.2	Model 1—Equally weighted portfolio $R_{p(\text{EW})} - r_f$	0.004 [1.768]	0.938 [15.300]	0.536 [6.180]	−0.251 [−2.457]	68.4
			Model 2—Value-weighted portfolio $R_{p(\text{VW})} - r_f$	0.005 [1.849]	1.007 [13.539]	0.264 [2.732]	−0.265 [−2.249]	61.4
Panel B2: Non-focus-increasing	166	11.2	Model 1—Equally weighted portfolio $R_{p(\text{EW})} - r_f$	**0.008** [2.144]	0.882 [13.265]	0.374 [2.784]	0.049 [0.394]	42.5
			Model 2—Value-weighted portfolio $R_{p(\text{VW})} - r_f$	0.006 [1.723]	0.669 [6.919]	0.112 [0.804]	0.345 [2.357]	40.7
Panel C1: Internally developed subsidiary	166	22.8	Model 1—Equally weighted portfolio $R_{p(\text{EW})} - r_f$	**0.005** [2.341]	1.013 [22.271]	0.526 [6.724]	−0.274 [−3.157]	71.8
			Model 2—Value-weighted portfolio $R_{p(\text{VW})} - r_f$	0.005 [1.724]	0.980 [8.489]	0.253 [2.020]	−0.226 [−1.416]	54.7

(continued)

Table 8 (continued)

	OBS	Average no. of firms in portfolio	Regression model	Constant $\hat{a}_i$	Europe market excess return $\hat{b}_i$	Europe small-minus-big return $\hat{s}_i$	Europe high-minus-low return $\hat{h}_i$	Adjusted $\overline{R}^2$ (%)
Panel C2: Previously acquired subsidiary	166	11.6	Model 1—Equally weighted portfolio $R_{p(\mathrm{EW})} - r_f$	0.004 [1.493]	0.754 [8.276]	0.385 [3.347]	0.033 [0.254]	45.6
			Model 2—Value-weighted portfolio $R_{p(\mathrm{VW})} - r_f$	0.006 [1.784]	0.585 [6.468]	0.055 [0.451]	0.265 [1.846]	34.5
Panel D: No M&A within 3-year	166	32.3	Model 1—Equally weighted portfolio $R_{p(\mathrm{EW})} - r_f$	**0.005** [2.176]	0.922 [18.304]	0.476 [6.457]	−0.175 [−1.956]	71.2
			Model 2—Value-weighted portfolio $R_{p(\mathrm{VW})} - r_f$	0.004 [1.544]	0.774 [13.544]	0.061 [0.745]	0.039 [0.396]	56.9

$R_{p,t} - r_{f,t} = a_p + b_p\left(R_{\mathrm{M},t} - r_{f,t}\right) + s_p\,\mathrm{SMB} + h_p\,\mathrm{HML} + \varepsilon_{p,t}$. This table presents calendar-time portfolio regressions using Fama and French (1993) three-factor model over the period after the spin-off completion month for a sample of parent firms that completed spin-offs from January 1989 to June 2005 in 12 European countries. Sample firms are included in a particular monthly portfolio from the month following $(t+1)$ the spin-off completion month ($t=$ ex-month), and the time series of calendar-time portfolio returns is from January 1993 to October 2006. R_{M} is the return on the value-weighted index of Europe in month t computed by Morgan Stanley International. $r_{f,t}$ is the 1-month Germany-EU Deutsche mark interest rate, observed at the beginning of the month and is obtained from DataStream (Series ECWGM1M). SMB is the return on small firms index, minus the return on large firms' index in month t, and it is computed as the difference between the Morgan Stanley International Europe Small Cap and the Morgan Stanley International Europe. HML is the return on value stocks index, minus the return on growth stocks index in month t, and it is computed as the difference between the Morgan Stanley International Europe Value and the Morgan Stanley International Europe Growth. Where required, index and stock returns have been converted into euros using DataStream exchange rate series. In regression model (1), the dependent variable is the excess return of the equally weighted portfolio of sample firms, $R_{p(\mathrm{EW})} - r_f$. In regression model (2), the dependent variable is the excess return of the value-weighted portfolio of sample firms, $R_{p(\mathrm{VW})} - r_f$ using total market value at the beginning of the month. The t-statistics for the regression coefficients are reported in brackets and use the heteroscedasticity-consistent standard errors of White's (1980). All significant intercepts at 5 % or better are marked in bold merger, exhibit higher and more significant long-term stock market performance in the 3 years following spin-offs.

Table 9 reports the calendar-time regression coefficient estimates for subsidiary firms.

The results for spun-off units mostly mirror the findings for parent firms, but are statistically more robust. Results for the whole sample presented in panel A show that the intercept is a highly significant monthly 0.7 % for the EW portfolio and a 1.2 % for the VW portfolio. Results for the VW portfolio imply that investing in a portfolio of spun-off firms would have earned an average risk-adjusted return of over 53 % over the 3-year holding period from the spin-off completion month. Results reported in panel B2 for non-focusing spin-offs, in panel C1 for internally developed subsidiaries and in panel D2 for spin-offs not involved in merger and acquisition activity, all show which spin-offs are creating value through long-term stock returns. Our findings for spin-offs do not confirm past results that long-term value creation is created through either takeover activity (e.g., Cusatis et al. 1993) or by undertaking focus-increasing spin-offs (e.g., Desai and Jain 1999).

4.7 *Alternative Measure of Long-Term Abnormal Stock Returns*

In this subsection, we examine long-term abnormal returns computed as buy-and-hold returns (BHARs) to check the robustness of the evidence provided by calendar-time regression tests and make our results comparable to previous research.[21]

Fama (1998) and Mitchell and Stafford (2000) argue that the BHARs methodology could be severely flawed because it assumes independence of multiyear abnormal returns for event firms, producing test statistics that are typically too large. The source of test statistics bias is the cross-correlation of event firms, since many corporate

[21] BHARs are obtained from two different approaches. In the first, we apply a matching firm methodology by selecting a control firm for each parent or subsidiary from the sample of firms that did not undertake a spin-off in the 5 years centered on the spin-off completion year (−2,. . .0,. . . +2), which is headquartered in the same geographic area [(1) UK and Ireland; (2) Nordic Countries (Denmark, Finland, Norway, and Sweden); and (3) Continental Europe (Belgium, Germany, Italy, Netherlands, Spain, and Switzerland)], has the same two-digit SIC code, and is closest in market value of equity (±30 %) and book-to-market ratio. If we do not find a matching firm in the same geographic area, we rely on the whole European data set to identify the closest firm by industry, market value of equity, and book-to-market ratio. If the matching firm stock return data are missing (e.g., because of merger, going private, etc.), we replace it with the second closest matching firm, and so on, if subsequent missing data occur. In the same way, if a parent or a subsidiary firm in sample disappears from the database, we replace it with returns time series of the matched firm. In the second approach, we use the firm's country market index as a benchmark. With this approach, missing stock return data for firms in sample are replaced with country market index returns from that point on.

Table 9 Calendar-time portfolio regressions for subsidiary firms

	OBS	Average number of firms in portfolio	Regression model	Constant $\hat{a}_i$	Europe market excess return $\hat{b}_i$	Europe small-minus-big return $\hat{s}_i$	Europe high-minus-low return $\hat{h}_i$	Adjusted $\overline{R}^2$ (%)
Panel A: Spin-off whole Sample	166	34.4	Model 1—Equally weighted portfolio $R_{p(\mathrm{EW})} - r_f$	**0.007** [3.125]	0.833 [16.749]	0.678 [6.846]	−0.233 [−2.509]	67.6
			Model 2—Value-weighted portfolio $R_{p(\mathrm{VW})} - r_f$	**0.012** [5.674]	0.777 [16.525]	0.100 [1.365]	−0.106 [−1.007]	61.8
Panel B1: Focus-increasing	166	23.7	Model 1—Equally weighted portfolio $R_{p(\mathrm{EW})} - r_f$	0.004 [1.621]	0.840 [14.107]	0.618 [5.188]	−0.214 [−1.914]	58.9
			Model 2—Value-weighted portfolio $R_{p(\mathrm{VW})} - r_f$	0.003 [0.845]	0.666 [8.665]	0.272 [1.848]	−0.137 [−0.908]	32.7
Panel B2: Non-focus-increasing	166	10.8	Model 1—Equally weighted portfolio $R_{p(\mathrm{EW})} - r_f$	**0.013** [4.699]	0.821 [12.354]	0.786 [6.357]	−0.279 [−1.782]	57.5
			Model 2—Value-weighted portfolio $R_{p(\mathrm{VW})} - r_f$	**0.016** [5.250]	0.883 [10.908]	0.108 [1.057]	−0.182 [−1.227]	48.2
Panel C1: Internally developed subsidiary	166	24.0	Model 1—Equally weighted portfolio $R_{p(\mathrm{EW})} - r_f$	**0.011** [4.087]	0.822 [14.439]	0.718 [6.242]	−0.237 [−2.385]	58.1
			Model 2—Value-weighted portfolio $R_{p(\mathrm{VW})} - r_f$	**0.013** [5.234]	0.827 [14.715]	0.049 [0.562]	−0.157 [−1.252]	52.5

Panel C2: Previously acquired subsidiary	166	10.4	Model 1—Equally weighted portfolio $R_{p(\text{EW})} - r_f$	−0.002 [−0.497]	0.843 [11.455]	0.560 [4.439]	−0.179 [−1.226]	48.2
			Model 2—Value-weighted portfolio $R_{p(\text{VW})} - r_f$	0.006 [1.548]	0.598 [6.426]	0.216 [1.303]	0.212 [1.194]	29.2
Panel D: No M&A within 3-year	166	32.3	Model 1—Equally weighted portfolio $R_{p(\text{EW})} - r_f$	**0.007** [2.972]	0.860 [16.648]	0.652 [6.126]	−0.215 [−2.255]	67.5
			Model 2—Value-weighted portfolio $R_{p(\text{VW})} - r_f$	**0.011** [5.512]	0.824 [16.396]	0.107 [1.332]	−0.113 [−1.021]	62.6

$R_{p,t} - r_{f,t} = a_p + b_p(R_{\text{M},t} - r_{f,t}) + s_p\,\text{SMB} + h_p\,\text{HML} + \varepsilon_{p,t}$. This table presents calendar-time portfolio regressions using Fama and French (1993) three-factor model over the period after the spin-off completion month for a sample of spin-offs completed from January 1989 to June 2005 in 12 European countries. Sample firms are included in a particular monthly portfolio from the month following ($t+1$) the spin-off completion month ($t=$ ex-month), and the time series of calendar-time portfolio returns is from January 1993 to October 2006. R_{M} is the return on the value-weighted index of Europe in month t computed by Morgan Stanley International. $r_{f,t}$ is the 1-month Germany-EU Deutsche mark interest rate, observed at the beginning of the month and is obtained from DataStream (Series ECWGM1M). SMB is the return on small firms index, minus the return on large firms' index in month t, and it is computed as the difference between the Morgan Stanley International Europe Small Cap and the Morgan Stanley International Europe. HML is the return on value stocks index, minus the return on growth stocks index in month t, and it is computed as the difference between the Morgan Stanley International Europe Value and the Morgan Stanley International Europe Growth. Where required, index and stock returns have been converted into euros using DataStream exchange rate series. In the regression model (1), the dependent variable is the excess return of the equally weighted portfolio of sample firms, $R_{p(\text{EW})} - r_f$. In the regression model (2), the dependent variable is the excess return of the value-weighted portfolio of sample firms, $R_{p(\text{VW})} - r_f$ using total market value at the beginning of the month. The t-statistics for the regression coefficients are reported in brackets and use the heteroscedasticity-consistent standard errors of White's (1980). All significant intercepts at 5 % or better are marked in bold actions are not random events, but typically cluster by industry and by time. Mitchell and Stafford (2000) examine three large samples of US mergers, equity offers, and share repurchases and show that BHARs exhibit average positive correlation in all three samples. The average positive correlation is then affecting the statistical inference of BHARs, which assumes their independence. They propose to correct standard t-statistics, by accounting for dependence in individual BHARs, and present evidence that abnormal returns show no statistical significance for the three event samples.

We are not aware of any attempt to examine the degree of BHARs cross-correlations using an international sample of corporate events. We follow the methodology proposed by Mitchell and Stafford (2000, Appendix, pp. 326–328) to account for cross-correlation of individual BHARs in our sample of European spin-offs and adjust the t-statistics accordingly. Our findings, however, differ from Mitchell and Stafford (2000). First, we uncover an average negative cross-correlation between individual BHARs of parent firms (−0.007) and a slightly positive cross-correlation between individual BHARs of spin-off firms (0.005). Second, by applying the proposed correction method, t-statistics become almost two times higher in the case of parent BHARs and about 19 % lower for subsidiaries.[22] Our findings show that similar corporate events in international markets are less likely to be clustered by industry and time, and the assumption of event independence is reasonable and would not significantly affect standard statistical inference.

Empirical results on long-term, abnormal returns, for European parent firms and subsidiary firms following the spin-off, highlight three relevant findings: (1) positive long-term stock returns are attributable to spun-off units; parents of spin-offs typically underperform benchmarks unless they are merged or taken over; (2) internally developed subsidiaries and units related to a parent's business activity are the spin-offs which generate higher and highly significant abnormal returns in the long term; (3) at the pro forma, combined firm level, the transactions which earn higher (and some statistically significant) abnormal returns are those that separate an internally developed subsidiary. Our evidence differs from past US studies, which find that either focus-increasing spin-offs (e.g., Daley et al. 1997; Desai and Jain 1999) or takeovers of either the parent or the subsidiary (Cusatis et al. 1993) are the spin-off transactions which generate higher long-term stock returns. The interesting empirical result emerging from long-term abnormal return tests is the clear consistency of BHARs evidence and the findings using the calendar-time portfolio regression approach.

4.8 Spin-Off Firms Long-Term Operating Performance

The previous section shows that internally developed subsidiaries and units operating in the parent industry are the spin-offs that outperform in the long-term, risk-

[22] Specifically, only three t-statistics of spin-off individual BHARs reduce their level of significance from 1 % to 5 %.

adjusted benchmarks. This section explores two issues: (1) whether post-spin-off efficiency improvements are also evident at the operating level and (2) whether measures of long-term operating performance are consistent with results of long-term stock returns. We compute two measures of operating performance, and our methodology follows early studies of post-spin-off operating performance (e.g., Daley et al. 1997; Desai and Jain 1999) and incorporates the suggestions of methodological papers such as Barber and Lyon (1996) and Lie (2001).[23]

Our main findings are summarized as follows[24]: (a) parent firms do not show any improvement in operating performance after the spin-off is completed. This result holds using either benchmark and adopting different statistical methods; (b) subsidiary firms show statistically significant improvements in operating performance starting in the spin-off completion year. The subsidiary operating efficient improvements are statistically higher than control firms' and median industry levels. Of various groups of spin-off firms, non-focusing and internally developed subsidiaries are those that show the higher and mostly significant levels of abnormal operating performance. For these two subgroups of corporate spin-offs, it is interesting to notice the clear link between long-term, excess stock returns and concurrent, fundamental (accounting) performance. These results are in contrast with findings of early US studies of corporate spin-offs in which the only subgroup of transactions that showed significantly improved operating performance after a spin-off was the focus-increasing one (e.g., Daley et al. 1997; Desai and Jain 1999). Furthermore, our results show that significant operating performance improvements are generated only at the subsidiary level and not within parent firms.

5 Conclusion

This study helps to increase our understanding of the decision to spin off a subsidiary and the economic consequences of spin-offs. We document that spin-off decisions in Europe are often triggered by a firm's governance earthquakes, such as an appointment of a new CEO or a takeover threat. These findings indicate that even in less active markets for mergers and corporate restructuring, breakup decisions are enforced by the monitoring activity of outside investors and capital

---

[23] The two measures of operating performance are the ratio of operating cash flow to the average of beginning and ending period book value of total assets (ROA) and the ratio of operating cash flow to total sales (ROS). To control for macroeconomic and industry effects, we adjust both ROA and ROS using two different benchmarks: (a) matched control firm and (b) median industry operating performance. Matched control firm is identified in the same way as described in Sect. 3.2. The median industry operating performance is obtained by selecting all European firms with the same two-digit SIC code and computing the median operating performance within the subset of firms with the closest market value of equity (±30 %).

[24] To save space we do not present tables reporting BHARs results, but they are available from the authors upon request.

markets. Our empirical study has shown that a significant component of stock price appreciation observed around spin-off announcement date is driven by the reverse of previous diversifying mergers. An implication of our research is that care should be used in spin-off studies by identifying the subsidiary's origin, a characteristic that appears to be more relevant than classifying spun-off units into focus-increasing and non-focus-increasing. Finally, we show that long-term efficiency improvement of spin-offs is generated mostly by internally developed subsidiaries and parent-related units (non-focusing). These findings contrast the US evidence, where focus-increasing spin-offs and spin-offs involved in subsequent mergers are those showing significant value creation and efficiency improvements.

In summary, our study shows that corporate spin-offs could be successful transactions when the parent firm is divesting an internally developed unit, and we suggest that our results are consistent with the growing view that a firm's corporate culture and an individual managers' style can play an important role in corporate behavior and economic performance.

Appendix 1: Variables Definitions

Variable	Definition	Data source
ACQUISITIONS	Total number of acquisitions completed by the firm in the year preceding the spin-off announcement date	Thomson One Banker
ANALYSTS FORECAST	Forecast error of mean analyst estimates of a firm's earnings per share in the year preceding the spin-off announcement date	I/B/E/S
ANALYST STD FORECAST	Standard deviation of a firm's earnings forecasts in the month preceding the spin-off announcement date	I/B/E/S
ANTIDIRECTOR RIGHTS	Index of aggregated shareholders' rights protection for the firm's country of incorporation	La Porta et al. (1998)
CEO CHANGE	Dummy that takes the value of 1 if the firm experienced a CEO turnover in the year before the spin-off announcement date and zero otherwise	LexisNexis
COMPENSATION PLAN	Dummy that takes the value of 1 if the firm experienced a change in management and board compensation plans in the year before the spin-off announcement date and zero otherwise	LexisNexis
COUNTRY DUMMY-NORDIC	Dummy that takes the value of 1 if the firm's country of incorporation is Denmark, Finland, Norway, or Sweden and zero otherwise	Own computations
COUNTRY DUMMY-BRITISH	Dummy that takes the value of 1 if the firm's country of incorporation is either United Kingdom or Ireland and zero otherwise	Own computations

(continued)

Variable	Definition	Data source
DIVERSIFICATION VALUE	The value of diversification discount computed as in Berger and Ofek (1995) by estimating the difference between the market value of the firm and the sum of the imputed value of all the firm's segments, based on the sales multiplier valuation method of the stand-alone firms	WorldScope, own computations
DIVESTITURES	Total number of asset sales completed by the firm in the year preceding the spin-off announcement date	Thomson One Banker
FOCUS	Dummy that takes the value of 1 if the spin-off subsidiary's two-digit primary SIC code is different from the parent firm's main SIC code and zero otherwise	Thomson One Banker, WorldScope, Amadeus
FOCUS PASTACQU	Dummy that takes the value of 1 if the spin-off subsidiary has a different two-digit primary SIC code from the parent firm and is originated from the parent firm's past acquisition and zero otherwise	Own computations
GOVERNANCE CHANGES	Dummy that takes the value of 1 if the parent firm experienced either a Management/Board turnover, or an outside shareholder pressure or a change in management compensation plans as reported in Table 4 in the 13-month period around the spin-off announcement date and zero otherwise	LexisNexis
GROWTH	Average annual growth rate of net sales of the company during the 3 years before the spin-off announcement	DataStream, own computations
HERFINDAHL	HERFINDAHL index in the year before the announcement of the spin-off computed as the sum of squares of each segment's sales revenue as a proportion of total sales revenue	WorldScope, own computations
PARENT MERGER DUMMY	Dummy that takes the value of 1 if the parent firm merged or has been involved in a full-control acquisition within the 3-year period following the spin-off completion month and zero otherwise	LexisNexis
PARENT MERGRESTR	Ratio of total number of corporate control transactions (mergers, acquisitions, and buy-outs) for all Western European firms with the same two-digit SIC codes as parent firms, over the total number of European corporate control transactions in the 12 months before the spin-off announcement date	Thomson One Banker
PREVIOUSLY ACQUIRED	Dummy that takes the value of 1 if the spin-off subsidiary originated from the parent firm's past acquisition and zero otherwise	LexisNexis
Q-PARENT INDUSTRY	Median Tobin's *Q* of all Western European firms with same two-digit SIC code as the parent firm at the end of month before the	DataStream, own computations

(continued)

Variable	Definition	Data source
	announcement date. Tobin's Q is estimated as the ratio of market value of equity, plus the book value of total assets, minus the book value of equity, over the book value of total assets	
Q-SPINOFF INDUSTRY	Median Tobin's *Q* of all Western European firms with same two-digit SIC code as the spin-off subsidiary at the end of month before announcement date. Tobin's Q is estimated as the ratio of market value of equity, plus the book value of total assets, minus the book value of equity, over the book value of total assets	DataStream, own computations
R&D	Average ratio of R&D expenses over total sales for the 3 years before the spin-off announcement date	DataStream, own computations
RELSIZE	Ratio of the subsidiary-firm market value to the parent-firm market value	DataStream, own computations
RELSIZE[2]	RELSIZE variable squared	Own computations
RESIDUAL STD	Residual standard deviation of the market-model adjusted daily stock returns in the spin-off estimation period (−220 to −21)	DataStream, own computations
SEGMENTS	Number of segments of the company at three-digit SIC code level in the year before the announcement of the spin-off	WorldScope
SPINOFF MERGER DUMMY	Dummy that takes the value of 1 if the subsidiary firm merged or has been involved in a full-control acquisition within the 3-year period following the spin-off completion month and zero otherwise	LexisNexis
SPINOFF MERGRESTR	Ratio of total number of corporate control transactions (mergers, acquisitions and buy-outs) for all Western European firms with same two-digit SIC codes as the spin-off subsidiary over the total number of European corporate control transactions in the 12 months before the spin-off announcement date	Thomson One Banker
STOCK RETURN	Total stock return (including cash dividends) net of country market index return in the year before the spin-off announcement date	DataStream, own computations.
TAKEOVER THREAT	Dummy that takes the value of 1 if the firm experienced a merger and/or controlling acquisition attempt in the year before the spin-off announcement date and zero otherwise	LexisNexis

[2] relsize squared

References

Ahn, S., & Denis, D. (2004). Internal capital markets and investment policy: Evidence from corporate spinoffs. *Journal of Financial Economics, 71*, 489–516.

Ahn, S., & Walker, M. D. (2007). Corporate governance and the spinoff decision. *Journal of Corporate Finance, 13*, 76–93.

Allen, J. W., Lummer, S. L., McConnell, J. J., & Reed, D. K. (1995). Can takeover losses explain spin-off gains? *Journal of Financial and Quantitative Analysis, 30*, 465–485.

Aron, D. J. (1991). Using the capital market as a monitor: Corporate spinoffs in an agency framework. *Rand Journal of Economics, 22*, 505–518.

Barber, B. M., & Lyon, J. D. (1996). Detecting abnormal operating performance: The empirical power and specification of test statistics. *Journal of Financial Economics, 41*, 359–399.

Berger, P., & Ofek, E. (1995). Diversification's effect on firm value. *Journal of Financial Economics, 37*, 39–65.

Berger, P., & Ofek, E. (1999). Causes and effects of corporate refocusing programs. *Review of Financial Studies, 12*, 311–345.

Brown, S. J., & Warner, J. B. (1985). Using daily stock returns: The case of event studies. *Journal of Financial Economics, 14*, 3–31.

Chemmanur, T., & Nandy, D. (2006). How do spin-offs increase efficiency? A look inside the black box. Unpublished working paper, Carroll School of Management, Boston College.

Chemmanur, T., & Paeglis, I. (2001). Why issue tracking stocks? Insights from a comparison with spin-offs and carve-outs. *Journal of Applied Corporate Finance, 14*, 102–114.

Chemmanur, T., & Yan, A. (2004). A theory of corporate spin-offs. *Journal of Financial Economics, 72*, 259–290.

Choi, Y. K., & Han, S. H. (2006). Internal capital markets and bank relationships: Evidence from Japanese corporate spin-offs. Unpublished working paper, University of Central Florida.

Comment, R., & Jarrell, G. A. (1995). Corporate focus and stock returns. *Journal of Financial Economics, 37*, 67–87.

Cusatis, P. J., Miles, J. A., & Woolridge, J. R. (1993). Restructuring through spin-offs, the stock market evidence. *Journal of Financial Economics, 33*, 293–311.

Daley, L., Mehrotra, V., & Sivakumar, R. (1997). Corporate focus and value creation: Evidence from spin-off. *Journal of Financial Economics, 45*, 257–281.

Denis, D. J., Denis, D. K., & Sarin, A. (1997). Agency problems, equity ownership, and corporate diversification. *Journal of Finance, 52*, 135–160.

Desai, H., & Jain, P. (1999). Firm performance and focus: Long-run and stock market performance following spin-offs. *Journal of Financial Economics, 54*, 75–101.

Dittmar, A., & Shivdasani, A. (2003). Divestitures and divisional investment policies. *Journal of Finance, 58*, 2711–2743.

Dodd, P., & Warner, J. B. (1983). On corporate governance. A study of proxy contests. *Journal of Financial Economics, 11*, 401–438.

Faccio, M., & Lang, L. (2002). The ultimate ownership of western European corporations. *Journal of Financial Economics, 65*, 365–395.

Fama, E. F. (1998). Market efficiency, long-term returns and behavioral finance. *Journal of Financial Economics, 49*, 283–306.

Fama, E. F., & French, K. R. (1993). Common risk factors in the returns on stocks and bonds. *Journal of Financial Economics, 33*, 3–56.

Galai, D., & Masulis, R. W. (1976). The option pricing model and the risk factor of stock. *Journal of Financial Economics, 3*, 53–81.

Gertner, R., Powers, E., & Scharfstein, D. (2002). Learning about internal capital markets from corporate spinoffs. *Journal of Finance, 57*, 2479–2506.

Gilson, S. C., Healy, P. M., Noe, C. F., & Palepu, K. G. (2001). Analyst specialization and conglomerate stock breakups. *Journal of Accounting Research, 39*, 565–582.

Habib, M. A., Johnsen, D. B., & Naik, N. Y. (1997). Spinoffs and information. *Journal of Financial Intermediation, 6*, 153–176.
Hite, G., & Owers, J. (1983). Security price reactions around corporate spin-off announcements. *Journal of Financial Economics, 12*, 409–436.
John, T. A. (1993). Optimality of spin-offs and allocation of debt. *Journal of Financial and Quantitative Analysis, 28*, 139–160.
John, K., & Ofek, E. (1995). Asset sales and increase in focus. *Journal of Financial Economics, 37*, 105–126.
Kaplan, S. N., & Weisbach, M. S. (1992). The success of acquisitions: Evidence from divestitures. *Journal of Finance, 47*, 107–138.
Krishnaswami, S., & Subramaniam, V. (1999). Information asymmetry, valuation and the corporate spin-off decision. *Journal of Financial Economics, 53*, 73–112.
La Porta, R., Lopez-de-Silanes, F., & Shleifer, A. (1998). Law and finance. *Journal of Political Economy, 106*(6), 1113–1155.
Lang, L. H. P., & Stulz, R. (1994). Tobin's q, corporate diversification, and firm performance. *Journal of Political Economy, 102*, 1248–1260.
Lie, E. (2001). Detecting abnormal operating performance: Revisited. *Financial Management, Summer*, 5–30.
Lins, K., & Servaes, H. (1999). International evidence on the value of corporate diversification. *Journal of Finance, 54*, 2215–2240.
Maxwell, W. F., & Rao, R. P. (2003). Do spin-offs expropriate wealth from bondholders? *Journal of Finance, 58*, 2087–2108.
McConnell, J. J., Ozbilgin, M., & Wahal, S. (2001). Spin-offs, ex-ante. *Journal of Business, 74*, 245–280.
Michaely, R., & Shaw, W. H. (1995). The choice of going public: Spin-offs vs. carve-outs. *Financial Management, 24*, 5–21.
Miles, J., & Rosenfeld, J. (1983). An empirical analysis of the effects of spin-off announcements on shareholder wealth. *Journal of Finance, 38*, 1597–1606.
Mitchell, M. L., & Stafford, E. (2000). Managerial decisions and long-term stock price performance. *Journal of Business, 73*, 287–329.
Mulherin, J. H., & Boone, A. L. (2000). Comparing acquisitions and divestitures. *Journal of Corporate Finance, 6*, 117–139.
Nanda, V., & Narayanan, M. P. (1999). Disentangling value: Financing needs, firm scope, and divestitures. *Journal of Financial Intermediation, 8*, 174–204.
Parrino, R. (1997). Spinoffs and wealth transfers: The Marriott case. *Journal of Financial Economics, 43*, 241–274.
Pyo, U. (2006). Enhancing managerial incentives and value creation: Evidence from corporate spin-offs. Unpublished working paper, Brock University.
Rajan, R., Servaes, H., & Zingales, L. (2000). The cost of diversity: The diversification discount and inefficient investment. *Journal of Finance, 55*, 35–80.
Rossi, S., & Volpin, P. F. (2004). Cross-country determinants of mergers and acquisitions. *Journal of Financial Economics, 74*, 277–304.
Schipper, K., & Smith, A. (1983). Effects of recontracting on shareholder wealth: The case of voluntary spin-offs. *Journal of Financial Economics, 12*, 437–467.
Scholes, M. S., & Williams, J. T. (1977). Estimating betas from nonsynchronous data. *Journal of Financial Economics, 5*, 309–328.
Seward, J. K., & Walsh, J. P. (1996). The governance and control of voluntary corporate spin-offs. *Strategic Management Journal, 17*, 25–39.
Slovin, M. B., Sushka, M. E., & Ferraro, S. R. (1995). A comparison of the information conveyed by equity carve-outs, spin-offs, and asset sell-offs. *Journal of Financial Economics, 37*, 89–104.
Veld, C., & Veld-Merkoulova, Y. V. (2004). Do spin-offs really create value? The European case. *Journal of Banking and Finance, 28*, 1111–1135.

Villalonga, B. (2004). Diversification discount or premium? New evidence from the business information tracking series. *Journal of Finance, 59*, 479–506.
Weston, J. F. (1989). Divestitures: Mistakes or learning. *Journal of Applied Corporate Finance, 2*, 68–76.
White, H. (1980). A heteroskedastic-consistent covariance matrix estimator and a direct test for heteroscedasticity. *Econometrica, 48*, 817–838.
Wruck, E. G., & Wruck, K. H. (2002). Restructuring top management: Evidence from corporate spin-offs. *Journal of Labor Economics, 20*, 176–218.

Alternative Specifications of Bank Lending in France and Germany: Theory, Evidence, and Policy Implications

Robert E. Krainer

1 Introduction

There is a large body of research going back at least to Schumpeter and revived by King and Levine (1993) arguing that finance plays an important role in the dynamic economic development of market economies.[1] The main idea underlying this view is that an advanced and efficient financial system: (1) enables firms to obtain external financing at the lowest cost for investment that facilitates the efficient production of existing goods and services, and even more important the development of new products; (2) facilitates the liquidation and redistribution of productive resources of firms producing the old products displaced by new innovations; and (3) at the same time provides savers with a wide variety of claims to future consumption. One of the mechanism by which this is accomplished in developed and efficient financial systems is by reducing the asymmetric information and moral hazard problems associated with decentralized production and investment in old and especially new companies. In this sense, advanced financial systems are powerful engines for the manufacturing of company information and facilitating the savings and investment process.

One of the first directions this research on "finance matters" took was to categorize developed countries on the basis of whether their financial system was market oriented (typically interpreted as stock market oriented) or bank oriented

[1] There is a minority view that the direction of causation is from economic development to financial development. For this view, see Robinson (1952) and Manning (2003). Moreover, Acemoglu et al. (2001), Rioja and Valev (2004), and Rousseau and Wachtel (2006) argue that the finance/growth link is becoming weaker over time for developed countries like the US.

R.E. Krainer (✉)
University of Wisconsin-Madison, 3110 Grainger Hall, 975 University Ave., Madison, WI 53706, USA
e-mail: rkrainer@bus.wisc.edu

T. Azarmi, W. Amann (eds.), *The Financial Crisis*,
DOI 10.1007/978-3-319-20588-5_3

(Mayer 1998). High-income countries were categorized in this way based on metrics such as the magnitude of their security market valuations of their publicly traded firms, and the magnitude of the assets and deposits of their banking sector all relative to aggregates such as population and GDP. On these metrics, the US was classified as a market-oriented financial system while France and Germany (the focus of this study) were classified as bank-based financial systems. Which financial system is better in terms of fostering economic growth? From the perspective of transferring resources from household savers to firm investors, the consensus answer from academic research was that neither enjoyed an advantage over the other. The only thing that seemed to matter is whether both types of financial orientations were based on the substructure of an efficient and flexible legal and political system that respected property rights and contracts (Levine 1998).

The role of finance in facilitating economic growth is the good side of finance. The less good side of finance is its role as a source and propagator of macroeconomic volatility, the most striking example of which was the recent Great Crisis beginning in 2007. Sharp swings in the optimism/pessimism and risk perceptions of banks, non-bank financial institutions, and other investors in marketable and non-marketable securities have historically resulted in economies overshooting and undershooting their long-run trend growth in output. Cyclical expansions are preceded by an abundance of finance available for consumption and investment while recessions are brought on by an evaporation of finance available for these expenditures.

Banks play a central role in the provision of finance to the real economy. To begin with they are the only financial intermediary whose deposit liabilities are an important component of transactions money. When they lend to households and firms they pay for these loans by creating liquidity in the form of demand deposit money. Their loan customers (for a commitment fee and interest payments) are given a new deposit account or an addition to a deposit account from which they can buy goods and services, as well as assets. For this reason, banks are well-positioned to reduce information asymmetries and moral hazard problems that separate savers and investors. One way they can do this is to monitor the deposit balances of their loan customers over time (Norden and Weber 2007). More generally, there is a large amount of research in banking that emphasizes the importance of bank screening and monitoring in the provision of finance particularly for households and small- to medium-sized firms where the returns are particularly opaque.[2] Because money is so important in facilitating trade in a market economy, banks have been subject to a great deal of regulation designed to control the risk-taking of their lending and capital structure decisions in order to prevent bankruptcy and the destruction of deposit money. For this reason also most governments in countries with advanced financial systems provide low cost deposit insurance for households and firms holding bank deposits.

---

[2] A small sample of this research would include Berger and Humphrey (1998), Berger and Udell (1994, 1995), Nakamura (1993), and Peterson and Rajan (1994).

These attributes of banks (i.e., the provision of liquidity in the form of deposit money and financial intermediation services) present society with a dilemma. Good banking based on careful screening and monitoring of firms spurs economic development and growth. Bad banking that takes the form of screening and monitoring tainted by changes in optimism and pessimism of bankers amplifies the business cycle. Bank stockholders want their banks to facilitate economic growth by taking risks in their lending decisions in the hope of earning high rates of return. On the other hand, bank depositors and society in general want their banks to be safe in order that they might have instantaneous access to liquidity in the form of checking account money to carry out economic transactions. Regulators have tried to accommodate both stockholders and depositors. But in order to understand existing regulation and whether or not it is effective, we need a model of how a bank should adjust its portfolio of assets and the financing of those assets as between debt (including deposits) and equity. We have, in previous work, developed such a model that makes no particular distinction between nonfinancial and financial enterprises. Both types of enterprises have assets (both real and paper) of varying degrees of risk. They also fund those assets with debt (including deposits) and equity claims. In the next section, we describe the model of asset adjustments and financing adjustments over time. In Sect. 3, we test certain implications of that model with balance sheet data for monetary financial institutions (MFIs) and banks in France and Germany, two countries that the finance literature classifies as bank-based financial systems.[3] In particular, the model in Sect. 2 argues that bank asset adjustments (including investments in loans) should be made to conform to the risk aversion of the bank's equity investors as communicated to managers by changing equity valuations. To test this prediction, we use non-nested hypothesis tests and omitted variables tests to compare an interest rate channel model to a stock market channel model of bank lending in France and Germany. Section 6 concludes and discusses some possible implications for the conduct of monetary policy that seemingly follows from the balance sheet adjustment model described in Sect. 2.

To preview the results, our non-nested hypothesis test and omitted variables tests find that a capital budgeting model based on equity valuations in France provides a better specification of bank lending than the typical demand factors of bank-lending rates and an income variable like GDP. For Germany, the results were mixed. For MFIs, we encountered a severe problem of autocorrelation in the residuals. When correcting for this autocorrelation with a Cochrane-Orcutt AR(1) process we ended up rejecting both the traditional demand-oriented model and the capital budgeting model described in Sect. 2. However, when we analyzed the banking subsector of German MFIs, we ended up with the same result as for France; namely, rejecting the traditional demand-oriented model of bank lending but not the stock market-oriented capital budgeting model in Sect. 2. These statistical results might suggest that a possible unconventional monetary policy would be to target the level of equity valuations in those countries in an attempt to reduce the volatility of their

[3] For a description of the data see the Appendix on Data Sources.

bank lending. This could be accomplished by imposing margin requirements on stock purchases and sales when stock market valuations are "irrationally" high/low, or, by the central bank directly buying/selling an index fund of bank and non-bank shares. Nevertheless, we emphasize in our conclusion that a great deal more research will have to be done in this area before this particular type of monetary policy can be implemented.

2 Optimal Balance Sheet Adjustments for Nonfinancial and Financial Enterprises[4]

To start things off, consider a risk-neutral entrepreneur/investor making an intertemporal consumption and real investment decision according to the textbook model of Fisher–Hirshleifer. While the focus of the model in the beginning is on real investments of nonfinancial firms, we will open it up below to financial investments like loans by banks. The entrepreneur's problem is described in Fig. 1. The horizontal axis in the figure measures the endowment of resources ($0P$ of wealth W_0) available to the investor to be allocated to starting a firm/economy, A_0, and current consumption measured as C_0. The vertical axis measures the expected future income, $\overline{X}$, generated from the investment in the assets of this firm/economy. The payoff in terms of $\overline{X}$ on the real investments in the firm/economy is described by a diminishing returns productive opportunity curve given by PO in the figure. The preference of the investor for current consumption and future expected income is given by the traditional convex indifference curve, IC, in the figure. The tangency between the indifference curve and productive opportunity curve defines the equilibrium in terms of current consumption, C_0, current investment in productive assets, A_0, and future expected income, $\overline{X}$. The financial claims underlying the productive assets are unlevered equity.

Now suppose this risk-neutral entrepreneur retires and bequeaths the unlevered equity of the firm/economy equally to his (or her) differentially risk-averse children, D and E. We assume that D is relatively more risk averse than E and for that reason an investment banker is called in to convert the unlevered equity of the start-up firm/economy into a debt and levered equity seasoned firm/economy. The same individual could hold both claims in different proportions but it will be easier to assume D and E specialize in one or the other. In this way, we set up a conflict of interest problem between the two types of investors that must be taken into account when the firm makes investment and financing decisions in the future. This ownership structure is pictured as an Edgeworth–Bowley box diagram in Fig. 2. The lower and upper horizontal sides of the box represent the economic book value of the real productive assets, A, of the firm/economy, while the left and right sides of

[4] This model has been successively developed in Krainer (1985, 1992, 2003, 2014).

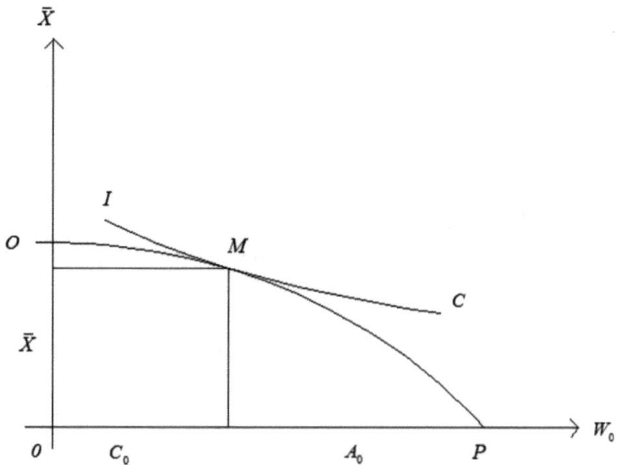

Fig. 1 Consumption and investment of a risk-neutral entrepreneur

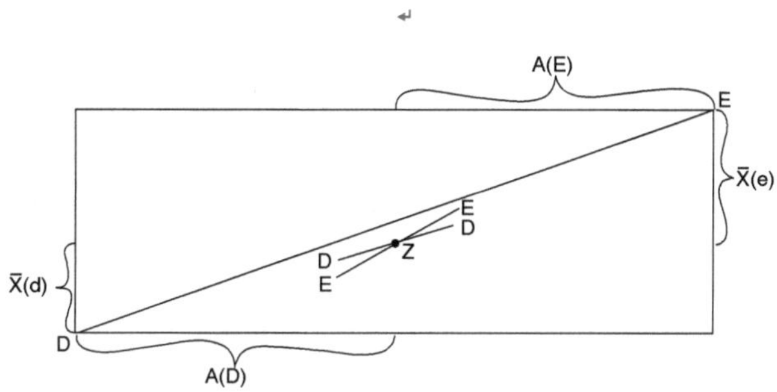

Fig. 2 Input and expected output sharing in a debt and equity economy

the box represent the future expected income, $\overline{X}$, generated on the assets. The variables $A(D)$ and $\overline{X}(D)$ represent the investment put up by debt (including deposits) investors and their expected return on that investment, while $A(E)$ and $\overline{X}(E)$ represent the same for equity investors. Point Z measures how investors D and E share the investment in the firm/economy and expected returns on that investment. Note that Z lies below the diagonal line in the box indicating that the expected rate of return on debt, $R(d) = \overline{X}(D)/A(D)$, is less than the expected rate of return on equity, $R(e) = \overline{X}(E)/A(E)$ reflecting the fact that security D is perceived to be safer than security E. The debt security is safer because it is a fixed claim on the income and assets of the firm that enjoys a legal priority in payment before the equity security.

Next, suppose that investors D and E perceive themselves to be price-takers in the capital market and hence $R(d)$ and $R(e)$ are constants in the "small" neighborhood around Z in Fig. 2. This is reflected in the diagram as schedules DD and EE being straight lines intersecting at Z. For small variations in D's investment of $A(D)$ in the firm/economy in and around point Z, the required money income on debt/deposits is:

$$\overline{X}\ (D) = R(d)A(D) \tag{1}$$

The expected money income, $\overline{X}$, generated on the fixed amount of assets, A, is:

$$\overline{X} = R\ [A(D) + A(E)] \tag{2}$$

Where R = the expected IRR earned on A.

The expected residual income (from the perspective of investor D) going to levered equity investors is then:

$$\overline{X}(E) = \overline{X} - \overline{X}(D) \tag{3}$$

Inserting the rhs of Eq. (2) into Eq. (3) and then dividing the result into Eq. (1) gives the following concave relationship between financial leverage, $A(D)/A(E)$, and the distribution of corporate income between investors D and E, i.e., $\overline{X}(D)/\overline{X}(E)$.

$$\frac{X(D)}{X(E)} = \frac{A(D)/A(E)}{\frac{R}{R(D)} + \left\{\frac{[R-R(d)]}{R(d)}\right\}A(D)/A(E)} > 0 \tag{4}$$

The linear approximation to Eq. (4) is given by the *dd* schedule in Fig. 3. Every point along the *dd* schedule in the figure represents varying combinations of $A(D)/A(E)$ and $\overline{X}(D)/\overline{X}(E)$ for which $R(d)$ is a constant. It can also be shown from Eq. (4) that *dd* schedules with a higher (or lower) constant yields $R(d)$ lie above (or below) the *dd* schedule shown in Fig. 3. Higher or lower constant debt yields will be indicated by $R'(d) > R(d)$ and $R''(d) < R(d)$, respectively.

Managers in the real world cannot directly observe the $R(d)$ underlying the *dd* schedule in Fig. 3. It is, however, possible to give a market valuation interpretation to the *dd* schedule presented in Fig. 3 which managers can observe. Toward this end, think of $R(d)$ as representing two rates of return which must be equal in equilibrium: (1) an expected yield, $R(d,\text{ER})$, delivered to investor D by the

Fig. 3 Financial markets and equilibrium

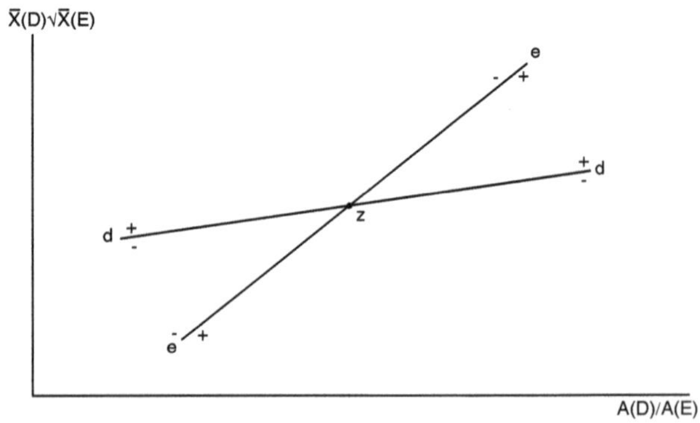

investment/lending decisions of the firm; and (2) a required yield, $R(d,\mathrm{RR})$, of debt investors that depends on their time and risk preferences and their demand for liquidity in the case of depositors. The market value of one unit of a perpetual debt claim is then:

$$P(d) = \frac{\overline{X}(d)}{R(d,\mathrm{RR})} \cdot \frac{1}{N(d)} \tag{5}$$

Where

$P(d)$ = the market value of one unit of debt.

$N(d)$ = the number of debt units.

Multiplying the numerator of the rhs of Eq. (5) by $A(D)/A(D)$ and defining the expected yield to be $R(d,\mathrm{ER}) = \overline{X}(D)/A(D)$ results in the market value of one unit of a debt security.

$$P(d) = \frac{R(d,\mathrm{ER})}{R(d,\mathrm{RR})} \cdot \frac{A(D)}{N(d)} \tag{6}$$

Equation (6) says the market price of one unit of a debt security is the book value of these securities scaled by $R(d,\mathrm{ER})/R(d,\mathrm{RR})$, which in effect is a Keynes–Tobin Q-factor for the debt security. Along an equilibrium *dd* schedule in Fig. 3, we have $R(d,\mathrm{ER}) = R(d,\mathrm{RR})$ and the market value of debt securities is then $P(d) = A(D)/N(d)$. Debt securities are zero NPV investments in equilibrium. It follows that when $R(d,\mathrm{ER}) \neq R(d,\mathrm{RR})$, then $P(d) \neq A(D)/N(d)$. To further understand this in terms of Fig. 3 suppose starting from some initial point on the *dd* schedule in Fig. 3, there suddenly is a negative shock that raises $R(d,\mathrm{RR})$ to $R'(d,\mathrm{RR}) > R(d,\mathrm{RR}) = R(d,\mathrm{ER})$. The required yield $R'(d,\mathrm{RR})$ is now according to Eq. (4) on a $d'd'$ schedule that lies above the old *dd* schedule in the figure, while $R(d,\mathrm{ER})$ because of frictions is still on the old *dd* schedule.[5] It is then the case that immediately after this negative shock $R(d,\mathrm{ER})/R'(d,\mathrm{RR}) < 1$, and therefore $P(d) < A(D)/N(d)$. In terms of Fig. 3, the expected yield $R(d,\mathrm{ER})$ is on the old *dd* schedule in the figure but the new required yield $R'(d,\mathrm{RR})$ is now on a $d'd'$ schedule above the initial *dd* schedule. Since $R(d,\mathrm{ER})$ is the expected yield on the original equilibrium *dd* schedule below the $d'd'$ schedule, it is now in the negative (−) zone of the $d'd'$ schedule where the market price of debt is below book value.

The equity market schedule *ee* can be derived in the same way. To see this, let $\overline{X}(E)$ be the income required by equity investors on an economic book value investment of $A(E)$ in the small neighborhood of Z in Fig. 2. Then for small variations in $A(E)$ we have:

---

[5] In other words, we assume that the managers of the firm cannot instantaneously change $R(d,\mathrm{ER})$ by instantly changing its investments for "time to plan" and "time to build" reasons. Consequently, market values of debt (and as we will see later, equity) securities can be temporarily different than book values.

$$\overline{X}(e) = R(e)A(E) \tag{7}$$

Total income generated on the firm's assets is again

$$\overline{X} = R\ [A(D) + A(E)] \tag{2}$$

From the perspective of equity investors the expected income available for debt investors is Eq. (2) minus Eq. (7), or

$$\overline{X}(D) = \overline{X} - \overline{X}(E) \tag{8}$$

Substituting the rhs of Eq. (2) into Eq. (8) and dividing the result by Eq. (7) yields the following:

$$\frac{\overline{X}(D)}{\overline{X}(E)} = \frac{R - R(e)}{R(e)} + \frac{R}{R(e)}\left[\frac{A(D)}{A(E)}\right] \tag{9}$$

or the equation for the *ee* schedule in Fig. 3. The *ee* schedule represents the combinations of $A(D)/A(E)$ and $\overline{X}(D)/\overline{X}(E)$ for which the rate of return on stock, $R(e)$, is a constant in the small neighborhood of point Z in Fig. 2. It can also be shown from Eq. (9) that *ee* schedules with higher (or lower) constant yields lie to the right (or left) on $e'e'$ (or $e''e''$) schedules relative to the reference *ee* schedule shown in Fig. 3. Higher equity yields will be indicted by $R'(e) > R(e)$, while lower yield by $R''(e) < R(e)$.

To get observable market valuations, we again think of yields in two different senses: (1) an expected yield labeled $R(e,\text{ER})$ delivered to investors by the firm's investment and financing decisions; and (2) a required yield, $R(e,\text{RR})$ that depends on the amount of perceived risk along with investors' time preference and risk aversion. Equilibrium in the stock market requires $R(e,\text{ER}) = R(e,\text{RR})$. The price of one perpetual share of stock is then:

$$P(e) = \frac{\overline{X}(E)}{R(e,\text{RR})} \cdot \frac{1}{N(e)} \tag{10}$$

Where

$P(e)$ = the market value of one share of stock.

$N(e)$ = the number of shares outstanding.

Multiplying the numerator of the rhs of Eq. (10) by $A(E)/A(E)$ and defining $R(e,\text{ER}) = \overline{X}(E)/A(E)$ results in:

$$P(e) = \frac{\overline{X}(E)/A(E)}{R(e,\text{RR})} \cdot \frac{A(E)}{N(e)} \tag{11a}$$

Or simply,

$$P(e) = \frac{R(e, \mathrm{ER})}{R(e, \mathrm{RR})} \cdot \frac{A(E)}{N(e)} \tag{11b}$$

Equations (11a) and (11b) indicate that equity investors require $R(e,\mathrm{RR})$ as a result of their time preference, risk aversion, and their assessment of risk. Managers in turn deliver $R(e,\mathrm{ER})$ with their investment and financing decisions. An equilibrium *ee* schedule is one where $R(e) = R(e,\mathrm{ER}) = R(e,\mathrm{RR})$. This implies from Eqs. (11a) and (11b) that in equilibrium stocks are zero NPV investments in that $P(e) = A(E)/N(e)$. When $R(e,\mathrm{ER}) \neq R(e,\mathrm{RR})$, then $P(e) \neq A(E)/N(e)$. What do the (+) and (−) sign around the *ee* schedule in Fig. 3 indicate? They indicate the direction of change in rates of return on equity securities and the direction of change in market valuations of equity due to the reciprocal nature of percentage rates of return and market valuations. To see this, in Fig. 3 we start from a point on the *ee* schedule where the Keynes–Tobin Q-ratio for stock is unity, namely, $R(e,\mathrm{ER}) = R(e,\mathrm{RR})$. Now suppose there is a favorable shock so that equity investors reduce the yield they require from $R(e,\mathrm{RR})$ along the initial *ee* schedule shown in the figure, to a new $R''(e,\mathrm{RR}) < R(e,\mathrm{RR})$ along a $e''e''$ schedule (not shown in the figure) which according to Eq. (9) lies to the left and above the initial *ee* schedule. On the assumption that frictions prevent managers from immediately adjusting the firm's real productive investments/loans that in turn generate $\overline{X}$, we then will have $R(e,\mathrm{ER}) > R''(e,\mathrm{RR})$ so that $P(e) > A(E)/N(e)$ occurs immediately after the positive shock. This can be seen in Fig. 3 in that a point on *ee* for $R(e,\mathrm{ER})$ lies to the right and below—i.e., in the (+) zone—of the new $e''e''$ schedule with the new constant $R''(e,\mathrm{RR})$. The opposite would be the case for a negative shock that would result in investors increasing $R(e,\mathrm{RR})$.

In Fig. 3, it can be seen that the *ee* schedule intersects the *dd* schedule at point *z* from below. This can be shown to follow from the positive risk premium $R(e) > R(d)$ when Z is below the diagonal line in Fig. 2. It is also the case that at the point *z* in Fig. 3 the capital market value of the firm's assets equals the economic book value of those assets. This condition defines the investment equilibrium and the financial market equilibrium for this economy in that the representative firm is delivering the returns that debt investors and equity investors require.

How do firms deliver returns to their investors in this model? The return generating process assumed in this model takes the following form.

$$\overline{X} = f(A) \;\; f'(A) > 0 \;\text{ and }\; f''(A) \leq 0 \tag{12}$$

$$\sigma(X) = g(A) \;\; g'(A) > 0 \;\text{ and }\; g''(A) \geq 0 \tag{13}$$

Expected returns go up at a diminishing rate with an increase in investment while operating risk (defined as the standard deviation of returns) accompanies those returns and goes up with investment.

With this model, it is possible to describe the ups and downs of the real economy. To see this, suppose the economy is at some initial equilibrium point *z* that is described by the intersection of a *dd* schedule and an *ee* schedule in Fig. 4. Now suppose there is a negative shock; for example, real estate prices falling for the first

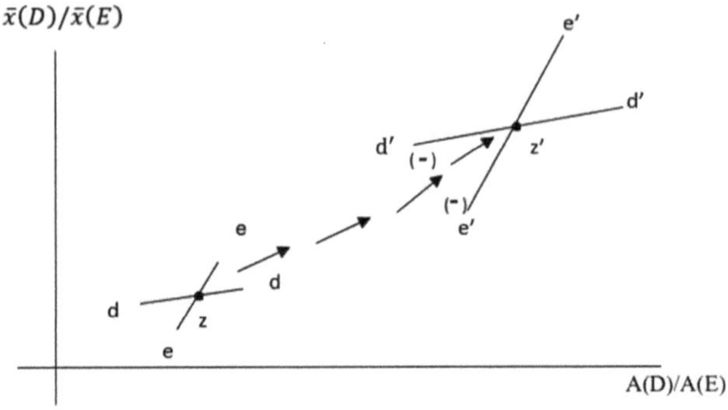

Fig. 4 Investment and financing adjustments for recessions

time in a long time. Both debt investors and equity investors in banks and nonfinancial enterprises react to this negative shock by raising their required rate of return from $R(d,\mathrm{RR})$ and $R(e,\mathrm{RR})$ to $R'(d,\mathrm{RR})$ and $R'(e,\mathrm{RR})$. This reaction by investors in the securities market shifts both the *dd* and *ee* schedules so that immediately after the shock they intersect at some z' point lying to the northeast of the old equilibrium at z. The reaction to the negative shock is immediate in the securities markets where market prices fall below book value. Market prices below book value present managers of firms with an arbitrage opportunity, namely, sell assets A back to the factor market at book value and use the proceeds to retire debt and mostly equity securities. This downsizing results in a recession. For manufacturing firms, this downsizing takes the form of reducing investment in tangible assets and employment. For banks, this downsizing takes the form of reducing their lending (that help finance investment) and employment.

What effect does this downsizing have on the returns and risk of firms? As firms downsize, the expected rate of return goes up according to the return generating process in Eq. (12) which of course is what investors are now demanding in the new riskier environment. Moreover, as investment goes down, operating risk also goes down by Eq. (13). As operating/portfolio risk goes down, a coalescing contract [described in Krainer (2014)] between debt investors and equity investors would have the firm increase their financial risk by financing relatively more of their assets with debt. Recessions then are characterized by a lower level of real investment and investment returns, a lower level of lending by banks and nonbank financial institutions, higher rates of return, lower operating and portfolio risk, and higher financial leverage and financial risk.[6] The opposite sequence of events would occur in response to a positive shock. In this case, a positive shock would reduce investors' required rates of return, thereby raising debt and equity market valuations above book value. Firm managers would then respond to the new arbitrage opportunity and buy assets (tangible assets and human capital for manufacturing firms,

[6] As the firm/economy moves closer to z' by downsizing, the difference between market and book values for both debt and equity securities becomes smaller. When the firm/economy reaches z' market values will equal book values and that will be the signal for managers to stop the downsizing. When at point z' the firm/economy is in a recession equilibrium according to this model.

and loans and human capital for banks) so that total returns would go up, rates of return on assets would go down, and operating risk would increase. In response to the increase in operating/portfolio risk via their investment/lending decisions, a coalescing financial contract between debt/deposit investors and equity investors would have the representative firm reduce its financial leverage and financial risk by financing the expansion in assets with equity. Expansions are then characterized by a higher level of real investment and investment returns, lower rates of return, higher amounts of operating/portfolio risk, and lower amounts of financial leverage and financial risk. In Krainer (1992, 2003, 2014), certain predictions from the theory for nonfinancial enterprises were empirically tested with balance sheet data for the G-7 countries. For the most part, these predictions from the theory were not rejected. In Krainer (2009), these balance sheet predictions were empirically tested for US banks. Again, the asset adjustment and financing adjustment predictions from the theory were not rejected for US banks.[7]

In the next section, we will test certain (but not all) predictions of this model against balance sheet data for banks in France and Germany.

3 Bank Lending in France and Germany

In the model of Sect. 2, we have two investors (debt/deposit investors and equity investors), two decisions (an asset adjustment decision and a financing adjustment decision), and two market equilibrium conditions (market value equals book value

[7] The financial leverage of nonfinancial enterprises that is predicted by this theory to be countercyclical is long-term financial leverage. What about short-term debt like bank loans that is predicted in this chapter to be procyclical? Are these two predictions contradictory? Bank loans are risky assets on the balance sheets of banks. As such the model predicts they will be procyclical. Bank loans are also liabilities on the balance sheets of bank loan customers such as nonfinancial enterprises and households. In the case of nonfinancial enterprises short-term bank debt in our model is more like equity than long-term debt. This is because short-term lenders like banks have the option of getting in or out of a loan to a borrowing company at book value at higher frequencies than long-term bondholders where the option is to get in or out at continually changing current market prices before the redemption date. When a short-term bank loan matures the decision by the bank to renew or not depends on the borrower (particularly small and medium size companies) presenting an acceptable business plan; that is, an operating plan and a financing plan. By continually requiring the borrowing firm to produce an updated business plan bank control of the business plan of the borrowing firm rivals that of equity holders and far exceeds that of long-term bondholders. Control rights are another way to distinguish among financial claims on firms. Equity claims contain the most control rights and long-term funded debt the least. Short-term bank loans are somewhere in-between but closer to equity. For that reason we include bank loans along with equity to be in the denominator of the leverage ratio of firms. Research by Dichev and Skinner (2002) indicates that banks exercise this control by setting covenants in loan agreements tightly so that they are frequently breached, roughly 30 % in their sample. Typically, the bank waives the resulting noncompliance but instead uses it as an opportunity to discuss the borrowing firm's business plan further. In this way, banks, like the board of directors representing stockholders, frequently monitor the ongoing business strategy of borrowing firms.

for both debt and equity securities). In previous work on this model (Krainer 1992, 2003, 2014), we have shown that in this $2 \times 2 \times 2$ economy where the two investors differ in terms of their risk aversion, it is optimal for the less risk averse equity investor to control the asset adjustment decision and the more risk averse debt investor through financial contracts to control the financing adjustment.[8] Each investor controls one side of the balance sheet. Thus, when the firm expands its risky assets in response to a positive shock that increases the market valuation of its equity, an optimal debt contract will have the firm reduce its financial risk by financing the expansion in risky assets at the margin with equity. The reason for this is that an increase in risky investment that causes a cyclical expansion in economic activity increases the firm's operating risk according to Eq. (13). Since relatively more risk-averse debt investors only get a fixed claim on the income of the firm they cannot benefit if the speculative investment is successful, but they can share in losses incurred if the outcome is unsuccessful. On the other hand, a negative shock that increases investor risk aversion and perception of risk driving market valuations of securities down will be the market signal for managers to downsize the assets of their firm, thereby reducing operating risk by Eq. (13) and creating a recession. The financial response of an optimal contract between debt and equity investors in this recession case is for the firm to increase financial risk by increasing financial leverage. In this way of linking financial policy to investment policy, no investor is exploited during a cyclical expansion or recession. The sharing of risk and return is equitable.

For banks this particular assignment of asset adjustment and financing adjustment decisions to equity investors and depositors is somewhat different. One reason for this is because the deposit liabilities of banks are systemically more important for the economic health of an economy than the debt liabilities of nonfinancial enterprises (Krainer 2002). Checks on demand deposit accounts are a generally accepted medium of exchange that facilitates economic transactions. If convertibility of deposit accounts breaks down because of bank failure, the real economy breaks down. As John Gurley (1961) picturesquely put it, "Money is a veil, but when the veil flutters, real output sputters." This is the result of the fact that the financial sector is highly interconnected due in part to the high degree of the layering and "round aboutness" of financial intermediation between ultimate household savers and ultimate firm investors in advanced financial systems. Bankruptcy in one part of the interconnected financial chain can cause bankruptcies in other parts of the chain. For this reason, government regulation takes over the contracting between bank stockholders and creditors including depositors. A second reason for this is that bank assets and returns are opaque and monitoring costs are subject to

[8] Why this particular assignment of decisions to claimants? In our model it is the case (as reflected in Fig. 1) that entrepreneur investors have a better understanding of the technology underlying the assets of the all equity firm they created than subsequent debt investors. In addition the variable residual nature of equity claims on the firm allows subsequent less risk averse investors to benefit from their (or their agent's) understanding of the technology. More risk averse debt investors can protect themselves with a financial contract that allows them to determine the financial strategy of the firm. For a numerical example on how the financial contract might work see Krainer (2014).

scale economies. Most depositors cannot be expected to adequately monitor the risk of bank loans and other forms of investment. The various Basle Accords are an attempt to provide guidelines to local regulators for the matching of financing decisions of banks to their investment decisions. The more risk taken on in the bank's portfolio decision, the less risk it can take on in its financing decision.

Government regulation in the form of the Basle Accord determines the financing adjustments of banks. What, then, determines their asset adjustments? In the balance sheet model of Sect. 2, the asset adjustments are made to conform to the changing risk aversion of the firm's equity investors. How do managers get information on the risk aversion of their stockholders? They get this information from the stock market. Changes in stock prices reflect changes in the risk aversion and/or perceptions of risk of bank shareholders. Thus, a positive external shock that triggers an increase in bank share valuations will, according to the model in Sect. 2, be the market signal for banks to increase their investments in risky loans. The net present value (NPV) version of the theory is for banks to make all loans that meet the criteria:

$$\mathrm{NPV} = -\Delta L_0 + \Sigma_t X_t/(1+\rho)^t \geq 0 \tag{14}$$

Where

ΔL_0 = bank investments in loans.

X = future expected cash flows on the bank's investment in risky loans.

ρ = The required rate of return of bank shareholders, or, $R(e,\mathrm{RR})$.

Section 2 and Eq. (14) is not the only model of the determinants of bank lending in the banking literature. The more traditional view is to analyze bank lending within a supply–demand framework. In a simple model, supply depends on the risk aversion of bank managers, a wealth constraint in the form of bank assets and reserves, and the relative expected rate of return on loans versus securities. The demand for loan finance by firms depends on the cost of loan finance relative to the cost of other funding sources of finance and the expected profitability of investment projects. Within this framework, there has been a tension in the literature between the relative importance of supply factors versus demand factors in the bank loan market. Much recent research before and after the Great Crisis starting in 2007 indicates that demand factors are relatively more important than supply factors.[9] This would seem to be especially true in bank-based financial systems where there often is a close and long-term relationship between a bank and its borrowing customers. Among other things this focus on the demand side of the bank loan market assumes that banks have a cushion of liquidity, or wholesale borrowing capacity, or an accommodating central bank that can be utilized to provide the funding for any unexpected loan demand of their borrowing customers. A

[9] Before the Great Crisis empirical work on demand models of bank lending included Calza et al. (2003), Eickmeier et al. (2006), and Frommel and Schmidt (2006) among others. After the Crisis work on these models include Sorensen et al. (2009), Kooths and Rieger (2009), Carpenter and Demiralp (2010), Campello et al. (2012), Kahle and Stulz (2011), among many others.

parsimonious reduced form specification of the demand hypothesis of bank lending would include interest rates charged on bank loans reflecting the cost of loan finance, and an income variable like GDP reflecting the profitability of firms and household income. This demand hypothesis can then be written as:

$$\Delta L_0 = \gamma(\text{GDP},\ R) \quad \gamma'(\text{GDP}) \gtrless 0 \quad \gamma'(R) < 0 \tag{15}$$

There is some disagreement about the derivative on GDP. The traditional argument is that γ' (GDP) is positive, reflecting the idea that higher incomes of firms and households imply a greater ability to service debt. On the other hand, Friedman and Kuttner (1993), Bernanke and Gertler (1995), and Calza et al. (2003) have argued that γ' could be negative. Their argument is that higher business and household incomes that accompany higher GDP could be used by financially conservative agents to pay down outstanding bank loans and increasingly finance their asset acquisitions from internally generated retained earnings. When the economy is in a recession and business profits and household incomes fall, firms and households will increase their borrowing from banks in order to smooth their intertemporal expenditures on assets and consumption.

The two views of bank lending given in Eqs. (14) and (15) potentially suggest different ways monetary policy might affect bank lending and ultimately the real economy. The demand view of bank lending in Eq. (15) is consistent with the pre-Great Crisis traditional view of monetary policy that works through an interest rate channel. When an economy slips into recession, central banks typically follow policies that reduce short-term interest rates and interest rate expectations in the hope that it will stimulate borrowing and spending, thereby pulling the economy out of the recession. That was pretty much the strategy followed by central banks up to and through the Great Crisis. The first policy initiative of central banks in response to the Great Crisis was to reduce interest rate expectations and short-term interest rates driving them down close to zero. For the most part, this policy did not work. The second policy initiative was to reduce long-term interest rates on government securities. This policy also did not provide the desired result of pulling the high-income economies out of recession. Finally, the third policy initiative followed by the US Federal Reserve was to buy private mortgage backed securities driving interest rates on home mortgages down in hopes of stimulating housing investments. At this point (June 2013), it is too early to tell whether and to what extent this policy will work. The common thread of conventional monetary policy is to work through debt markets and interest rates. Now it is true that targeting interest rates in debt markets will have an indirect effect on many things, including exchange rates, commodity prices, and even the stock market. But while central banks can have considerable and precise influence on short-term interest rates and interest rate expectations, the indirect effects on exchange rates, commodity prices, and the stock market is much less predictable. On the other hand, the capital budgeting model of bank lending expressed in Eq. (14) would have the central bank directly targeting stock valuations as one goal of their monetary policy. According to the balance sheet adjustment model of Sect. 2, this goal of monetary policy could possibly be an effective way to stabilize bank lending and the real economy.

Consequently, it is important to find out statistically which of the two models more accurately captures the intertemporal movements of bank lending. For the remainder of this chapter, we will compare the two parsimonious specifications of bank lending expressed in Eqs. (14) and (15) for France and Germany using non-nested hypothesis tests and omitted variables tests.[10]

The linear regression specifications for the two non-nested hypotheses are:

$$\text{H1} \quad \Delta L_0 = a_0 + a_1(\text{SP, bk}) + a_2(\text{SP}) + u \tag{16}$$

Where,

ΔL_0 = the real investment in loans by monetary financial institutions (MFI).

(SP,bk) = the real stock market valuations of bank equity which is taken to be a proxy for the required rate of return of bank shareholders, or, $R(e,\text{RR})$.

(SP) = the real stock market valuations of shares in general which is taken to be a proxy for the expected rate of return, $R(e,\text{ER})$; or, $\Sigma_i X_i$ from Eq. (14).

u = random error term.

For the traditional view of bank lending the linear specification is taken to be:

$$\text{H2} \quad \Delta L_0 = b_0 + b_1(\text{GDP}) + b_2(R) + e \tag{17}$$

Where,

GDP = real GDP, a proxy for business and household income that shifts the demand curve for loans.

R = the real interest rate on bank loans, a proxy for the cost of loan finance.

e = random error term.

The data used to proxy these variables are described in the Appendix on Data Sources. We also present in Tables 1 and 2 certain descriptive statistics for the variables used in the regressions for France and Germany.

Table 1 Descriptive statistics for France

	Mean	Median	Maximum	Minimum	Std. dev.
$\Delta(L,\text{MFI})$	589.7	359.3	4917.3	−1289.8	1308.8
Δ(SP,bk)	0.897	1.020	13.927	−17.546	4.565
(SP,250)	5.491	5.000	10.401	3.034	2.091
Δ(GDP)	1.523	1.518	4.443	−1.714	1.451
(R,ST)	6.606	5.931	12.038	2.994	2.722
(R,LT)	6.097	5.313	10.938	2.410	2.586
$\Delta(\text{Tier1}/A)\times 100$	0.039	0.039	0.796	−0.805	0.003
$N=68$					

[10] Two hypothesized specifications H1 and H2 for an economic variable is said to be non-nested if it is not possible to derive either one from the other by means of a set of parametric restrictions.

Table 2 Descriptive statistics for Germany

	Mean	Median	Maximum	Minimum	Std. dev.
Δ(*L*,MFI)	24.122	24.840	122.62	−47.31	35.10
Δ(*L*,Banks)	6.881	7.031	87.45	−31.15	19.28
Δ(SP,bk)	3.246	6.038	73.75	117.46	33.56
Δ(SP,CDAX)	2.413	2.467	81.25	−78.00	23.32
Δ(Tier1/*A*)mfi × 100	0.02	0.02	0.30	−0.022	0.08
Δ(Tier1/*A*)Banks × 100	0.0035	0.0000	0.0060	0.001	0.002
Δ(GDP)	0.501	0.500	2.900	−2.100	0.807
Δ(*R*,Ave)	5.722	5.715	9.093	2.924	1.625
N = 88					

4 Bank Lending in France

Table 3 below presents the regression results for the two specifications of Monetary Financial Institutions (hereinafter MFIs) investments in private loans in France, Δ(*L*,MFI). This variable is defined to be the change in the real stock of French MFI loans to the private sector. For the H1 specification, MFI investments in real private loans depends on the real market valuations of bank equity shares, (SP,bk), reflecting the cost of capital ρ in Eq. (14) or *R*(*e*,RR) in Eq. (10). We also included $(\text{SP,bk})^2$ to test for nonlinearities. Our proxy for future expected cash flows, $\Sigma_t X_t$ in Eq. (14) or *R*(*e*,ER) in Eqs. (11a) and (11b), of bank loan customers is taken to be the real value of the SBF index of 250 French stocks traded on the Paris Bourse and indicated in the regressions as (SP,250). We obtained roughly the same results for the CAC 40 index which is less representative of French industry than the (SP,250) index we use. For the demand-oriented H2 specification of MFI investments in private loans, the explanatory variables include real GDP (reflecting business revenues and household income), a short-term business loan rate indicated by (*R*,ST), and a long-term interest rate (*R*,LT) reflecting an alternative source of funding from long-term investors like insurance companies and pension funds. To both specifications, we add a dummy variable (DV,2001/3,4) reflecting the September attack on the financial district in New York City. In preliminary regressions, we also added dummy variables for the 1990 reunification of Germany and the adoption of the Euro in 2000 but neither dummy variable for those events were statistically significant so they were not included in the results reported in Table 3.

Before concluding the discussion of the factors determining French (and later German) MFIs investments in loans to the private sector, it would be useful to consider other possible explanatory variables not particularly related to H1 and H2. In this connection, there is the question whether a bank's lending is in any way influenced by the equity capital position of the bank particularly since the introduction of the Basle Accord on risk-based capital requirements. This is a contentious issue between regulators and the regulated. By and large, bankers argue that higher equity capital requirements will increase the cost of capital of banks which in

Table 3 France quarterly: 1990:1–2006:4

H1												
$\Delta(L,\text{MFI})_t$	=	−	1344.81 (−5.90/00)	+	$63.82\Delta(\text{SP,bk})_{t-4}$ (3.11/00)	+	$.34(\text{SP, bk})_t^2$ (3.72/00)	+	$265.03(\text{SP,250})_t$ (5.21/00)	−	1279.0(DV,2001/3,4) (−3.39/00)	−	$49{,}764.2\Delta(\text{Tier1}/A)_t$ (−1.06/.29)
$\overline{R}^2 = 0.61$; DW = 2.11												
H2												
$\Delta(L,\text{MFI})_t$	=		2157.5 (4.65/.00)	+	$153.56\Delta(\text{GDP})_{t-2}$ (2.29/.03)	−	$260.601(R,\text{ST})_t$ (−5.22/.00)	+	$528.02\Delta(R,\text{LT})_t$ (2.82/.01)	−	884.0(DV,2001/3,4) (−2.05/.04)	−	$63{,}169.3\Delta(\text{Tier1}/A)_t$ (−1.14/.26)
$\overline{R}^2 = 0.391$; DW = 1.55												
***J*-test results**												
$\Delta(L,\text{MFI})_t$	=	−	1222.49 (−4.67/.00)	+	$67.82\Delta(\text{SP,bk})_{t-4}$ (4.06/.00)	+	$.31(\text{SP, bk})_t^2$ (3.47/.00)	+	$228.96(\text{SP,250})_t$ (3.77/.00)	−	1174.22(DV,2001/3,4) (−2.86/.01)	+	$0.15\Delta(L,\text{H2})$ (1.05/.30)
$\Delta(L,\text{MFI})_t$	=		135.33 (0.30/.77)	+	$31.78\Delta(\text{GDP})_{t-2}$ (.44/.66)	−	$19.70(R,\text{ST})_t$ (−.36/.72)	+	$160.52\Delta(R,\text{LT})_t$ (.97/.34)	−	150.32(DV,2001/3,4) (.17/.86)	−	$.93\Delta(L,\text{H1})$ (6.16/.00)

$\overline{R}^2$ = adjusted coefficient of determination; DW = Durbin–Watson statistic

Newey–West computed *t*-scores and *P*-values are given in the parentheses beneath the estimated coefficients turn will result in less bank lending and less real investment financed by bank lending. Their position has some empirical support in the work of Kashyap et al. (2010) and Baker and Wurgler (2013) for the US, and Brun et al. (2013) for France based on the so-called empirical "low risk" anomaly in empirical asset pricing that shows over long periods of time and across different samples that low beta stocks earn higher expected returns than high beta stocks. On the other side of this argument, Admati et al. (2011) invoking Modigliani–Miller argue that the cost of capital of banks is little affected by changes in the equity capital ratio. To see whether the equity capital leverage ratio matters or not, we will include in the regressions for both H1 and H2 an equity capital ratio measured as the ratio of tier 1 capital to total assets or Tier1/*A*.

To sum up, bank lending in France according to H1 depends on two stock market variables: (SP,bk) (and $(\text{SP,bk})^2$) both reflecting the required rate of return of bank shareholders or *R*(*e*,RR) from Eq. (10); and (SP,250) reflecting the expected rate of return on bank loans, or *R*(*e*,ER) from Eqs. (11a) and (11b). The expectation is that the estimated coefficient on the stock market variables will be positive. For H2, the demand specification argues that bank lending in France depends on an income variable measured as real GDP; and two interest rate variables: a short-term business loan rate (*R*,ST) and a long-term rate on private debt (*R*,LT). As stated above, the estimated coefficient on the GDP variable can either be positive or negative while the coefficients on (*R*,ST) and (*R*,LT) are expected to be negative and positive, respectively. To both specifications, we add a dummy variable (DV,2001/3,4) reflecting the attack on the financial center in New York City in September 2001 (Brounen and Derwall 2010). The estimated coefficient on this variable is expected to be negative. Finally, we add to both H1 and H2 an equity leverage variable, Tier1/*A*. The estimated coefficient on this leverage measure is expected to be negative or zero depending on whether the "low risk" anomaly in bank stocks or the Modigliani–Miller proposition is empirically dominant.

The next thing to decide is whether these explanatory variables from the two specifications are measured as levels or first differences. A related question is whether these explanatory variables (except for the dummy variable) are contemporaneous with Δ(*L*,MFI) or lagged. If they are lagged, how many quarters are they to be lagged? Theory provides no guidance here. Therefore, we will use statistical criteria to determine the form of the explanatory variables. The statistical test we will use to determine whether an explanatory variable is to be measured in levels or first differences, or, the lag structure is to minimize the Akaike Information Criteria. On the basis of minimizing the Aikaike criteria, the following specification of the explanatory variables for H1 was chosen.

$$\Delta(\text{SP},\text{bk})_{t-4} \qquad (\text{SP},\text{bk})_t^2 \qquad (\text{SP},250)_t$$

For H2, the specification for the explanatory variables turned out to be:

$\Delta(\mathrm{GDP})_{t-2}$ $\quad$ $(\mathrm{R,ST})_t$ $\quad$ $(\mathrm{R,LT})_t$

The lowest Akaike score for the equity leverage variable included in both specifications was $\Delta(\mathrm{Tier1}/A)_t$.

The results for the regression specification of MFI lending in H1 and H2 are presented in Table 3. The top part of the table reports the OLS estimates for the coefficients on the explanatory variables, the Newey–West t-scores/P-values, the adjusted coefficient of determination, and the Durbin–Watson statistic for both specifications. In the first regression of the table testing H1 it can be seen that the estimated coefficients on $\Delta(\mathrm{SP,bk})_{t-4}$, $(\mathrm{SP,bk})_t^2$, and $(\mathrm{SP},250)_t$ are all positive as predicted by the theory in Sect. 2 above and all are statistically significant. Moreover, Fig. 5a, b indicates that the CUSUM and CUSUM of Squares plots of the recursive residuals all lie within the critical 5 % significance lines indicating that we cannot reject the hypothesis that the estimated coefficients of the explanatory variables are stable over the sample period 1990/1 to 2006/4. The estimated coefficient on (DV,2001/3,4) is negative and statistically significant as expected. Finally, the estimated coefficient on $\Delta(\mathrm{Tier1}/A)_t$ is negative but not significantly different than zero lending support to the Modigliani–Miller view of the effects of capital structure on bank lending. This regression fails to reject H1.

The OLS evidence for the H2 model of bank lending is presented in the second regression in Table 3. The estimated coefficients on $\Delta(\mathrm{GDP})_{t-2}$ is positive and statistically significant at the 5 % level. Of more interest for purposes of monetary policy is the relationship between the short-term interest rate on business loans and borrowing. As can be seen from the table, there is a strong statistically significant negative relationship between the interest rate on short-term business loans, (R,ST), and MFI lending to the private sector. This is support for the traditional hypothesis that monetary policy influences MFI lending through a short-term interest rate channel. The positive and statistically significant estimated coefficient on the long-term interest rate variable, (R,LT), is consistent with the view that firms trade-off short-term borrowing from banks against long-term borrowing from long-term investors like insurance companies and pension funds. Increases in long-term rates have firms shifting their borrowing from these long-term sources of finance to MFIs. Similarly, reductions in long-term rates have firms shifting away from short-term borrowing from MFIs toward long-term borrowing from insurance companies and pension funds. As was the case for H1 the estimated coefficient on $\Delta(\mathrm{Tier1}/A)$ while negative was not statistically significant indicating that financial structure is irrelevant in the lending decisions of MFIs. In this respect, our results differ from (Brun et al. 2013). One slight difference between the two specifications is that the attack on the financial district in New York City in September 2001 had a statistically significant negative effect on MFI lending under H1, but the effect was much weaker under H2. Finally, the CUSUM and CUSUM of Squares plot of the recursive residuals in Fig. 6a, b indicate that we are unable to reject the hypothesis that the estimated coefficients in the H2 specification of MFI lending are stable over the sample period.

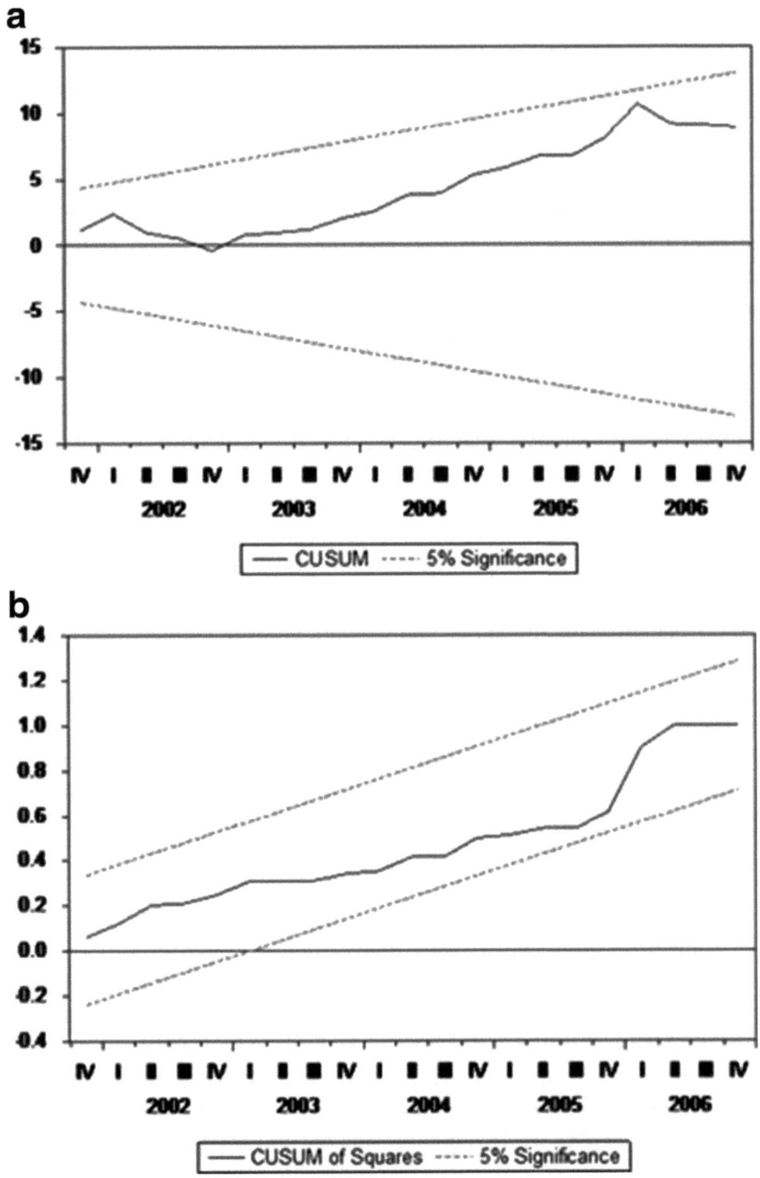

Fig. 5 France: H1 monetary financial institutions

To summarize, we have two specifications of MFI lending that carry with them possibly different implications for the conduct of monetary policy. The specification labeled H2 emphasizes the interest rate channel. If the central bank wishes to influence MFI lending, the policy implication is to vary short-term interest rates to achieve the desired result. Up to the Great Crisis that began in 2007 the data were

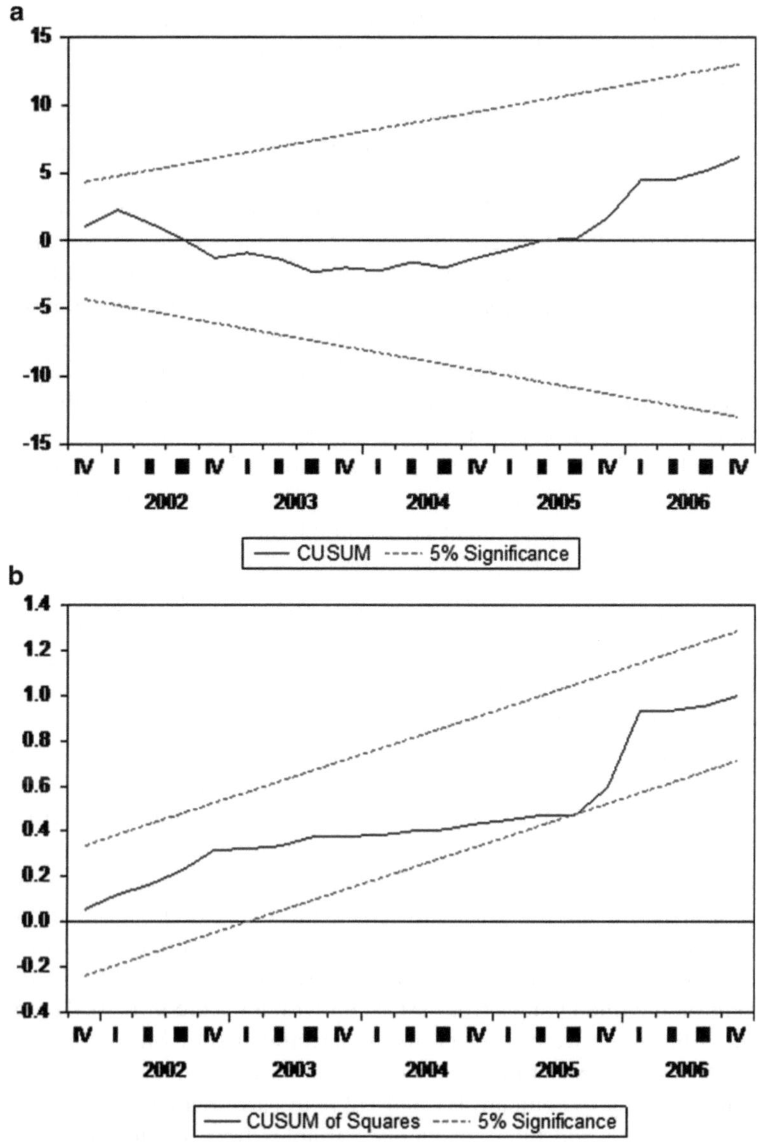

Fig. 6 France: H2 monetary financial institutions

consistent with this hypothesis. Central banks followed the policy implications of this specification during the Great Crisis by reducing short-term interest rates, but the results on MFI lending and economic recovery were minimal. The other specification labeled H1 emphasized the stock market channel. Presumably, this hypothesis states that if the central bank for some reason wishes to influence bank lending it must first influence stock prices. The data over the sample period move in a way that is also consistent with this hypothesis. The end result is that we have two specifications of MFI lending that receive statistical support over the 68 quarters prior to the crisis when each is on the table by itself. The question we now address is whether there are ways to statistically differentiate among these two specifications that carry with them possibly different implications for the conduct of monetary policy.

A second way to compare H1 and H2 is to carry out the *J*-type of a non-nested hypothesis test developed by Davidson and MacKinnon (1981, 1993) and further described in the Journal of Econometrics 1983 special issue.[11] To test H1, we first run the regression in H2 in Table 3 and then collect the fitted values of $\Delta(L,\text{H2})$. In the second step, these fitted values from the regression in H2 are included as an explanatory variable in the regression for H1. If the estimated coefficient on the fitted values of $\Delta(L,\text{H2})$ are statistically significant, then reject H1. If this estimated coefficient is not statistically significant, then we cannot reject H1. The procedure is then repeated for H2 by first running the regression in H1 and then taking the fitted values from $\Delta(L,\text{H1})$ and inserting them as an explanatory variable in the regression for H2. If the estimated coefficient on the fitted values from $\Delta(L,\text{H1})$ are statistically significant then reject H2, otherwise do not reject H2. There are four possible outcomes: (1) reject H2, fail to reject H1; (2) reject H1, fail to reject H2; (3) reject both H1 and H2; and (4) finally, fail to reject both H1 and H2. If both H1 and H2 are rejected as in (3), then neither model is useful in explaining MFI lending. If it is not possible to reject both H1 and H2 as in (4), then the data are not rich enough to discriminate among the two specifications of MFI lending.

The results of this *J*-test for the two specifications for MFI lending in France are presented in the bottom half of Table 3. There it can be seen that the estimated coefficient on the fitted values of $\Delta(L,\text{H2})$ in the H1 regression is only .15 with a *t*-score of 1.05. In other words, the demand specification variables in H2 adds very little if any explanatory power to MFI lending after taking account of the stock market variables in H1. On the other hand, the fitted values from the $\Delta(L,\text{H1})$ specification add a great deal of explanatory power to MFI lending after taking account of the income and interest rate variables contained in H2. The estimated coefficient on the fitted values from H1 is .93 with a *t*-score of 6.16. Therefore, on the basis of the *J*-test we can reject the H2 specification of MFI lending based on interest rates and not reject the H1 specification based on stock market valuations.

Still another way to compare H1 and H2 is to carry out an "omitted variables" test. To do this, we add the explanatory variables from H2 to the stock market explanatory variables in H1 to get an unrestricted regression specification for H1. It is then possible to see whether adding the demand variables from H2 makes a significant contribution to explaining $\Delta(L,\text{MFI})$ over and above the explanatory variables from H1. The Null hypothesis is that the additional regressors from the H2 specification are not jointly significant and therefore do not belong to the H1

[11] Since the equity leverage variable $\Delta\left(\frac{\text{Tier1}}{A}\right)_t$ was not significantly different from zero in the OLS test of H1 and H2, we dropped it from the non-nested hypothesis test in the bottom half of Table 3.

specification of MFI lending. The test for this is an F-statistic and an associated P-value. The result for this omitted variables test for the H1 specification of MFI lending is as follows: when adding $\Delta(\text{GDP})_{t-2}$, $(R,\text{ST})_t$, and $(R,\text{LT})_t$ to the H1 specification, the F-statistic is .39 with an associated probability of .76. What this says is that adding the GDP and the two interest rate variables from the H2 specification of MFI lending to the stock market variables in specification H1 results in a failure to reject the Null hypothesis that H2 belongs to the H1 specification. In other words, GDP and the two interest rate variables are not omitted variables from the H1 specification of MFI lending. On the other hand, when the stock market variables $\Delta(\text{SP,bk})_{t-4}$, $(\text{SP, bk})_t^2$, and $(\text{SP,250})_t$ from the H1 specification are added to the H2 specification of income and interest rates, the F-statistic becomes 12.3 with a probability of .00 indicating that the three stock market variables are omitted variables from the H2 specification of MFI lending. The omitted variables test like the J-test rejects the H2 hypothesis of MFI lending.

In summary, an analysis of MFI investments in private loans from 1990/1 to 2006/4 indicates that the stock market view in H1 reflecting both the required yield of bank shareholders and the expected yield on MFI investment in loans captures the lending decisions of French MFIs better than the H2 specification containing GDP and the two interest rate variables. Even though France is a bank-based financial system in terms of banking assets relative to population and GDP, it would appear that the stock market plays an important role in allocating financial capital to firms and households. We now move on to Germany to see which of these two specifications provides the better description of MFI lending.

5 Bank Lending in Germany

The German economy is the largest in the Euro area. Germany is also the country most closely associated with a bank-oriented financial system in the sense that banks are closely linked to non-financial enterprises. These links historically arose through their direct ownership of equity shares in non-financial enterprises and their indirect control over the voting rights of shares placed with them through trusteeships. This ownership and control of equity shares give German banks a dominant position over that part of the supervisory boards elected by shareholders. As such banks in Germany have considerable influence over the management of non-financial enterprises in terms of their operating decisions and financing decisions which in turn enables them to overcome the problems associated with asymmetric information. For these institutional reasons, it would seem a priori that German banks should be more predisposed to accommodate the informed loan requests of their borrowing customers than banks in other countries, particularly banks in market-based financial systems. The end result is that the H2 specification should fit the intertemporal data on bank loans better than the stock market-oriented

H1 specification. As we will see below, this is partly true in that H1 does not clearly dominate the H2 specification of MFI lending like it did in the case of France.

In the empirical work, we will study bank lending over the period 1985/1 to 2006/4. One problem with this sample time period is that Germany was two separate countries up to 1990. For this sample time period, German reunification will be accommodated with a dummy variable for the year 1990. Slope dummies were not successful so they were not included in the regressions. In France, the attack on the financial district in New York City on 11 September 2001 was a statistically significant event in terms of bank lending. In Germany, it was not so DV2001/3,4 will not be included in the comparison between H1 and H2. Similarly, the creation of the Euro bloc in 2000 was not a significant event in France, so it was not included in the French regressions. It turns out that it was a significant event in the German data so DV2000 was included in the regression tests.

For the sample time period 1985/1 to 2006/4, the best OLS specification of MFI lending, $\Delta(L,\text{MFI})$, for H1 was again obtained by minimizing the Akaike Information Criteria. Using this procedure to select the form of the explanatory variables, we obtained the change in the real market value of bank equity shares lagged two quarters, $\Delta(\text{SP,bk})_{t-2}$, and the contemporaneous change in the real value of the CDAX index of general stock prices, $\Delta(\text{SP,CDAX})_t$. The bank share price variable will proxy for the equity cost of capital for German MFIs and the general share price variable will proxy for the expected returns on MFI loans. Both are expected to be positively related to MFI investments in private loans. In addition to the two dummy variable DV90 and DV2000, we add the equity leverage ratio that by the Akaike Information Criteria is specified as $\Delta(\text{Tier1}/A)_t$. The sign on the coefficients of the two dummy variables is expected to be positive, while the sign on the equity leverage variable is expected to be negative or zero. For H2, the specification that minimized the Akaike Information Criteria was the change in real GDP lagged three quarters and the change in the average interest rate on short-term and long-term debt also lagged three quarters, respectively, labeled $\Delta(\text{GDP})_{t-3}$ and $\Delta(R,\text{Ave})_{t-3}$. For a more detailed description of the data, see the Appendix on Data Sources. To the H2 specification we also add DV90, DV2000, and $\Delta(\text{Tier1}/A)_t$.

Our first comparison of H1 and H2 is for the sample time period 1985/1 to 2006/4 and is given in Table 4. The first thing to note is that for both specifications we encountered a severe problem of first-order serial correlation in the residuals. The existence of serial correlation will not affect the estimated coefficients but it will impart an upward bias to the estimated *t*-scores overstating the true statistical significance of the estimated coefficients. To overcome this problem, we implemented a Cochrane–Orcutt procedure that transform the data in H1 and H2 with an AR(1) process. This AR(1) process is included in both the H1 and H2 regressions. One cost of correcting the serial correlation problem with the Cochrane–Orcutt procedure is that we can no longer use the CUSUM and CUSUM of Squares diagnostic to test for the intertemporal stability of the estimated coefficients or carry out an omitted variables test on the two specifications of MFI lending. In any event for the variables of interest in the H1 specification it can be seen that the estimated coefficients on $\Delta(\text{SP,bk})_{t-2}$ and $\Delta(\text{SP,CDAX})_t$ are both

Table 4 Germany quarterly 1985:1–2006:4

H1															
$\Delta(L,\text{MFI})_t$	=		23.12 (3.69/.00)	+	$0.20\Delta(\text{SP,bk})_{t-2}$ (2.61/.01)	+	$0.33\Delta(\text{SP,CDAX})_t$ (2.46/.02)	+	113.22(DV,90) (46.28/.00)	+	41.07(DV,2000) (1.98/.05)	–	$0.13\Delta(\text{Tier1}/A)_t$ (−5.99/)		
$\overline{R}^2 = 0.49$; DW = 2.15; AR(1) = 0.58															
H2															
$\Delta(L,\text{MFI})_t$	=		21.62 (3.34/.00)	+	$3.56\Delta(\text{GDP})_{t-3}$ (1.42/.16)	–	$23.56(R,\text{Ave})_{t-3}$ (−2.85/.01)	+	95.10(DV,90) (19.43/.00)	+	59.54(DV,2000) (4.21/00)	–	$0.13\Delta(\text{Tier1}/A)_t$ (−5.24/00)		
$\overline{R}^2 = 0.49$; DW = 2.10; AR(1) = 0.57															
***J*-test results**															
$\Delta(L,\text{MFI})_t$	=	-	4.42 (−1.03/.31)	+	$0.15\Delta(\text{SP,bk})_{t-2}$ (2.00/.05)	+	$0.12\Delta(\text{SP,CDAX})_t$ (1.04/.30)	–	12.28(DV,90) (−.42/.67)	–	58.30(DV,2000) (−2.11/.04)	+	$440.78\Delta(\text{Tier1}/A)_t$ (.11/.91)	+	$1.17\Delta(L,\text{H2})$ (7.99/00)
$\Delta(L,\text{MFI})_t$	=	-	5.21 (−.73/.47)	+	$7.53\Delta(\text{GDP})_{t-3}$ (.72/.47)	–	$20.80\Delta(R,\text{Ave})_{t-3}$ (−2.16/.03)	–	0.95(DV,90) (−.13/.90)	–	31.69(DV,2000) (−1.11/.27)	–	$1814.45\Delta(\text{Tier1}/A)_t$ (−.42/.68)	+	$1.03\Delta(L,\text{H1})$ (5.83/.00)

$\overline{R}^2$ = adjusted coefficient of determination; DW = Durbin–Watson statistic

Newey–West computed *t*-scores and *P*-values are given in the parentheses beneath the estimated coefficients positive as predicted by the capital budgeting model of bank lending, and the Newey–West calculated t-statistics indicate that both estimated coefficients are statistically significant. These results are consistent with the stock market signaling theory described in Sect. 2. It is also the case that the estimated coefficient on DV90 (reflecting German reunification) is positive and highly significant, while the estimated coefficient on DV2000 reflecting the birth of the Euro area is positive and statistically significant at the 5 % level. Finally, and quite different than was the case for France, the estimate coefficient on $\Delta(\text{Tier1}/A)_t$ is negative and statistically significant indicating that MFI lending in Germany was strongly influenced by the equity leverage rate in the run-up to the Great Crisis.

We had more difficulty verifying the H2 specification. The estimated coefficient on $\Delta(\text{GDP})_{t-3}$ while positive is not statistically significant at the 5 % (or 10 %) level of significance. The estimated coefficient on the interest rate variable, $\Delta(R,\text{Ave})_{t-3}$, was negative and statistically significant. As in the case for H1, the estimated coefficients on the two dummy variables DV90 and DV2000 were both positive and statistically significant, and the estimated coefficient on the equity leverage variable $\Delta(\text{Tier1}/A)_t$ was negative and statistically significant. At this point, the best OLS evidence for H2 based on minimizing the Akaike Criteria seems less strong than the evidence for H1.

In the second half of the table, we analyze the question of model specification further by carrying out a non-nested hypothesis test. In doing this, we first run the regression in H2 and obtain the computed values of $\Delta(L,\text{H2})$. We then insert the computed values from $\Delta(L,\text{H2})$ as an additional explanatory variable in the regression describing H1. As can be seen the estimated coefficient on the computed values from $\Delta(L,\text{H2})$ in the regression $\Delta(L,\text{H1})$ is 1.172 with a t-statistic of 7.99. We therefore reject H1. Reversing this procedure we run the regression for H1 and obtain the computed values for $\Delta(L,\text{H1})$. We then take the computed values from $\Delta(L,\text{H1})$ and insert them as an additional explanatory variable in the regression describing H2. Again, it can be seen the estimated coefficient on the computed values from $\Delta(L,\text{H1})$ in the regression $\Delta(L,\text{H2})$ is 1.032 with a t-statistic of 5.83. We therefore reject H2. The results of the J form of the non-nested hypothesis test are that neither model of MFI lending is valid in the presence of the other. This is not an uncommon result when applying the J-test to time series models with autocorrelated errors (see Bernanke et al. 1988).

One approach to this problem is to simply ignore the autocorrelation and perform the J-test on regressions without a correction such as the Cochrane–Orcutt procedure (see Pesaran and Deaton 1978; Bean 1981; Wisley and Johnson 1985; Johannes and Nasseh 1985). We choose not to follow this approach. Fortunately, Germany also has balance sheet data for the commercial bank component of MFIs and as we will see in Table 5 below there is no evidence of first-order serial correlation in the residuals for this sector. Our strategy for selecting the exact specification for H1 and H2 will be the same as the one previously used for MFIs, namely, minimize the Akaike Criteria. Using this procedure for H1, we regress $\Delta(L,\text{Banks})_t$ on $\Delta(\text{SP},\text{bk})_{t-2}$, $\Delta(\text{SP},\text{CDAX})_{t-4}$, and $\Delta(\text{Tier1}/A)_t$. The dummy variables DV90 and DV2000 remain the same. For the H2 specification,

Table 5 Germany quarterly, 1985:1–2006:4

H1															
$\Delta(L,\text{Banks})_t$	=		5.34 (3.63/.00)	+	$.09\Delta(\text{SP,bk})_{t-2}$ (3.47/.00)	+	$.15\Delta(\text{SP,CDAX})_{t-4}$ (1.59/.12)	+	90.25(DV,90) (30.19/.00)	+	38.91(DV,2000) (9.47/00)	–	$3926.80\Delta(\text{Tier1}/A)_t$ (−4.03/00)		
$\overline{R}^2 = 0.49$; DW = 2.01															
H2															
$\Delta(L,\text{Banks})_t$	=		3.82 (1.88/.06)	+	$3.85\Delta(\text{GDP})_t$ (2.02/.05)	–	$1.54\Delta(R,\text{Ave})_{t-3}$ (−.54/.59)	+	91.02(DV,90) (29.57/.00)	+	41.42(DV,2000) (9.72/.00)	–	$3994.53\Delta(\text{Tier1}/A)_t$ (−3.67/00)		
$\overline{R}^2 = 0.46$; DW = 1.90															
***J*-test results**															
$\Delta(L,\text{Banks})_t$	=		.84 (0.26/.79)	+	$0.07\Delta(\text{SP,bk})_{t-2}$ (1.61/.11)	+	$.15\Delta(\text{SP,CDAX})_t$ (2.32/0.02)	+	18.97(DV,90) (0.40/.69)	+	5.66(DV,2000) (.22/.82)	–	$799.85\Delta(\text{Tier1}/A)_t$ (−.38/71)	+	$.78\Delta(L,\text{H2})$ (1.59/.12)
$\Delta(L,\text{Banks})_t$	=	–	1.37 (−0.67/.50)	+	$2.88\Delta(\text{GDP})_{t-2}$ (1.63/.10)	–	$3.55\Delta(R,\text{Ave})_{t-3}$ (−0.41/.68)	–	2.015(DV,90) (−0.09/.93)	–	.17(DV,2000) (4.50/.00)	–	$178.76\Delta(\text{Tier1}/A)_t$ (−.12/.91)	+	$.95\Delta(L,\text{H1})$ (2.96/0.00)

$\overline{R}^2$ = adjusted coefficient of determination; DW = Durbin–Watson statistic

Newey–West computed t-scores and P-values are given in the parentheses beneath the estimated coefficients we regressed $\Delta(L,\text{Banks})$ on $\Delta(\text{GDP})_t$ and $\Delta(R,\text{Ave})_{t-3}$ along with $\Delta(\text{Tier1}/A)_t$, DV90 and DV2000.

The OLS results for H1 and H2 are presented in Table 5 for the sample period 1985/1 to 2006/4. For the H1 specification, the estimated coefficients on the two stock market variables are positive as predicted by theory but only the $\Delta(\text{SP,bk})_{t-2}$ proxy for the bank's equity cost of capital is statistically significant. The estimated coefficient for the proxy of the expected return on bank loans, $\Delta(\text{SP,CDAX})_{t-4}$, just misses significance at the 10 % level. All the other variables DV90, DV2000, and $\Delta(\text{Tier1}/A)_t$ are as predicted. In the case of H2, the estimated coefficient on $\Delta(\text{GDP})_t$ is positive and statistically significant at the 5 % level. The result for $\Delta(R,\text{Ave})_{t-3}$ is less encouraging. While the sign of the estimated coefficient is negative as predicted, it is not significantly different from zero. As was the case for H1, the signs and significance of the estimated coefficients on DV90, DV2000, and $\Delta(\text{Tier1}/A)_t$ were as predicted. Finally, it should be noted that the estimated Durbin–Watson statistic for both H1 and H2 indicates an absence of first-order autocorrelation thus enabling us to carry out the *J*-test and other specification tests. In this connection, one of these tests is the CUSUM and CUSUM of Squares plots. These are presented for the H1 and H2 specifications of bank lending in Figs. 7 and 8. There it can be seen in both figures that the recursive residuals from both the H1 and H2 specifications of bank lending fall within the 5 % boundary lines indicating that the coefficients are stable through the sample period.

The results for the *J*-test are presented in the second half of Table 5. Again the procedure is to run the regression in H2 and obtain the fitted values for $\Delta(L,\text{H2})$. We then include the fitted values of $\Delta(L,\text{H2})$ as an additional explanatory variable in the regression describing H1. From the table it can be seen that the estimated coefficient on the fitted values from $\Delta(L,\text{H2})$ in the regression $\Delta(L,\text{H1})$ is .779 with a *t*-score of 1.589. This *t*-score indicates that the coefficient on $\Delta(L,\text{H2})$ in the regression $\Delta(L,\text{H1})$ is not significant at the 5 (nor 10) % level of significance. We therefore fail to reject at both the 5 (and 10) % level of significance the model specification in H1. The procedure is then reversed by first running the regression in H1. The fitted values from $\Delta(L,\text{H1})$ are then included as an additional explanatory variable in the regression describing H2. It can be seen in the table that the estimated coefficient on the fitted values from $\Delta(L,\text{H1})$ in the regression $\Delta(L,\text{H2})$ is .953 with a *t*-score of 2.964. Since the fitted values of $\Delta(L,\text{H1})$ are a statistically significant (at the 1 % level) explanatory variable in the $\Delta(L,\text{H2})$ regression, we reject H2. The *J*-test indicates that H1 is a better specification of bank lending than H2.

To test these results further, we carry out an omitted variables test on both the H1 and H2 specification of bank lending. Beginning with H1, we add the explanatory variables $\Delta(\text{GDP})_t$ and $\Delta(R,\text{Ave})_{t-3}$ from H2 to get an unrestricted regression for the H1 specification of bank lending. Again, the output of this test is an *F*-statistic and *P*-value testing whether the estimated coefficients on these two additional regressors from H2 are jointly zero. In this case, the *F*-statistic is 1.46 and the associated probability is .24. We therefore reject the hypothesis that $\Delta(\text{GDP})_t$ and $\Delta(R,\text{Ave})_{t-3}$ are omitted variables from the H1 specification. On the other hand,

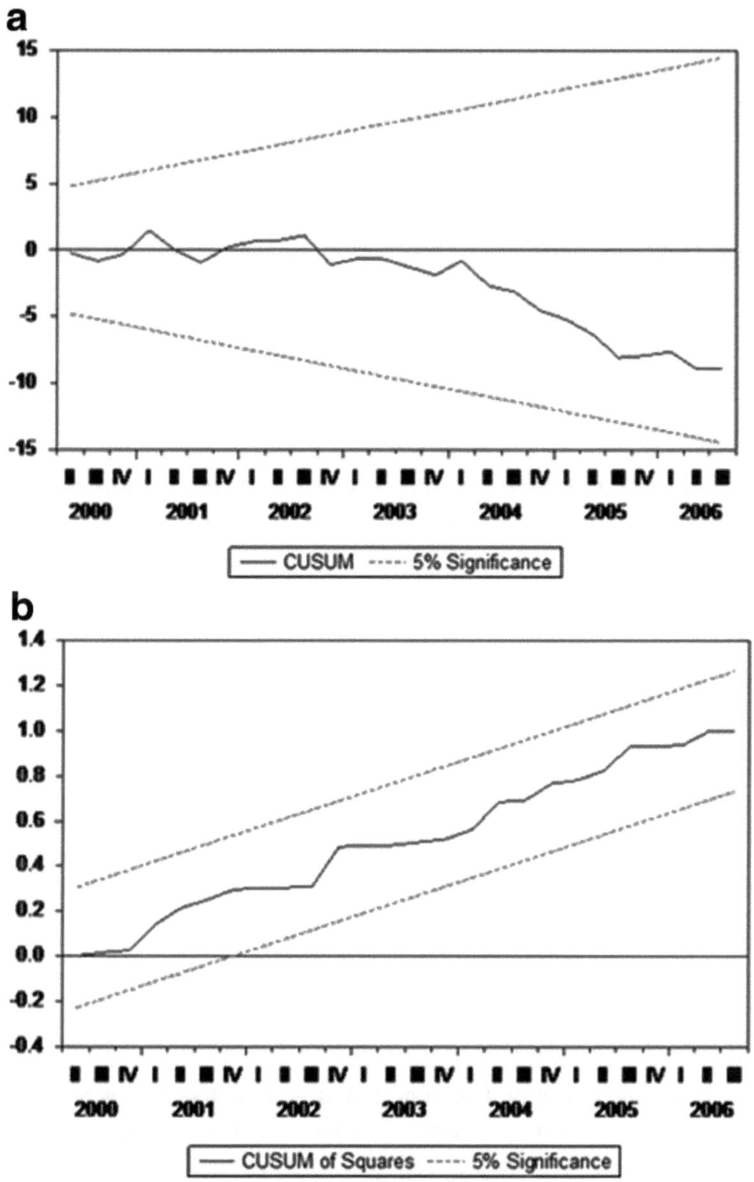

Fig. 7 Germany: H1 commercial banks

when $\Delta(\text{SP,bk})_{t-2}$ and $\Delta(\text{SP,CDAX})_{t-4}$ are added to the H2 specification of bank lending, the F-statistic is 4.39 with a probability of .016. We therefore cannot reject (at the 5 % significance level) the hypothesis that these two stock market variables from H1 are omitted variables from the H2 specification of bank lending. These results from the omitted variables test confirm the results from the J-test; namely,

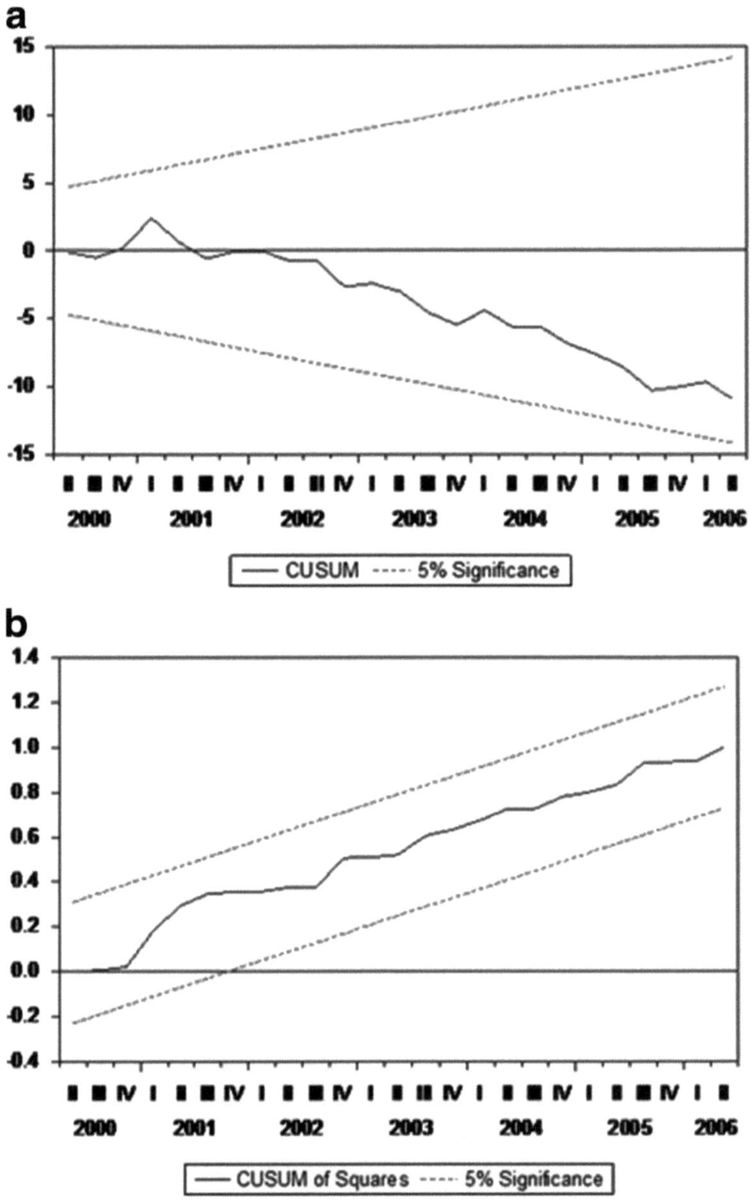

Fig. 8 Germany: H2 commercial banks

commercial bank investments in private loans are relatively better described by H1 than H2.

The results of our comparisons between the demand-oriented H2 specification of bank lending and the stock market H1 specification of bank lending in Germany are somewhat mixed. For the broader set of monetary financial institutions, neither specification worked well due in part to autocorrelation in the residuals which we corrected with a Cochrane–Orcutt AR(1) procedure. We did, however, achieve some success with the commercial bank sector of monetary financial institutions. There we were able to reject the demand-oriented model of bank lending in H2 and not reject the H1 specification based on stock valuations. Even though customer relationships are very important in a bank-based financial system like that in place in Germany, it would appear that stock market valuations play an important role in allocating loan finance to borrowers over the sample period of 1985–2007.

6 Summary and Policy Implications

In this chapter, I compare two models of bank lending in France and Germany, countries that are frequently classified as having bank-oriented financial systems. One model was based on capital budgeting theory that is typically not used by economists when modeling bank investments in private loans. The capital budgeting model argues that bank investments in paper assets like private loans must meet a cost of capital hurdle just like the tangible investments of nonfinancial firms. That cost of capital hurdle was proxied by changes in the real market valuations of bank shares. An increase (or decrease) in the market valuation of bank shares, Δ(SP,bk), reflects a decrease (or increase) in the equity cost of capital for banks. Other things remaining equal, banks should then make a larger (or smaller) investment in loans. The other ingredient in the capital budgeting decision for banks is the expected future cash returns on private loans. These expected cash returns were proxied with the real value of general share prices (SP,250) for France and (SP,CDAX) for Germany. An increase (or decrease) in general share valuations reflect the stock markets assessment of changing expected future cash returns of borrowers. Other things equal an increase (or decrease) in these expected returns should increase (or decrease) bank investments in loans. In effect, the capital budgeting model of bank lending takes the view that equity share valuations reflect all the relevant information about the future prospects of bank loan customers, and the risk aversion and risk perceptions of bank shareholders. This specification of bank lending was labeled H1. The alternative specification labeled H2 was based on traditional supply and demand analysis. This traditional view of bank lending in Europe for institutional reasons focused attention on the demand side of the market. Historically, European banks have had a close relationship to their loan customers, and because of this close relationship they go to great lengths to accommodate their loan requests by typically carrying excess liquidity or having access to managed liabilities including central bank funding. Loan demand by borrowers were assumed to depend negatively on the cost of loan finance (an interest rate variable R) and positively on an income variable (like GDP) reflecting the ability of borrowers to service loans. Other variables not unique to H1 or H2 included the equity leverage ratio, Δ(Tier1/A), and dummy variables for exogenous events like the reunification of Germany in 1990, the formation of the Euro area in 2000, and the attack on the financial district in New York City in 2001.

We purposely chose to compare parsimonious versions of H1 and H2. Our reason is that while it is possible to pump-up the explanatory power of both specifications with additional variables, those additional variables would be extraneous to the theoretical core of both specifications. We are, therefore, following the caution to be wary of economists bearing free parameters.

Our basis for comparing H1 and H2 consisted of carrying out non-nested hypothesis tests and omitted variables tests. There are not many examples of these kinds of econometric tests in the empirical finance literature. The usual practice is to pose a standalone model where the null hypothesis is to reject or not reject it. As standalone models of bank lending in the case of France both H1 and H2 were not rejected by the data. Which model is better? This is the question answered by the non-nested hypothesis test and the omitted variables test. The clearest results in this chapter were for France where both tests decisively rejected the H2 specification based on the demand for loans from borrowers and were unable to reject the H1 capital budgeting specification based on stock market valuations for banks and nonfinancial enterprises. This would suggest that future model development on bank lending in France could fruitfully focus on H1.

The results for Germany were mixed. The standalone regression specification for MFI lending in Table 4 provided slightly more support for H1 than H2 if one simply counts the number of statistically significant estimated coefficients with the correct theoretical sign. This can be seen in the top half of the table where the estimated coefficients on both stock market variables in H1 were positive and statistically significant. For H2, the positive estimated coefficient on ΔGDP was not statistically significant at the 5 % significance level and the negative estimated coefficient on changes in the bank lending rate Δ(*R*,Ave) was statistically significant. Unfortunately, the non-nested hypothesis tests ended up rejecting both H1 and H2. The same was true for the omitted variables tests in that the demand variable of ΔGDP and interest rates, Δ(*R*,Ave), were omitted variables in the H1 regression, and both stock market variables from H1 were omitted variables in the H2 regression. Part of the problem was the fact that the residuals from both the H1 and H2 regressions were highly autocorrelated which we eliminated with a Cochrane–Orcutt AR (1) correction. This is a well-known problem with non-nested hypothesis test that has previously arisen when comparing model specifications for intertemporal consumption expenditures, investment expenditures, and money demand. This also is probably one reason why non-nested hypothesis tests are not frequently used in finance and economics in that the test rejects too many theories. Fortunately, the Bundesbank publishes balance sheets for the commercial bank sector of German MFIs. When we carried out our comparison of the H1 and H2 regressions for German commercial banks, there was no evidence of first order autocorrelation in the regression residuals. We then implemented non-nested hypothesis test and omitted variables tests on the H1 and H2 specifications of lending by commercial banks in Table 5. Both tests rejected the H2 specification of bank lending at the 5 % significance level and failed to reject the H1 specification. However, both the rejection of H2 and the failure to reject H1 for German commercial banks were not as decisive as they were for French MFIs.[12]

What is the practical policy significance of the H1 and H2 specifications for bank lending? Conventional monetary policy assumes that some version of H2 is correct and consequently there is an interest rate channel in bank lending. According to this line of reasoning, if the central bank during a recession wants to increase bank lending in the hope of stimulating consumption and investment spending, they use various instruments of monetary policy to reduce interest rates. The usual strategy is to target some risk-free market rate and/or administered interest rate and then let private investors arbitrage the target rate change out to interest rates that are relevant for spending decisions by households and firms such as the bank loan rate and bond yields. But suppose that H1 is the correct specification for bank lending. What implications might this have for monetary policy? It might be argued that nothing should change. The central bank would still target a risk-free rate and/or an administered rate and then let private investors arbitrage the rate change out to stock market valuations which then would influence bank lending and spending by households and firms. The economic reasoning behind this is that in an efficient market all yields are linked together so that exogenous shocks in one market will be felt in all markets.

Unfortunately, the arbitrage channel from target rate to the yields relevant for lending in H2 and then spending decisions has been exceedingly slow and erratic during the Great Crisis. Because of this slowness, some central banks (particularly the Federal Reserve and to a lesser extent the ECB) have aggressively pursued what has come to be called "non-standard policy" initiatives. Some of these non-standard policies have been aimed at providing liquidity support to the banking system and include the Term Auction Facility (TAF) and the Troubled Asset Relief Program (TARP) in the US, and the lengthening of the maturity profile of repo loans to banks and the providing of unlimited liquidity to banks in the Euro area. Carpenter et al. (2013) estimate that without the liquidity support programs in place in the US and the Euro area, business loans would have been 23 % less in the US, while without the liquidity provisions by the ECB Euro area loans to nonfinancial enterprises would have been 4 % less. Besides these liquidity provisions to banks, non-standard policy during the Great Crisis included the direct purchase of public and private securities by the ECB and the commercial paper funding facility of the Federal Reserve.

The above non-standard policy initiatives were thought to work through an interest rate channel. What might a non-standard policy initiative be when there is a stock market channel? One standard policy instrument some central banks once had (and used) to influence stock prices was to impose credit controls for the buying

[12] It should also be noted that the standalone specification for H1 in the top half of Table 5 for commercial banks was not as supportive of the capital budgeting model of bank lending as the standalone specification for MFI lending in Table 4 in that the positive estimated coefficient on (SP,CDAX) was not statistically significant at the 5 % significance level.

and selling of stock. These credit controls or margin requirements could be varied over time and linked to the stock market cycle. When stock prices are rising above their intrinsic value on a tide of investor optimism, the central bank could raise margin requirements on stock purchases and at least prevent borrowed money from financing the stock market bubble. Similarly, when stock prices are falling below their intrinsic value driven by investor pessimism, the central bank could lower margin requirements and encourage stock investing with borrowed money. This policy would again rely on private investors implementing the central bank's policy through their buying and selling decisions. One problem with this approach is that some investors can borrow abroad, and thereby thwart the central bank's policy of dampening any speculative increase in stock prices with borrowed money.

Moving further along the nontraditional policy spectrum would be for the central bank itself to buy and sell a well-diversified portfolio of equities. This proposal is not new having been previously suggested by Tobin and Brainard (1977), Fischer and Merton (1984), and Krainer (2003, 2013). Moreover, there are actual cases where governments have directly intervened in the stock market to stabilize the market and the economy. For example, in the 1997/1998 Asian Crisis the Hang Seng stock index in Hong Kong fell 40 % over the period June 1997 to June 1998 as a result of massive short selling in the spot and futures markets by foreign hedge funds.[13] These foreign hedge funds could and did borrow abroad to finance their portfolio strategy. In response to this sharp decline in the stock market, the Hong Kong monetary authority believing stocks were undervalued in August 1998 purchased 118 billion HK dollars of stock over 10 consecutive trading days to reverse this downward trend. At the time this policy was criticized as being socialistic in that Hong Kong had just recently reverted to China. In any event the value of their investment at the end of 1999 was 200 billion HK dollars for a gain of 69 % not counting the dividends received over that period. After this successful speculative gain, the policy was then criticized on the grounds that this large capital gain would be used to reduce a large government budget deficit partly the result of the recession thereby hiding wasteful government outlays.

The Hong Kong government's experiment of carrying out open market purchases of equities was highly successful in terms of earning a handsome profit and stemming the decline in equity prices and reviving GDP growth from −5.9 % in 1998 to 2.9 % in 1999 and 7.7 % in 2000. This profitable stock market intervention by the Hong Kong monetary authority in 1998 appears to have been a "one off" policy. Would a more continuous policy of buying and selling stocks by the government be desirable? What might a more continuous policy of open market operations in a broad index of equities like the market portfolio look like? To begin with it would seem that such a policy should be based on the intrinsic value of the market as a whole, and therefore be linked to the aggregate earnings of the business sector. If the permanent earnings of the business sector grow at an annual rate of 2.5 % on average over long periods of time, fundamental stock valuations should

[13] For a detailed description of this episode see Goodhart and Dai (2003).

grow at roughly the same rate abstracting from changes in time preference and risk aversion. Large deviations of market valuation from intrinsic valuation serve no socially useful purpose and potentially can amplify the fluctuations in real economic activity. One possibility then is for the central bank to bracket the long-run average growth rate of stocks with a $\pm\alpha$-percent filter. The magnitude of that filter would presumably depend in some way on the magnitude of the transitory earnings of firms that the stock market is tracking. In this setup, if stocks fall below the lower filter band in an investor flight to safety, the central bank would buy the market portfolio and drive it up to the lower filter band. Conversely, if stocks rose above the upper α-percent filter on a wave of exuberant optimism, the central bank would sell the market portfolio until the market reached the upper filter band. In this way, the central bank would limit the fluctuations in the stock market which in turn would limit fluctuations in bank lending and real economic activity.

Setting aside political considerations, would a policy of conducting some open market operations in a diversified portfolio of equities be feasible? Would the ECB or the Federal Reserve have enough resources to limit fluctuations in the stock market? The example of Hong Kong indicates that central banks can drive stock prices up with their purchases. Moreover, the ECB and the Federal Reserve have shown in the Great Crisis that they can drive the yield of short-term financial securities practically to zero. Could they do the same with equities? Since both of these large central banks have access to almost unlimited quantities of their currency, the answer would seem to be: Yes. But what about preventing share prices from rising above some upper filter band? We have less evidence on this. Yet, it would seem that a central bank credibly committing to some upper and lower filter bands on the stock market could probably rely on private investors keeping the market within the targeted bands. Still other problems remain. If the central bank would trade in the stock market, would that change the composition of private investors in the market? In other words, would the mix of noise traders and informed traders change? If informed traders would leave the market then the noise traders would determine relative share prices which would have implications for the efficient allocation of capital across different sectors of the economy. The answer to this question is crucial in that possible misallocation of resources would have to be weighed against any benefits of stabilizing the economy. Finally, how would managers of financial and nonfinancial enterprises react in terms of their asset and financing adjustments if central banks became a significant shareholder in their company? The model in Sect. 2 had managers arbitraging the differences between the financial market value of the firm and the factor market value (i.e., economic book value) of the firm. Would this arbitrage mechanism work in the same way if the central bank was an investor in the firm's securities? In this connection would the central bank be considered a permanent or transitory investor? All of these are important questions that would have to be answered before central banks could consider conducting some open market operations in equities. And yet, if our results were found to hold for other Euro area countries, the payoff of conducting open market operations in equities could possibly be substantial. One problem the ECB will always face with its current instruments of monetary policy is that the economic problems facing individual countries within the Euro Area are different. One policy may not fit all. What might be a good policy for France and Germany may not be a good policy for Italy and Spain at any given point in time. That being the case it would be possible for the ECB to have different stock market targets for the different countries within the Euro area depending on their given economic condition. However, these are only conjectures requiring additional research. The turbulent times unleashed on the world economy by the Great Crisis has led to new ways to think about banks, bank regulation, monetary policy, and the links between finance and the economy. For the financial economist, this is an exciting period with much work remaining to be done.

Acknowledgments I would like to thank Colin Mayer, Henri Pages, Natacha Valla, Hubert Kempf, Ted Azarmi, Mathias Moerch, and seminar participants at the 31st SUERF Colloquium & Baffi Finlawmetrics Conference for helpful suggestions and comments on earlier versions of this paper. They are not responsible for any errors that might remain. I am grateful for the financial support provided by the Banque de France and Hochschule Heilbronn. The views expressed in this paper are not necessarily those of the Banque de France.

Appendix on Data Sources

France

MFI	Monetary financial institutions excluding the Banque de France and mutual funds. MFIs include resident credit institutions and other resident credit institutions that issue deposits and/or close substitutes, and grant credit and/or make investments in securities.
(*L*,MFI)	The stock of MFI loans outstanding to other Euro area residents. This variable is deflated by the French consumer price index. Source: Banque de France. Pre-1999 data converted into euros at the fixed irrevocable exchange rate between French francs and euros.
(Equity)	The total stock of equity capital and reserves of French MFIs. Source: Banque de France. Pre-1999 data converted at the fixed irrevocable exchange rate between French francs and euros.
A	The stock of total assets of MFIs in France. Source: Banque de France. Pre-1999 data converted at the fixed irrevocable exchange rate between French francs and euros.
(SP,bk)	Quarterly index of French bank share prices deflated by the consumer price index in France. Source: DataStream, Code: SBFNNKZ.
(SP,250)	Quarterly index of general share prices of 250 stocks traded on the Paris bourse. This stock series was deflated by the consumer price index in France. Source: Datastream, Code: FSBF250.
(GDP)	Real gross domestic product in France. Nominal GDP was deflated by the consumer price index for France. Source: Banque de France.

(*R*,LT) Real interest rate on medium to long-term loans to business. The nominal interest rate was deflated by the percentage rate of change in the French consumer price index. Monthly rates were averaged to obtain quarterly rates. Source: Banque de France, Business Conditions Division.

(*R*,ST) Real interest rate on overdraft facilities. The nominal rate was deflated by the percentage rate of change in the French consumer price index. Monthly rates were averaged to obtain quarterly rates. Source: Banque de France, Business Conditions Division.

Germany

MFI Monetary financial institutions excluding the Deutsche Bundesbank and mutual funds. These are financial institutions that issue deposits or close substitutes for deposits, and grant credit and/or make investments in securities.

(*L*,MFI) The stock of MFI loans outstanding to non-MFI borrowers. This variable is deflated by the German producer price index (2000 = 100) seasonally adjusted. Source: Deutsche Bundesbank, Time series key OU0083. Pre-1999 data converted at the fixed irrevocable exchange rate between DMs and euros.

(*L*,Banks) The stock of commercial bank loans outstanding to non-MFI borrowers. This variable is deflated by the German producer price index seasonally adjusted. Commercial banks comprise the subgroup of big banks, regional banks, other commercial banks, and branches of foreign banks. Source: Deutsche Bundesbank, Time series key OU0783. Pre-1999 data converted at the fixed irrevocable exchange rate between DMs and euros.

(*A*,MFI) The stock of total assets of MFIs. Source: Deutsche Bundesbank, Time series key: OU0308. Pre-1999 data converted at the fixed irrevocable exchange rate between DMs and euros.

(*A*,Banks) The stock of total assets of commercial banks. Source: Deutsche Bundesbank, Time series key: OU0749. Pre-1999 data converted at the fixed irrevocable exchange rate between DMs and euros.

(Equity) Total equity capital. For MFIs this variable was obtained from the Deutsche Bundesbank, time series key OU0322. For commercial banks, this variable was obtained from the Deutsche Bundesbank, Time series key OU1543. Pre-1999 data converted at the fixed irrevocable exchange rates between DMs and euros.

(SP,bk) Quarterly index of large German bank share prices deflated by the German producer price index. Source: Datastream, DS banks, Code BANKSBD (PI).

(SP, CDAX)	The CDAX stock price index of all ordinary and preference shares officially listed on the Frankfurt stock exchange of companies domiciled in Germany. The series is deflated by the German producer price index. Source: Deutsche Bundesbank S 300, Time series key WU 001a.
Δ(GDP)	The change in real GDP in Germany. Source: Deutsche Bundesbank, Time series key jbb000.
(*R*,Ave)	The average yield on German debt securities of all maturities. Monthly data were averaged to obtain quarterly data. The average yields were deflated by the percentage change in the German producer price index. Source: Deutsche Bundesbank, Time series key WU0017.

References

Acemoglu, D., Johnson, S., & Robinson, J. (2001). The colonial origins of economic development: An empirical investigation. *American Economic Review, 91*, 1369–1401.

Admati, A., DeMarzo, P., Hellwig, M., & Pfleider, P. (2011). *Fallacies, irrelevant facts, and myths in the discussion of capital regulation: Why bank equity is not expensive*. Stanford GSB Research Paper No. 2065.

Baker, M., & Wurgler, J. (2013). *Do strict capital requirements raise the cost of capital? Banking regulation and the low risk anomaly*. NBER Working Paper No. 19018.

Bean, C. (1981). An econometric model of manufacturing investment in the U.K. *Economic Journal, 91*, 106–121.

Berger, A., & Humphrey, D. (1998). Efficiency of financial institutions: International survey and directions for future research. In P. Harker & S. Zenios (Eds.), *Performance of financial institutions*. Cambridge: Cambridge University Press.

Berger, A., & Udell, G. (1994). Did risk-based capital allocate bank credit and cause a "credit crunch" in the United States? *Journal of Money, Credit, and Banking, 26*, 585–628.

Berger, A., & Udell, G. (1995). Relationship and lines of credit in small firm finance. *Journal of Business, 68*, 351–382.

Bernanke, B., Bohn, H., & Reiss, P. (1988). Alternative nonnested specification tests of time series models. *Journal of Econometrics, 37*, 293–326.

Bernanke, B., & Gertler, M. (1995). Inside the black box: The credit channel of monetary policy transmission. *Journal of Economic Perspectives, 9*, 27–48.

Brounen, D., & Derwall, J. (2010). The impact of terrorist attacks on international stock markets. *European Financial Management, 16*, 585–598.

Brun, M., Fraisse, H., & Thesmar, D. (2013). *The real effects of bank capital requirements*. HEC Paris Research Paper No. FIN-2013-988.

Calza, A., Gartner, C., & Sousa, J. (2003). Modelling the demand for loans to the private sector in the Euro area. *Applied Economics, 35*, 107–117.

Campello, M., Giambona, E., Graham, J., & Harvey, C. (2012). Access to liquidity and corporate investment in Europe. *Review of Finance, 16*, 323–346.

Carpenter, S., & Demiralp, S. (2010). *Money, reserves, and the transmission of monetary policy: Does the money multiplier exist?* Finance and Economics Discussion Series. Division of Research & Statistics and Monetary Affairs, Federal Reserve Board, Washington, DC.

Carpenter, S., Demiralp, S., & Eisenschmidt, J. (2013). *The effectiveness of the non-standard policy measures during the financial crisis: The experience of the Federal Reserve and the European Central Bank*. Finance and Economics Discussion Series. Division of Research & Statistics and Monetary Affairs, Federal Reserve Board, Washington, DC.

Davidson, R., & MacKinnon, J. (1981). Several tests for model specification in the presence of alternative hypotheses. *Econometrica, 49*, 781–793.

Davidson, R., & MacKinnon, J. (1993). *Estimation and inference in econometrics*. Oxford: Oxford University Press.

Dichev, I., & Skinner, D. (2002). Large sample evidence on the debt covenant hypothesis. *Journal of Accounting Research, 40*, 1091–1193.

Eickmeier, S., Hofmann, B., & Worms, A. (2006). *Macroeconomic Fluctuations and bank lending: Evidence for Germany and the Euro area*. Deutsche Bundesbank Discussion Paper, Series 1: Economic Studies, No. 34/2006.

Fischer, S., & Merton, R. (1984). Macroeconomics and finance. *Carnegie-Rochester Conference Series on Public Policy, 21*, 57–108.

Friedman, B., & Kuttner, K. (1993). Economic activity and the short-term credit markets: An analysis of prices and quantities. *Brookings Papers on Economic Activity, 2*, 193–283.

Frommel, M., & Schmidt, T. (2006). *Bank lending and asset prices in the Euro area*. Unpublished paper available on the SSRN.

Goodhart, C., & Dai, L. (2003). *Intervention to save Hong Kong: The authorities counter-speculation in financial markets*. Oxford: Oxford University Press.

Gurley, J. (1961). Review of M. Friedman's A program for monetary stability. *Review of Economics and Statistics, 43*, 307–308.

Johannes, J., & Nasseh, A. (1985). Income or wealth in money demand: An application of non-nested hypothesis tests. *Southern Economic Journal, 51*, 1099–1106.

Kahle, K., & Stulz, R. (2011). *Financial Policies, investment, and the financial crisis: Impaired credit channel or diminished demand for capital*. Dice Center Working Paper 2011-3.

Kashyap, A., Stein, J., & Hanson, S. (2010). *An Analysis of the impact of substantially heightened capital requirements on large financial institutions*. Harvard University Working Paper.

King, R., & Levine, R. (1993). Finance and growth: Schumpeter might be right. *Quarterly Journal of Economics, 108*, 717–737.

Kooths, S., & Rieger, M. (2009). *Caught in the U.S. subprime meltdown 2007/2008: Germany loses its wallet but escapes major harm*. Unpublished manuscript available at http://ssrn.com/abstract=1425530

Krainer, R. (1985). *The financial system and the coordination of economic activity*. New York: Praeger.

Krainer, R. (1992). *Finance in a theory of the business cycle*. Oxford: Blackwell.

Krainer, R. (2002). Banking in a theory of the business cycle: A model and critique of the basle accord on risk-based capital requirements for banks. *International Review of Law and Economics, 21*, 413–433.

Krainer, R. (2003). *Corporate finance, governance, and business cycles: Theory and international comparisons*. Amsterdam: North-Holland.

Krainer, R. (2009). Portfolio and financing adjustments for U.S. banks: Some empirical evidence. *Journal of Financial Stability, 5*, 1–24.

Krainer, R. (2013). Towards a program for financial stability. *Journal of Economic Behavior and Organization, 85*, 207–218.

Krainer, R. (2014). Financial aspects of business cycles: An analysis of balance sheet adjustments of U.S. nonfinancial enterprises over the twentieth century. *Journal of Money, Credit, and Banking, 46*, 371–407.

Levine, R. (1998). The legal environment, banks, and long-run economic growth. *Journal of Money, Credit, and Banking, 30*, 596–613.

Manning, M. (2003). *Finance causes growth: Can we be so sure?* Contributions to Macroeconomics 3, at http://www.bepress.com

Mayer, C. (1998). Financial systems and corporate governance: A review of international evidence. *Journal of Institutional and Theoretical Economics, 154*, 144–165.

Nakamura, L. (1993). Recent changes in commercial banking: Information and lending. *Financial Markets, Institutions, and Instruments, 2*, 73–88.

Norden, L., & Weber, M. (2007). *Checking account information and credit risk of bank customers.* Unpublished manuscript available at SSRN.

Pesaran, M., & Deaton, A. (1978). Testing non-nested nonlinear regression models. *Econometrica, 46*, 677–694.

Peterson, M., & Rajan, R. (1994). The benefits of lending relationships: Evidence from small business data. *Journal of Finance, 49*, 3–37.

Rioja, F., & Valev, N. (2004). Does one size fit all? A reexamination of the finance and growth relationship. *Journal of Development Economics, 74*, 429–447.

Robinson, J. (1952). The generalization of the general theory. In *The rate of interest and other essays*. London: Macmillan.

Rousseau, P., & Wachtel, P. (2006). *What is happening to the impact of financial deepening on economic growth?* Unpublished manuscript available on SSRN.

Sorensen, C., Ibanez, D., & Rossi, C. (2009). *Modelling loans to non-financial corporations in the Euro area*. European Central Bank Working Paper No. 989.

Tobin, J., & Brainard, W. (1977). Asset prices and the cost of capital. In B. Balassa & R. Nelson (Eds.), *Economic progress, private value, and public policy*. New York: North-Holland.

Wisley, T., & Johnson, S. (1985). An evaluation of alternative investment hypotheses using nonnested tests. *Southern Economic Journal, 52*, 422–430.

Toward Banking Union in Europe: An Interim Assessment

Christian Schmidt

1 Introduction

The financial crisis has exposed critical gaps in the architecture of financial stability in the euro area. While finance and banking have become increasingly cross-border, the European architecture for safeguarding financial stability remains largely decentralized.[1] This results in a mismatch between market structures and institutional arrangements that has been associated with an inclination of national authorities to favor domestic financial institutions and to view the competition among banks in Europe as a proxy for competition among member states and their respective national interests (Véron 2013a).

During the crisis, it became fully apparent that regulators and policymakers did not have robust tools to resolve ailing internationally active banks. Authorities were often confined to two alternatives: corporate bankruptcy—as chosen for instance by the US authorities in September 2008 in the case of Lehman Brothers—and an injection of public capital—as chosen by the Dutch, Belgian, and Luxembourg authorities in the case of Dexia (e.g., Schoenmaker 2013). Government support has at times been successful in avoiding financial contagion within internationally interconnected banking systems. But the expectation of assistance via publicly funded bailouts amplifies moral hazard, possibly leading to excessive risk taking. Moreover, in the euro area, it has nurtured the "doom-loop," the fatal feedback

[1] The sequence of financial events that started in the summer of 2007 is a series of crises, from the subprime crisis to the banking and economic to the fiscal or the European debt crisis. As none of these terms is fully satisfactory or has been universally adopted, the paper simply refers to "the crisis."

C. Schmidt (✉)
Financial Market Authority of Liechtenstein, Landstrasse 109, Postfach 279, 9490 Vaduz, Liechtenstein
e-mail: christian.schmidt@llb.li

T. Azarmi, W. Amann (eds.), *The Financial Crisis*,
DOI 10.1007/978-3-319-20588-5_4

between bank and sovereign creditworthiness that evolved into a salient feature of the crisis.

In order to revive and deepen financial integration in Europe, to break the toxic interactions between weak banks and weak sovereigns, and to build a more resilient policy infrastructure for Europe's financial system, the European Commission in September 2012 proposed a Single Supervisory Mechanism (SSM) led by the European Central Bank (ECB). This set of proposals was a first step toward an integrated "banking union" which includes further components such as a single rulebook, common deposit protection, and a Single Resolution Mechanism (SRM).

Plans have advanced rapidly. The regulation for the SSM is already in place, and the ECB is expected to take over responsibility for bank supervision in the euro area in November 2014. With regard to the SRM, a political compromise was reached in December 2013. The compromise consists of a draft regulation on the Single Resolution Mechanism and a decision by euro-area member states committing them to negotiate, by 1 March 2014, an intergovernmental agreement on the functioning of the single resolution fund. The European Parliament is due to agree on the SRM in a first reading before the end of the Parliament's current legislative term in May 2014. There are, however, differences between the Council and the Parliament, meaning that no deal before the European elections in May 2014 is a distinct possibility. With respect to the deposit guarantee scheme, European leaders have decided for the time being to proceed by stronger harmonization of national legislation, rather than by establishing a centralized European system.

This chapter reviews the main elements of the banking union and addresses some of the challenges on the way forward. The chapter is organized as follows: Sect. 2 discusses the changing banking landscape and the current fragmentation of European markets, Sect. 3 reviews the main elements of the envisaged banking union, and Sect. 4 analyzes some of the challenges on the way toward an eventual full-fledged banking union.

2 The Changing Banking Landscape in Western Europe

Financial integration in the European Union (EU) is defined as a situation in which there are no frictions that discriminate between economic agents in their access to—and their investment of—capital, particularly on the basis of their location (Coeurè 2013a). This means that financial integration is achieved when there is equal market access. In such a setting, one would expect to see significant cross-border holdings of financial assets, along with a convergence of asset prices and yields across borders.

Financial integration in Europe began several decades ago, in 1957, with the Treaty of Rome, which already contained basic principles for the creation of a single European market for financial services. However, until the mid-1980s, when efforts to promote an EU internal market intensified, the European Community's policies to integrate Europe's financial markets had remained relatively timid, and financial systems had remained predominantly national.

In 1988, the Second Banking Directive established the "single European passport," which allows banks to exercise the right of establishment and freedom to provide services across borders. In practice, this means that banks which have been granted authorization to conduct their business by the supervisory authorities of a member state may also pursue their business in all other member states without requiring further authorization. This principle of mutual recognition is not confined to EU member states but also applies to banks from third countries which have been granted authorization in an EU member state. Moreover, the Second Banking Directive established that foreign branches are subject to home-country supervision only. The objective is to allow a bank from one member state to enter the domestic market of other member states without the need to report to multiple supervisors. A bank operating across borders via subsidiaries, in contrast, is subject to host-country supervision in each and every member state in addition to home-country supervision on a consolidated basis.

The European passport and the single market in financial services were intended to cut through existing barriers that insulated national markets. However, continued discretionary powers of national supervisory authorities and the possibility accorded to the member states of prohibiting cross-border provision of services on general interest grounds prevented companies and individual investors from drawing full benefit from the single market for financial services. European financial markets integrated significantly after the introduction of the euro and before the outbreak of the crisis in 2007, particularly the interbank market in the euro area, and prices of bonds and other securities converged, but retail banking integration was lagging behind the ultimate objective of providing a single market for financial services in Europe (Kleimeier and Sander 2007).

Retail banking in Europe is generally still constrained by national borders, though small countries make an important exception. The total assets of foreign-owned branches and subsidiaries generally constitute only a small part of the total assets of the domestic banking system (see Fig. 1). On average, in euro-area member countries, slightly less than a quarter of total bank assets are foreign owned. Since 2008, the share of foreign asset ownership has fallen slightly in the euro area. Only in the smaller member states of Central and Eastern Europe is a significant part of the banking system foreign owned. Moreover, Trichet (2008) reports that the extent of cross-border lending to nonbank entities is quite small, constituting less than 6 % of total loans to nonbanks. While this share has grown from an average of about 3 % in the early years of the monetary union, the rate of increase is very slow.

Even if retail banking remains fragmented, the banking sector has been a central driver of financial integration in Europe, through cross-border interbank loans and deposits and the area-wide market in which banks are major cross-border purchasers of securities issued by other banks (Allen et al. 2011). A wave of high-profile cross-border mergers of universal banks contributed to the increasing number of banking groups serving retail customers in several member states. Among the

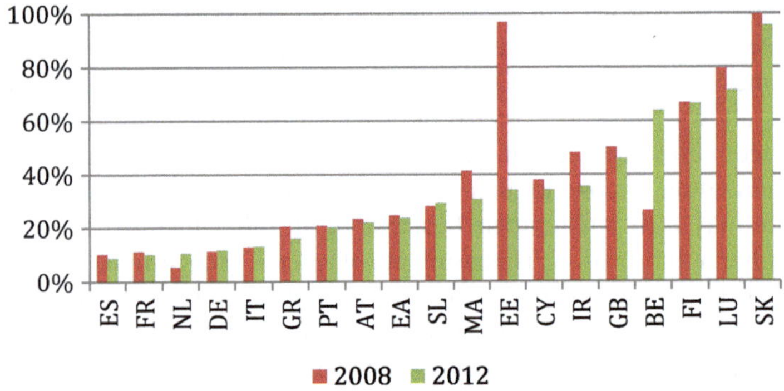

Fig. 1 Percentage of the euro area banking system that is foreign owned (ECB, EBF) (the percentage is calculated as the total assets of foreign owned subsidiaries/branches as % of total banking assets)

most high-profile cases were the takeover of Erste Bank in Austria and Hypobank in Germany by the Italian Bank Unicredito, the takeover of Abbey National in the UK by the Spanish bank Santander, and the takeovers of the Dutch ABN AMRO Bank in 2009 by Fortis, Royal Bank of Scotland, and Banco Santander. Major universal banking groups provide services on a cross-border basis. In doing so, they exploit diversification opportunities for banks' loan portfolios, given that risk and return differ across national banking markets, thereby allowing customers to choose banking products from their country of choice. This brings European banks to a dimension commensurate with the boundaries of an integrated European market.

The crisis has reversed much of the initial progress in financial integration. Monetary transmission channels ceased to function normally as the interbank market froze. The ECB lowered rates from 3.25 % in July 2008 to 0.25 % in November 2013, but only in some euro area countries have firms been able to take full advantage of the decline in key interest rates. Firms located in peripheral euro area economies have faced increasing funding costs as the crisis has escalated, with small and medium-sized firms hit harder (see Fig. 2).

European banking markets fragmented along national lines. Cross-border universal banking groups retrenched to national markets and stopped working as channels for integration of retail banking markets. Between year-end 2007 and mid-year 2013, cross-border claims of both German and French banks to banks in troubled peripheral countries declined by about 50 % (see Fig. 3). Banks in troubled economies have also cut their exposures to banks in core European countries. To a large extent, these figures reflect the collapse in the euro area interbank market due to the lack of trust among banks, which was replaced by the extraordinary measures introduced by the ECB, especially the Long-Term Refinancing Operations (LTRO). It reflects the concerns of creditor banks about the declining creditworthiness of these regions. Market participants demanded a premium for counterparties that were located in the peripheral European economies in return for the higher perceived risk and reduced their exposures to the banks in the region.

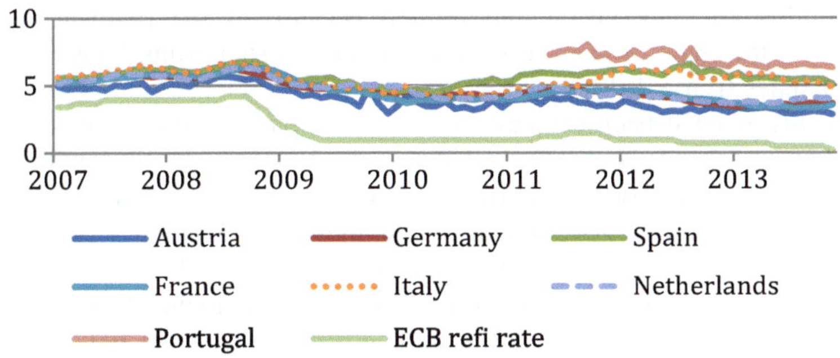

Fig. 2 Interest rates on new corporate loans (1–5 years) (ECB)

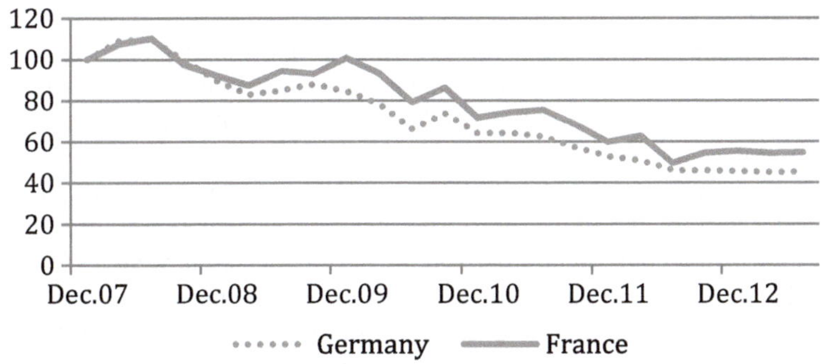

Fig. 3 Cross-border claims of German and French banks to peripheral European Economies (Cyprus, Greece, Ireland, Italy, Portugal, Spain) (Index Q4 2007 = 100) (BIS)

The reduction of flows between banks is also due to a decline of cross-border lending within banking groups, from the parent company to the subsidiary and the other way around (Enria 2013a). This development has been encouraged by supervisors: Home supervisors pushed banks to de-risk in foreign jurisdictions and refocus on domestic markets, while host supervisors have often adopted measures to increase the amount of capital and liquid assets that is expected to remain on the balance sheet of local subsidiaries (Enria 2013b). Moreover, the decline of flows within banking groups also reflects the increasing willingness of bank managers to get a closer matching of assets and liabilities in each jurisdiction, given that the adverse sovereign-bank link has made risks much more country-specific than they used to be before the crisis.

Finally, the mergers and acquisitions that have accompanied the restructuring of the EU banking sector have occurred almost exclusively on a national scale, which contributed to the fragmentation of the banking market. In a number of cases, cross-border groups have been divided along national lines to make them amenable to restructuring with national tools. The option to unite forces and provide an integrated support mechanism was discarded as incompatible with the national responsibility for supervision and refuted because of the political sensitivity involved in the issue of using taxpayers' money in supporting banks from other member states (Enria 2013c).

Bank losses have been primarily borne by taxpayers through bailout and the restructuring of fragile banks. Even if state-aid rules often involved burden sharing with the private sector, burden sharing applied exclusively to subordinated debt and only marginally reduced government capital injections. Over the September 2008–December 2011 period, EU governments committed a total of nearly 4.5 trillion euros, i.e., 37 % of the EU GDP (IMF 2013a). The amount of taxpayer money effectively used amounted to 1.7 trillion euros, or 13 % of EU GDP. Direct government support measures were normally complemented by action to restructure the affected banks. According to the IMF, 10–15 % of the EU banking system is currently under the State Aid Framework and undergoing some forced restructuring.

The European banking sector has grown disproportionally large relative to the size of the economy (see Figs. 4 and 5). The largest, systemically relevant banks in Europe are large relative to national GDP. At the end of 2012, the total assets of Deutsche Bank, for example, represented some 76 % of national GDP, Banco Santander accounted for 123 % of GDP, and ING for 195 % of GDP. At the same time, total assets of the entire euro area banking system represented more than 400 % of euro area GDP. In comparison, in 2011 bank assets were 78 % and 174 % of GDP in the USA and Japan, respectively. EU banking systems are thus large relative to GDP and represent excessive contingent liabilities for EU national governments. Moreover, the financial system in the EU and other advanced economies has become more interconnected across borders. Cross-border financial assets and liabilities have increased very substantially to reach more than 600 % of GDP on average per euro-area country (Sapir and Wolff 2013). In the UK, the figure is over 1000 %.

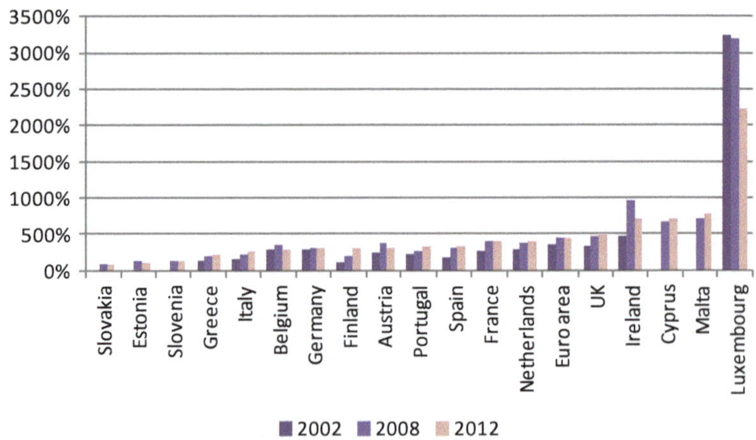

Fig. 4 Total bank assets/national GDP in euro-area countries (EBF, Eurostat)

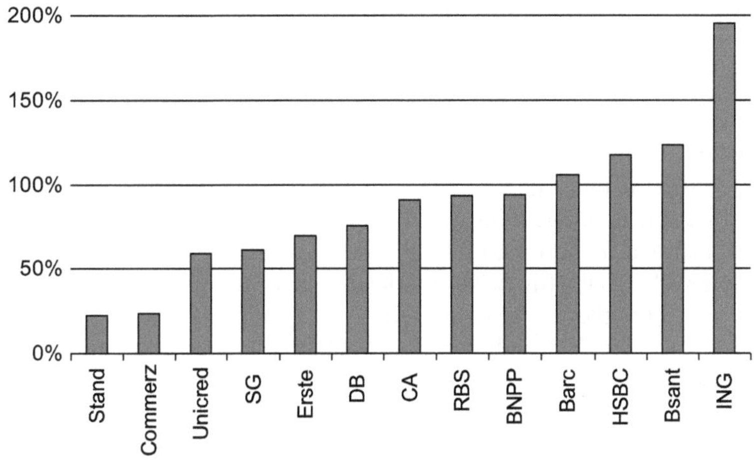

Fig. 5 Large EU banks relative to national GDP (2012) the following banks are included in the chart: Standard Chartered, Commerzbank, Societe Generale, Erste Bank, Deutsche Bank, Royal Bank of Scotland, Banque Paribas, Barclays, HSBC, Banco Santander, ING)

A salient feature of the crisis is the strong interdependence between banks and sovereigns. The feature surfaced most dramatically in Ireland. During the crisis, the Irish government pumped 64 billion euros into its ailing banks, an effort which eventually forced the country into an EU-IMF bailout and quickly transformed a banking crisis into a sovereign debt crisis. The dynamic ("doom loop") has unfolded with variations in other peripheral countries as well (see, e.g., Herring 2013; Merler and Pisani-Ferry 2012; Mody and Sandri 2011). Because of the decentralized financial stability framework in the euro area, the home country is individually responsible for its banking system. Given the size of the largest banks and more broadly the banking systems across the euro area, this implies that the fiscal consequences of rescuing banks are potentially very large. When the creditworthiness of the domestic banking system declines, e.g., due to financial problems of a systemically relevant bank, government bonds also decrease in value because of the perceived risk of having to bail out its bank(s). This causes losses to all holders of its debt, including banks. Moreover, when a country's creditworthiness declines, its prospects for growth and the profitability of most of its firms decline as well. Thus, loan losses are likely to rise, putting further strain on the capital positions of banks in that country. Any doubt about sovereign solvency, therefore immediately affects domestic banks. The two-way bank-sovereign interdependence constitutes one of the specific features of the crisis that renders it especially fragile. The banking union aims to break the toxic interactions between weak banks and weak sovereigns in order to ease the crisis in the euro area and to advance and deepen the single market in financial services.

3 Elements of the Banking Union

The banking union is one of the four building blocks toward a genuine Economic and Monetary Union, together with fiscal, political, and economic integration (Van Rompuy 2012). The banking union aims at building an integrated financial framework to safeguard financial stability and minimize the cost of bank failures. It consists of three main building blocks: (1) the Single Supervisory Mechanism (SSM), which is a framework for single supervision, being complemented by the Single Rulebook; (2) the Single Resolution Mechanism (SRM), designed to govern decision making at the EU level as well as the relationships among the European Commission, the Single Resolution Board (SRB, the new agency for bank resolution), the ECB, and national resolution authorities, and for which the Bank Recovery and Resolution Directive (BRR) is an important precondition, as it lays out a harmonized toolbox of resolution powers; and (3) a common system of deposit protection.

3.1 *Single Supervision and Rulebook*

At the core of the banking union is the Single Supervisory Mechanism (SSM). The SSM will give the ECB full responsibility for the prudential supervision of all credit institutions (banks) in the euro area. Before taking up its responsibilities, as is expected for November 2014, the ECB is required to conduct a balance-sheet assessment of the banks.

The scope of the ECB's future responsibilities is broad, covering more than 6000 credit institutions established in the euro area. The fact that all credit institutions in the euro area fall within the scope of the SSM—although a differentiated approach regarding the conduct of supervision is envisaged—is an essential element of the mechanism. The crisis has illustrated that not only larger banks can pose systemic risks. Due to interlinkages, smaller but more numerous regional institutions can also be systemic as a group and thus destabilize countries and regions. That was the case of the Spanish cajas (savings and loan banks), most of which collapsed and were reorganized as commercial banks, and which threatened both the solvency of the Spanish government and the credibility of the local supervisors (Illueca et al. 2013; Garicano 2012).

It is expected that the ECB will directly supervise around 130 credit institutions, representing almost 85 % of total banking assets in the euro area. All other ("less significant") credit institutions in the participating countries will continue to be supervised by the national supervisory authorities. The ECB can, however, decide at any time to exercise direct supervision of any one of these credit institutions in order to ensure consistent application of high supervisory standards. The ECB also has responsibility for the "less significant" institutions in the sense that national authorities are obliged to perform their supervisory tasks in line with regulations, guidelines, and general instructions issued by the ECB. The ECB will be able to require national authorities to notify the ECB of any material supervisory procedure, conduct further assessment, and/or transmit to the ECB draft supervisory decisions. The ECB will retain power to request information and to conduct investigations and on-site inspections.

The ECB will be able to use all the microprudential tools a supervisor typically has at its disposal, from licensing and carrying out early interventions in the case of financial distress of a bank to sanctioning powers. The ECB may, for instance, conduct all necessary investigations and on-site inspections, adopt guidelines, recommendations, and regulations, and obtain all the information that is necessary from the financial institutions in the participating member countries, as well as persons belonging to those entities and third parties to whom the financial institution has outsourced operational functions or activities (ECB 2013b). The ECB also has macroprudential tasks and tools, like the power to apply higher capital requirements for capital buffers, although overall they are limited and remain to a large extent the responsibility of national authorities. However, the regulation allows both the national authorities and the ECB to take action, and close collaboration on macroprudential issues is required.

Non-euro area member countries will be able to participate in the SSM through the establishment of "close cooperation." Close cooperation essentially requires non-euro member states that wish to join the SSM to adopt the necessary legal framework and cooperate with the ECB along the lines codified in the SSM regulation. This means, in particular, that the national authorities, like those authorities within the euro area, will be bound to abide by guidelines and requests issued by the ECB and will be responsible for providing the adequate information (Darvas and Wolff 2013).

Liechtenstein and the Banking Union

Liechtenstein does not have the possibility to "opt-in" to the SSM. Liechtenstein is a member state of the European Economic Area (EEA).[2] The three largest banks of the country have a market share of more than 80 % of the domestic market; they are headquartered in Liechtenstein, considered to be domestically systemic, and maintain branches and subsidiaries in various European countries. There is no possibility, and little reason, for Liechtenstein to join the banking union at this time. However, one needs to be alert to the risk of a split regime, which could trigger volatility in deposits in periods of stress, as savers could have an incentive to move to banks under a more reliable supervisory scheme.

[2] The European Economic Area was established on 1 January 1994 following an agreement between the member states of the European Free Trade Association (EFTA) and the EU. Specifically, it allows Iceland, Liechtenstein, and Norway to participate in the EU internal market without a conventional EU membership. In exchange, they are obliged to adopt all EU legislation related to the single market, except laws on agriculture and fisheries.

The SSM Regulation provides specific safeguards that aim to mitigate potential conflicts of interest between the ECB's monetary policy function and its supervisory function, in particular as regards ensuring the differentiated functioning of the Governing Council in relation to its monetary policy and supervisory functions. Decision-making within the SSM rests on three bodies (e.g., Buch et al. 2013): (1) The ECB Governing Council has the ultimate decision power. Deliberations of the ECB Governing Council on supervisory matters will be strictly separated from its monetary policy work, including separate agendas and meetings. (2) At the center of the SSM governance structure, a Supervisory Board will be established to plan and carry out the ECB's supervisory tasks, undertake preparatory work, and propose complete draft decisions for adoption by the ECB's Governing Council. It will be composed of a Chair, a Vice-Chair (to be chosen from among the members of the ECB's Executive Board), four ECB representatives, and one representative of each participating country. The four ECB representatives shall not perform duties directly related to the monetary functions of the ECB. The staff involved in carrying out supervisory tasks will be organizationally separate and subject to separate reporting lines. (3) A Mediation Panel will be established to resolve differences of views expressed by the national authorities regarding an objection of the Governing Council to a draft decision by the Supervisory Board.

The ECB will be accountable to the European Parliament and the Council of Ministers. The ECB shall submit an annual report on its tasks and activities with regard to bank supervision to the EU council, the European Parliament, the European Commission, and the Eurogroup, and the Chair of the Supervisory Board shall present the report to the European Parliament and the Eurogroup in the presence of representatives from participating Member States. In addition, the European Parliament may request to hear the Chair of the Supervisory Board. Furthermore, the national parliaments of the participating Member States may invite the Chair of the Supervisory Board to exchange views on a particular credit institution in the country. Finally, national parliaments may also request the ECB to reply to questions related to supervisory matters.

Single banking supervision requires a single set of rules. The Single Rulebook, which is overseen by the EBA, is thus an important complement of the banking union. It aims to provide a single set of harmonized prudential rules that financial institutions throughout the EU must respect. European banking legislation is currently based on regulation that leaves room for significant divergences in national rules. This has created a regulatory patchwork leading to legal uncertainty, enabling institutions to exploit regulatory loopholes, distorting competition, and making it burdensome for firms to operate across the single market. If national discretions were to remain, they would complicate enormously the task of the SSM, which would then be required to enforce different rules for the banks falling within its responsibility. The objective of a true single rulebook is still far from being reached, but Europe is getting closer. The Capital Requirements Regulation, which transposes the new global standards on bank capital (Basel III) into EU law, is the first time a large part of the prudential standards for banks has been adopted through a Regulation. The EBA is drafting a large number of technical standards: 35 technical standards were completed in 2013 and 67 are expected in 2014 (Enria 2013c). A significant number of technical standards are also envisaged in the draft Recovery and Resolution Directive and in other pieces of European legislation in the pipeline.

3.2 *Single Resolution Mechanism and Bank Recovery and Resolution Directive*

The crisis has demonstrated the need to expand resolution powers available for credit institutions. During the crisis, authorities were often confined to two alternatives: corporate bankruptcy—as chosen, for instance, by the US authorities in September 2008 in the case of Lehman Brothers—and an injection of public capital—as chosen, for example, by the Dutch, Belgian, and Luxembourg authorities in the case of Dexia (Cihák and Nier 2009). This experience demonstrated the need to expand resolution tools so that banks could undergo resolution in a way that preserved asset values and systemic business functions and minimized contagion.

The SRM and the BRR aim to reduce the costs of bank resolution, make banks resolvable without necessarily using taxpayer funds, and hence induce bank creditors to exert more market discipline. In this respect, it is important to note that the European Commission adapted temporary state aid rules, applicable as of 1 August 2013 (European Commission 2013a). The modified state-aid regime thus de facto introduces bail-in of junior debt as a precondition for accessing public funds for bank recapitalization (Merler and Wolff 2013).

In the SRM Regulation and the BRR Directive, there are three phases to bank crisis management: (1) preparation and prevention, (2) early intervention, and (3) resolution. In the preparation and prevention phase, banks will be required to draw up recovery plans—at entity and group level—detailing measures and actions that they will adopt to restore viability in stress. In turn, supervisory authorities will prepare resolution plans, explaining how a bank will be resolved while protecting systemic functions and financial stability and minimizing the potential burden for taxpayers. If the resolution authorities identify a significant impediment to a resolution, they will have the power to request that the institution address or remove this impediment. Supervisors will have powers to intervene if the financial situation or solvency of an institution is deteriorating. They may require an institution to implement recovery plan measures or require it to remove or replace management. If these measures are insufficient, a supervisor may request that a special manager be appointed to replace the management of the institution. A special manager has all the powers given to management by the company's constitutional documents and by national law. The manager's actions may include an increase of capital, a corporate reorganization, or a takeover of the institution or another viable institution.

Resolution begins when a bank is failing or likely to fail without any possibility of restoring its viability with a private sector or supervisory action and when a resolution is necessary in the public interest, i.e., basically to preserve financial stability and vital systemic functions (Huertas 2013; Micossi et al. 2013). A resolution authority is expected to have a harmonized minimum set of resolution tools including:

- A sale of business tool: this enables authorities to sell part of the business without shareholder consent
- A bridge institution tool: this allows authorities to transfer all or part of the business to an entity owned by the authorities, which continues to provide essential financial services pending onward sale or entity wind down
- An asset separation tool: this enables the transfer of "bad" assets to a separate vehicle or bad bank
- A bail-in tool: this allows equity and debt to be written down and is intended to ensure that most unsecured creditors of an institution bear appropriate losses

According to the IMF (2012), bail-in is a statutory power (as opposed to contractual arrangements, such as contingent capital requirements) to restructure the liabilities of a distressed financial institution by writing down its unsecured debt and/or converting it to equity. If the resolution authority has decided to apply bail-in, the existing hierarchy of claims that applies in the case of insolvency is respected (see Fig. 6). This means that the bank's losses are first fully absorbed by equity. After this, the subordinated debt is written down in full. If the losses have not been fully compensated, the remaining losses are for the account of (senior) unsecured debt: Their claims are partly or fully written down or converted into equity. Bail-in in principle applies to all the institution's unsecured and uninsured debt. The directive allows though for exceptions: interbank or other debt with an original maturity of less than 1 month; secured debt; savings deposits covered by a deposit guarantee scheme (i.e., deposits under 100,000 euros); liabilities such as salaries, pensions, and taxes; client assets; and some derivative instruments. Deposits of natural persons and small- and medium-sized entities above 100,000 euros will benefit from preferential treatment ensuring that they do not suffer any loss before other unsecured creditors (preferred deposits). Moreover, member states can choose

Fig. 6 Envisaged bail-in sequence (European Commission 2013a)

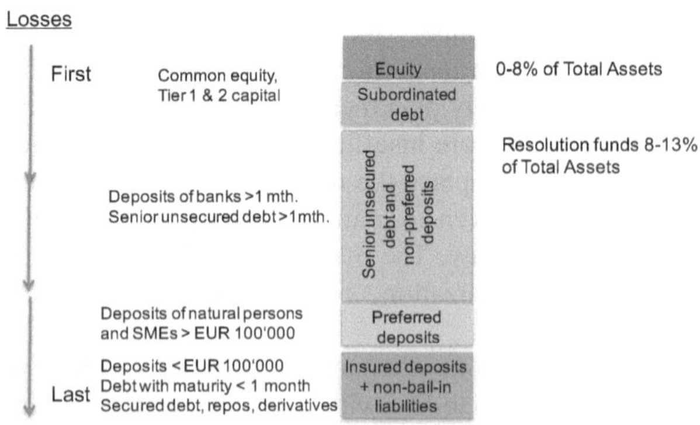

to exclude them fully. Bail-in legislation is due to be adopted in the member states by 2016.

The BRR Directive mandates that at least 8 % of the bank's total liabilities should be subject to bail-in. Should losses exceed the amount of total liabilities subject to bail-in, recourse will be made to the member state's resolution fund. The maximum amount that such a resolution fund can contribute will be capped at 5 % of the failed bank's total liabilities. This could bring the total contribution by the private sector (investors in the bank's obligations subject to bail-in and banks via contributions to the resolution fund) to 13 % of the failed bank's liabilities (Huertas and Nieto 2013).

European authorities hope that the bail-in requirement will minimize the fiscal costs of filling in any resulting capital shortfalls. An analysis by the services of the European Commission (2013b) suggests that European banks hold substantial bail-in liabilities. Based on publicly available data for 45 European banks, the analysis suggests that the "bail-in buffer" for different types of banks ranges between 11 % and 26 % of total assets before one would need to bail-in preferred deposits. Total bail-in liabilities, including preferred deposits, amount to roughly 50 % of total assets. In a counter-factual "back-testing" exercise, the chapter compares the state aid given to banks in the past crisis to the loss-absorbing capacity of the European banking sector, including bail-in liabilities. The results suggest that the enhanced loss-absorbing capacity—through the write-down of capital instruments, bail-in and contributions from resolution funds—of an average European bank would have been sufficient to replace the average state aid given to EU banks in the past crisis.

The political compromise reached within the Council in December 2013 foresees a single resolution fund that would be financed by risk-based bank levies raised at the national level. A levy on banks will gradually fill a fund of 55 billion euros (1 % of insured deposits) over 10 years. During this decade, each country will be responsible for the funding of a "compartment" that gradually shrinks as revenues from the bank levy rise. For governments to tap the fund, a two-thirds majority of members will need to give their approval, with votes weighted by their contribution to the ECB's capital base. For much of the 10-year transition phase, the problematic link between bank and sovereign balance sheets will thus remain in place. The fund's target size of 55 billion euros is fairly small—the Spanish bank bailout alone cost nearly 40 billion euros. European authorities hope that the bail-in requirement will minimize the fiscal costs of filling in any resulting capital shortfalls. But the fund, nonetheless, represents a gradual mutualization of resolution costs, in which levies on German banks could pay for a bailout of their Greek peers.

4 Deposit Guarantee Scheme

Deposit guarantee schemes (DGSs) reimburse a limited amount of deposits to depositors whose bank has failed. The European Commission does not envisage a single supranational DGS for the banking union at this time. The priority is to reach an agreement on a common network of national DGSs.

Deposit guarantees in the EU are provided by a variety of national deposit guarantee schemes (IMF 2013b). These schemes vary greatly in their coverage, contributions, fund sizes, and organizational setup. Some countries, such as Austria and Germany, have more than one scheme. Most schemes have access to limited prepaid funds in relation to the total amount of deposits covered, reflecting the current lack of common EU funding standards. Many national DGSs have limited prefunding or rely on ex post funding mechanisms. Some countries, such as Austria, Italy, and the UK, rely exclusively on ex post funding.

In July 2010, the Commission proposed to strengthen existing rules in the area of deposit guarantee schemes. Bank deposits up to 100,000 euros are guaranteed in all member states. The reform aims to ensure faster pay-outs to depositors, shortening the time period from 20 working days to 7 working days after the bank failure. The proposal also suggests a significant level of ex ante funding. The details are still being discussed in negotiations. The Commission aims for a minimum of 1 % of covered deposits to be collected from banks over a 10-year period. In case of insufficient funds, the DGS will collect immediate ex post contributions from the banking sector, and, as a last resort, it will have access to alternative funding arrangements such as loans from public or private third parties. There will also be a voluntary mechanism of mutual borrowing between the DGSs from different EU countries.

5 Challenges and Outlook

The first steps toward a banking union have been taken, yet challenges remain, and it is unclear how they will be met. First and foremost, the transfer of supervisory authority over most of Europe's banking system from national authorities to the ECB in November 2014 is preceded by an assessment of the banks' financial soundness. This assessment is an essential element of the preparations for the SSM, and its quality will be the first and crucial test of the credibility of the ECB in its supervisory capacity and of the banking union endeavor more broadly. Second, the banking union will remain incomplete. The bail-in legislation will come due in 2016 only, and the deposit guarantee scheme is far away on the horizon. The transition to a bail-in regime will be difficult; it will probably lead to higher bank funding costs and increase interconnectedness of the financial sector. Third, how to effectively regulate and supervise cross-border financial firms remains a fundamentally unsettled question. Fourth, the European macroprudential framework will be affected by the SSM. Questions relate with regards to the institutional cooperation of the national supervisory authorities, the ECB and the ESRB, but also to the relationship of macroprudential policy with monetary and fiscal policy. Fifth, the multitude of financial reforms will affect the European financial system's contribution to economic growth in multiple ways, which on the whole remain poorly understood. The euro area economy is currently characterized by weak and uneven growth, and the banking union seems unlikely to change that, at least in the short-term.

5.1 Challenges Related to the ECB's Comprehensive Assessment

The handover of supervisory authority over most of Europe's banking systems in November 2014 by the ECB will be preceded by a comprehensive assessment of the banking system. The assessment will be carried out by the ECB and the participating national supervisory authorities. The comprehensive assessment is an essential element of the preparations for the SSM, and its quality will be the first and crucial test of the credibility of the ECB in its supervisory capacity and of the banking union endeavor more broadly (Véron 2013c).

The sheer logistical and technical magnitude of the exercise that the ECB will have to perform is a challenge. It will require sufficient capacity to reach an informed judgment on the true capital needs of each banking group included in the scope of the assessment. The enormity of the challenge is compounded by the complex structures of many European banks as well as the near-complete lack of supervisory experience of the ECB until the creation of the SSM. Reflecting this, the assessment will be carried out in close cooperation with the national supervisory authorities, which will execute the exercise at the national level, on the basis of centrally developed data requirements and methodology and will be supported by private sector experts (consultants, auditors, etc.).

The assessment will comprise three pillars (ECB 2013a): (1) a supervisory risk assessment, addressing key risks in the banks' balance sheets, including liquidity, leverage, and funding; (2) an asset quality review, examining the asset side of bank balance sheets as at 31 December 2013, which will comprise credit and market exposures, and on- and off-balance sheet exposures will be covered; (3) a stress test that aims to provide a forward-looking view of banks' shock absorption capacity under stress. Together, these three pillars aim to provide a wide-ranging, in-depth review of banks' balance sheets. The EBA and the ECB will be working in close cooperation. The ECB is the competent supervisory authority and has the mandate to conduct the asset quality review and a stress test for the banks under its responsibility; the EBA has to define the broad framework for asset quality reviews and to initiate and coordinate the stress test at the EU level.

If capital shortfalls are identified against a capital benchmark, the ECB will require banks to adopt "corrective measures." The ECB will monitor and enforce the implementation of those measures. The capital benchmark is set at 8 % Common Equity Tier 1, which will constitute a minimum capital requirement for all of the banks covered by the comprehensive assessment.[3] The leverage ratio will be used as a backstop measure, providing supplementary information for assessing the outcomes. Ahead of the publication of the results, financial institutions will have prepared strategies for their possible restructuring in case of vulnerabilities. Banks that have viable business models but are in need of more capital will be required to obtain such additional resources within an appropriate time frame, roughly 6 months. Banks are expected to raise capital in the market, retain profits, undertake capital accretive sales and restructuring, engage in liability management exercises as appropriate, and/or raise capital from other sources.

If this turns out to be insufficient, national authorities will be the first to step in. As the bail-in tool will not yet be applicable at the time, the comprehensive assessment/stress test will be conducted; national funds, including national resolution funds or government support, will be tapped, in full respect of EU state aid rules. If national backstops are not sufficient, instruments at the European level will be available as appropriate. First, the European Stability Mechanism (ESM) can provide through its normal procedures financial assistance for the recapitalization of financial institutions in the form of a loan to a member state, after appropriate bail-in, in full respect of state aid rules. Second, the direct recapitalization instrument with its 60 billion euros ESM exposure limit could also be used when adopted according to euro area and national procedures following the establishment of the SSM.

One may speculate on the ECB's approach in the comprehensive assessment, whether it will be "rigorous," exposing a number of problem banks, or "forbearing," so that flashpoints would be avoided, but with the danger that a perceived "zombification" of the banking sector in the euro area would continue (e.g., Véron 2013d). The ECB certainly has powerful incentives to conduct the assessment in a rigorous manner, given the obvious linkages between its reputation as a supervisor and its credibility as a monetary institution. Those member states that insist on the credibility of euro area monetary policy should in principle be supportive of such rigor and be aligned with the ECB in this respect. However, each member state will find itself at political and financial risk if the ECB detects significant levels of undercapitalization in banks headquartered in its territory.

Market expectations will eventually be important also for the success of the ECB's comprehensive assessment. If capital shortfalls—and the information package provided by the ECB/EBA to market participants—end up being below the values that the markets at the time of the publication of the results expect, the

[3] The threshold can be decomposed into Common Equity Tier 1 ratio of 4.5 %, and in addition, the 2.5 % capital conservation buffer. An add-on of 1 % will be requested to take into account the systemic relevance of the banks considered significant under the SSM Regulation.

exercise is likely to be perceived as "forbearing." If the capital shortfalls exceed market expectations, markets will probably interpret the assessment as rigorous. If banks would be able to finance the capital shortfalls by issuing new equity or the like, markets would probably interpret the tests as "forbearing," given that, apparently, at least at this time, analysts expect the number of such problem banks to be in the double digits and the corresponding financial shortfall to be very large, possibly higher than 100 billion euros.

5.2 *Potential Drawbacks of Creditors' Bail-In*

The move away from bailout to bail-in in the EU has been undertaken in response to costly government support of banking systems. The bail-in tool is one of the four instruments for bank resolution in Europe. The Financial Stability Board (FSB) has included bail-in as one of the key attributes of effective resolution regimes (FSB 2011). Bail-in allows debt owed by a bank to creditors to be written down or converted to equity. It can be used in the event of a failure of a systemic bank. By replicating how creditors would incur losses if the bank had gone bankrupt, bail-in reduces the value and amount of liabilities of the failed bank. It thereby avoids a situation in which taxpayers would have to provide funds to cover these liabilities, while allowing for the critical functions of the bank to continue uninterrupted, either in a new entity such as a bridge bank or in the same, albeit significantly restructured franchise. Successful bail-in can help reduce the public cost of bank rescues and contingent liabilities and help remove the implicit guarantee for too-big-to-fail banks. A credible bail-in regime should also reduce moral hazard and improve market discipline and help decouple the link between sovereign and bank funding. Nonetheless, the transition to a steady state may prove challenging, particularly in the current crisis context.

Bank funding costs are likely to rise in a bail-in regime. The bail-in rules transfer risk from taxpayers to unsecured creditors. In this way, they counterbalance the perceived implicit risk subsidy from which some very large or highly interconnected institutions have benefited, leading to excessively low funding costs, particularly in good times. As a result of this increased risk, holders of bail-in liabilities may be expected to ask for a higher return (e.g., Coeurè 2013b). Analyst estimates vary, but a survey suggests that under a bail-in regime, investors would demand around 90 basis points more for a senior bond issued by a single A-rated bank.[4] The investors surveyed also expect that the implementation of a bail-in framework will lead to an increase in price differentials across issuers with diverse credit quality.

A comparison of the incremental cost of existing contingent capital instruments—which have characteristics broadly similar to future bail-in instruments—

[4] Financial Times, European bank bail-in will cost +87 basis points, 25 October 2010.

versus senior debt of the same issuer suggests that bail-in costs could come to an average of 500 basis points (Le Leslé 2012). In steady times, it would cost on average 160 basis points more to issue bail-in debt versus similar-maturity senior unsecured debt but with wide variations among banks—stronger issuers may pay less and weaker issuers are expected to pay more. The availability of bail-in instruments as well as their acceptance would also dictate issuance costs.

Building a market for bail-in debt is going to be challenging. Limited investor appetite and uncertainty regarding the future regulatory framework may hamper the ability of weaker banks, or banks headquartered in weaker sovereigns, to fund themselves. In turn, weaker banks, in most need of bail-in instruments to reduce the likelihood of bailout, will also experience the most difficulty in finding private sector investors willing to purchase bail-in securities. Moreover, investor preferences are shifting away from euro area banks' senior unsecured debt, which would be subject to bail-in. Long-term investors, such as insurance companies, are likely to adjust their portfolios' composition in line with the upcoming Solvency II requirements. Bank covered bonds will increase due to their preferential capital treatment, while unsecured debt will probably decline. Similarly, the punitive treatment of equity should discourage insurers from purchasing bank debt with contingent capital or bail-in features, which may hamper the development of these new asset classes.

The scope of application of bail-in, and hence its effectiveness, is reduced by high and rising levels of asset encumbrance and, conversely, low levels of unsecured funding. Between 2007 and 2012, the issuance of unsecured debt declined by approximately 20 % (Houben and Slingenberg 2013). Analyst estimates and definitions of asset encumbrance levels in Europe vary, but averages range between 15 % and 25 % of funded liabilities (or assets), with some banks reporting higher levels (Le Leslé 2012). Shifts in the funding mix may further reduce policymakers' ability to maneuver in a resolution. Higher balance sheet encumbrance reduces available assets during liquidation and increases potential costs for governments of protecting depositors if they must enter a full bailout or complete insufficient deposit guarantee schemes.

For banks that cannot raise sufficient senior unsecured debt, there are basically two options (Smolders 2012): holding more equity and/or subordinated debt or contracting the balance sheet. The advantage of the first option is that losses will initially be borne by other capital providers so that senior unsecured creditors will be better protected against a possible bail-in, and higher funding costs can to some extent be limited. On the other hand, the cost of capital will rise, and raising or building additional capital is a difficult exercise for many banks in the current market conditions. There will be banks that could be forced to reduce their balance sheets (the second option) to meet the minimum requirement of bail-in liabilities. The resultant deleveraging would have negative consequences for the availability of credit and for the economic recovery.

There may also be legal issues with shareholder rights, as the ordinary shareholder suffers a massive dilution when debt is converted. Alternatively, the bank may need ordinary shareholder permission to issue such debt. Another issue is legal enforceability of the discretion of the supervisor to trigger the write-down or conversion. In many common law jurisdictions, such as under English law, the courts have jealously protected their rights to hear claims of judicial review of any decision made under powers given to a public body, where any individual or group can show that they suffered as a result of that decision (PWC 2011). So ordinary shareholders, for example, who have seen their holdings reduced by the execution of conversion of bail-in capital into equity, may feel aggrieved and seek to have the decision reviewed by the courts.

A related uncertainty is whether one can override the national bankruptcy regime in question. Resolution authority, unlike supervision, is not explicitly referred to in the European treaties (Véron 2013b). Moreover, any special resolution regime for banks is defined as an alternative to insolvency. Thus, a genuine European bank resolution regime would require a matching European insolvency regime, at least for banks if not for other companies. But insolvency is a national competence under current treaties—unlike in the USA, where bankruptcy is one of a limited list of explicitly federal competences. Therefore, it is argued that a sustainable banking union cannot be completed within the legal framework defined by the current European treaties.

Finally, there are concerns regarding the impact on financial stability of the bail-in regime. In practice, a bail-in regime could lead to less rather than more financial stability. The concern is that as soon as professional investors, other banks, and large depositors become aware that a bank has problems, they will no longer wish to fund the bank in order to escape a possible future bail-in. This would exacerbate the bank's problems and moreover could lead to other banks or even other parts of the financial sector, like insurance companies, experiencing funding problems and cause a systemic crisis. The bail-in regime will increase interconnectedness of the financial system, which has been identified as a causal factor of the crisis.

5.3 Supervising and Regulating Multinational Firms

The crisis has brought a sense of urgency to another longstanding challenge: the deficiencies of nationally based supervision and resolution of multinational financial firms. Indeed, effective cooperation among financial supervisors was virtually absent in the case of the Icelandic banks. Many savers in the EU deposited their money with the Icelandic banks. In violation of agreements of the European Economic Area (EEA), Iceland protected only Icelandic depositors and failed to cooperate with foreign supervisory and resolution authorities. Some host countries paid their domestic savers for political reasons, outside of multilateral agreements for deposit protection. Likewise, when Fortis collapsed in September 2008, conflicts of interest between Dutch and Belgian authorities following the takeover of ABN AMRO by Fortis increased the cost of the rescue operation (Schoenmaker 2013).

The presence of two or more supervisory authorities with diverging interests—in the home country of multinational groups and in the country hosting a subsidiary—can complicate effective oversight (e.g., Pistor 2012; D'Hulster 2009). Home-country supervisors may have little incentive to policy subsidiaries abroad unless they are "systemic" from the perspective of the group. Host-country supervisors have this incentive but may have little information about subsidiaries' parent banks. Home–host cooperation becomes particularly difficult in the event of a failure of a multinational bank resulting in a direct conflict of interest over how to share the fiscal burden of bank resolution. Indeed, it is the anticipation of such a situation that drives the diverging interests of home and host supervisors, both in normal times and during crisis management. In bank resolution, the primary responsibility of national authorities is toward domestic taxpayers, ignoring cross-border externalities (e.g., if rescuing the parent bank helps the subsidiary, and vice versa). As a result, too little capital is likely to be invested in a failing multinational banking group.

In the banking union, the home–host coordination problems are addressed by centralizing supervision at the ECB. Supervisory standards are expected to improve in quality, independence of supervision should increase, and implementation of regulation should become more harmonized and consistent. The fear of a "home bias" should diminish, and compliance cost for cross-border banks should eventually fall. However, as only common supervision at the ECB is to be established in the first phase, a mismatch between decision-making power and responsibility for the consequences of supervisory decisions is created (Vienna Initiative 2 2013). National authorities will not be responsible for supervision of domestic banks but will still bear the fiscal or financial stability consequences that may arise from supervisory failures. With little influence on decisions, it will be hard to explain to domestic taxpayers why their money should be used in the resolution of cross-border banks, should all the mechanisms for avoiding this fail.

A strong and clear mechanism is needed to handle conflicts of interest between home and host countries given that the ECB will represent both. The SSM moves the coordination between home and host countries participating in the banking union from supervisory colleges to the ECB and to the decision-making body of the SSM. But this does not automatically eliminate potential conflicts of interest within the ECB's supervisory board. One of the possible conflict of interests is intra-bank-group support across borders in a crisis situation, when host countries' representatives may feel that their national financial stability is threatened. Finally, the SSM does not address supervisory coordination problems with respect to multinational banks for which either the parent or the subsidiary is located outside the area covered by the SSM (Berglöf et al. 2012).

5.4 Macroprudential Approaches

Events since 2007 have revealed embarrassing blind spots in the precrisis understanding of the financial system not only by policymakers but also by the academic community (Véron 2012). Thus, there has been an understandable drive to introduce a more comprehensive and joined-up approach to financial regulation. This has resulted in an emphasis on "macroprudential" approaches and institutions. In Europe, the European Systemic Risk Board (ESRB) was set up with the mandate to oversee risk in the financial system as a whole. The ESRB was established in 2010, following the 2009 De Larosière Report, which resulted in the establishment of the European System of Financial Supervision (ESFS), a network of national supervisors working in tandem with new European Supervisory Authorities (ESAs), and the ESRB.

The primary objective of macroprudential policy and supervision is to limit or mitigate systemic risks with the goal of maintaining financial stability and minimizing the incidence and impact of disruptions in the provision of key financial products and services that can have adverse consequences for the real economy and broader implications for economic growth (IAIS 2013). The rationale for macroprudential intervention rests on the presence of three sets of systemic externalities (IMF 2013c). These arise through: (1) the tendency of the financial system to amplify adverse aggregate shocks; (2) macrofinancial feedback mechanisms that result in an overexposure to such adverse aggregate shocks; and (3) linkages within the financial system that increase the vulnerability of the system to idiosyncratic or aggregate shocks.

The European macroprudential framework operates at two levels. At the EU level, the ESRB has a legal responsibility for macroprudential oversight and the prevention and mitigation of systemic risks to the EU financial system. To this aim, the ESRB can issue warnings and recommendations, which are subject to a (nonbinding) "comply or explain" mechanism. At the national level, authorities are responsible for macroprudential oversight of their national financial system. At the beginning of 2012, the ESRB proposed the establishment of macroprudential authorities or bodies at the national level, arguing that for efficient national macroprudential supervision, there needs to be a clearly defined scope for action; the ESRB therefore recommends a legislative basis for this. It is to define the aims of macroprudential supervision, appoint one or more competent authorities, and specify transparency and accountability obligations.

In the SSM, the ECB has macroprudential powers for banks, but not over financial holding companies and mixed financial holding companies (ECB 2013b). The SSM regulation stipulates that the ECB, according to the procedures foreseen in Union law, may apply certain measures addressing systemic or macroprudential risks. These measures include applying higher requirements for capital buffers, in particular countercyclical buffer rates. Macroprudential instruments which are not specified in Union law, such as loan-to-income and loan-to-value ratios, will remain the sole responsibility of national authorities. The established independence and financial stability expertise of the ECB are expected to help build a strong institutional framework among SSM countries and provide capacity to implement macroprudential instruments against national political pressure while taking into account interactions with monetary policy.

National authorities will be allowed to retain macroprudential powers under the SSM—providing flexibility to tailor solutions to local conditions—but in close cooperation with the ECB. Either party that takes such a step needs to inform and consult with the other party ahead of time, under modalities described in the EU Council draft regulation of the SSM. Cooperation will be critical to ensure flexibly to macrofinancial developments in particular countries or asset markets, and coherence and effectiveness of measures, and mechanisms would need to be in place to ensure effective decision making and "will to act" (IMF 2013d).

The modalities for coordination between the ECB and the ESRB in the area of macroprudential policies will need to be clearly spelled out. There will be some overlap between the tasks of the ESRB and of the ECB in the area of banking and covering euro area countries. The ESRB remains the only EU-wide in charge of macroprudential supervision and will continue to coordinate macroprudential oversight between countries participating in the SSM and those remaining outside. Ensuring macroprudential oversight at the EU level will also remain important for nonbanks and markets, which will not be covered by the SSM. The ECB is expected to coordinate closely with the ESRB, and will implement warnings and recommendation issued by the ESRB, in close cooperation with national authorities.

5.5 *Banking Union and Uneven Economic Growth*

Finally, an important and open question is how the banking union might affect the ability of the financial sector to contribute to overall economic growth. At least in the short term, the envisaged banking union will probably not be able to separate the banking from the sovereign risk and thus break the "doom loop." For a long time period, national funds will shoulder the largest part of the costs of bank failures. With only a limited number of large banks in an individual country, national funds might be insufficient in the case of one of them facing a problem (Wolff 2013).

Continued financial fragmentation risks underline real economic divergences in Europe. The banks in Europe may thus face different funding conditions for an extended period. Banks in countries with weaker public finances will probably continue to pay a risk premium because of their location. Banks in countries with larger banking systems compared to GDP will be put at a structural disadvantage. Banks in Germany will benefit from the value of the best state guarantee that the German government provides. As a result, interest rates on credit are likely to be different for a long time. A company in Europe's South may not be able to access affordable credit. Yet, without credit, the recovery will not come and the downward dynamics observed in Europe's South will continue.

Failure to agree on a strong banking union puts the emphasis on crisis prevention. The ECB, as single supervisor, is likely to apply high supervisory standards—for instance, in terms of capital requirements, liquidity ratios, risk management capabilities—in order to strengthen the resilience of the euro area banking system, even in the face of a big shock, and to minimize the risks of bank crises. This could lead over the coming years to a further deleveraging and restructuring of the banking system.

References

Allen, F., Beck, T., Carletti, E., Lane, P. R., Schoenmaker, D., & Wagner, W. (2011). *Cross-border banking in Europe: Implications for financial stability and macroeconomic policies*. London: Center for Economic Policy Research.

Berglöf, E., de Haas, R., & Zettelmeyer, J. (2012). *Banking union: The view from emerging Europe*. Accessed January 29, 2014, from http://www.voxeu.org

Buch, C., Körner, T., & Weigert, B. (2013). *Towards deeper financial integration in Europe: What the banking union can contribute*. Accessed December 1, 2013, from http://www.sachverstaendigenrat-wirtschaft.de

Cihák, M., & Nier, E. (2009). *The need for special resolution regimes for financial institutions – The case of the European Union*. IMF Working Paper WP/09/200.

Coeurè, B. (2013a, March 12). *The way back to financial integration*. Speech at the conference on International Financial Integration and Fragmentation: Drivers and Policy Responses, organized by the Banco de Espana und the Reinventing Bretton Woods Committee, Madrid.

Coeurè, B. (2013b, September 30). *The implications of bail-in rules for bank activity and stability*. Opening speech at conference on Financing the Recovery After the Crisis – The Roles of Bank Profitability, Stability and Regulation, Bocconi University, Milan.

D'Hulster, K. (2009). *Cross border banking supervision: Incentive conflicts in supervisory information sharing between home and host supervisors*. World Bank Policy Research Paper No. 5871.

Darvas, Z., & Wolff, G. B. (2013). *Should non-euro area countries join the single supervision mechanism*. Working Paper 2013/5. Corvinus University of Budapest.

ECB. (2013a). *Note comprehensive assessment*. Accessed December 5, 2013, from http://www.ecb.europa.eu

ECB. (2013b, April). The single supervisory mechanism: A pivotal step towards a banking union. In *Financial integration in Europe*. ECB.

Enria, A. (2013a). Establishing the banking union and repairing the single market. In F. Allen, E. Carletti, & J. Gray (Eds.), *Political, fiscal and banking union in the Eurozone* (pp. 47–65). Philadelphia: FIC Press.

Enria, A. (2013b, September 26). *The new role of the European Banking Authority in the Banking Union*. Speech at the ESE Conference in Frankfurt.

Enria, A. (2013c, November 18). *The single market after the banking union*. Speech at the AFME and EBF Banking Union in Europe Conference, Brussels.

European Commission. (2013a). *State aid: Commission adapts rules for banks*. Press release. Accessed December 12, 2013, from http://europa.eu

European Commission. (2013b). *Bail-in tool: A comparative analysis of the institutions' approaches*. Working Paper. Accessed December 26, 2013, from http://www.thetimes.co.uk

Financial Stability Board. (2011). *Key attributes of effective resolution regimes for financial institutions*. Accessed December 29, 2013, from http://www.financialstabilityboard.org

Garicano, L. (2012). *Five lessons from the Spanish cajas debacle for new euro-wide supervisor.* Accessed December 29, 2013, from www.voxeu.org

Herring, R. J. (2013). The danger of building a banking union on a one-legged stool. In F. Allen, E. Carletti, & J. Gray (Eds.), *Political, fiscal and banking union in the Eurozone?* Philadelphia: Wharton Financial Institutions Center.

Houben, A., & Slingenberg, J. W. (2013). *Collateral scarcity and asset encumbrance: Implications for the European financial system.* Banque de France Financial Stability Review No. 17, pp. 197–206.

Huertas, T. F. (2013). Banking Union. *Bank of Spain Financial Stability Journal*, V31, 31–45.

Huertas, T. F., & Nieto, M. J. (2013). *A game changer: The EU banking recovery and resolution directive.* www.voxeu.org

IAIS. (2013). *Macroprudential policy and surveillance in insurance.* Accessed January 29, 2014, from www.iaisweb.org

Illueca, M., Norden, L., & Udell, G. F. (2013). *When good intentions go wrong: Effects of bank deregulation and governance on risk taking.* www.voxeu.org

IMF. (2012). *From bail-out to bail-in: Mandatory debt restructuring of systemic financial institutions.* IMF Staff Discussion Note SDN/12/03.

IMF. (2013a). *European Union: Publication of financial sector assessment program documentation.* Technical note on progress with bank restructuring and resolution in Europe. IMF Country Report No. 13/67. Accessed December 12, 2013, from http://www.imf.org

IMF. (2013b). *European Union: Publication of financial sector assessment program documentation.* Technical note on deposit insurance. IMF Country Report No. 13/66. Accessed December 28, 2013, from http://www.imf.org

IMF. (2013c). *Key aspects of macroprudential policy.* Accessed January 29, 2014, from http://www.imf.org

IMF. (2013d). *European Union: Publication of financial sector assessment program documentation.* Technical note on macroprudential oversight and the role of the ESRB. IMF Country Report No. 13/70. Accessed February 3, 2014, from http://www.imf.org

Kleimeier, S., & Sander, H. (2007). *Integrating Europe's retail banking market: Where do we stand?* Centre for European Policy Studies.

Le Leslé, V. (2012). *Bank debt in Europe: "Are funding models broken?"* IMF Working Paper WP/12/299.

Merler, S., & Pisani-Ferry, J. (2012, April). *Hazardous tango: Sovereign-bank interdependence and financial stability in the euro area.* Bank of France Financial Stability Review No. 16.

Merler, S., & Wolff, G. B. (2013). *Ending uncertainty: Recapitalization under European central bank supervision.* Bruegel Policy Contribution Issue 2013/18.

Micossi, S., Bruzzone, G., & Carmassi, J. (2013). *The new European framework for managing bank crises.* CEPS Policy Brief No. 304.

Mody, A., & Sandri, D. (2011). *The Eurozone crisis: How banks and sovereigns came to be joined at the hip.* IMF WP/11/269.

Pistor, K. (2012). *Host's dilemma: Rethinking EU banking regulation in light of the global crisis.* Columbia Law and Economics Working Paper No. 378.

PWC. (2011). *The trillion dollar question: Can bail-in capital bail out the banking industry.* Accessed January 29, 2014, from http://www.pwc.com

Sapir, A., & Wolff, G. B. (2013, September 14). *The neglected side of banking union: Reshaping Europe's financial system.* Note presented at the informal ECOFIN, Vilnius. Accessed November 29, 2013, from http://www.bruegel.org

Schoenmaker, D. (2013). *Governance of international banking.* Oxford: Oxford University Press.

Smolders, N. (2012). *Bail-in: An alternative to bail-outs of banks?* Rabobank Special Report 2012/15. Accessed January 29, 2014, from https://economics.rabobank.com

Trichet, J.-C. (2008). *European financial integration.* Speech at the 23. Internationales ZinsForum Zinsen 2009, Frankfurt am Main. Accessed January 29, 2014, from http://www.bis.org

Van Rompuy, H. (2012). *Towards a genuine economic and monetary union*. Accessed December 29, 2013, from http://ec.europa.eu

Véron, N. (2012). *Financial reform after the crisis: An early assessment*. Bruegel Working Paper 2012/01. Accessed November 29, 2013, from http://www.bruegel.org

Véron, N. (2013a). *Banking nationalism and the financial crisis*. Accessed November 29, 2013, from http://www.bruegel.org

Véron, N. (2013b). *A realistic bridge towards European banking union*. Bruegel Policy Contribution Issue 2013/09.

Véron, N. (2013c). *An encouraging start for the ECB's Big Bank Review*. Accessed December 29, 2013, from http://www.bruegel.org

Véron, N. (2013d). *The ECB's big moment*. Accessed December 29, 2013, from http://www.bruegel.org

Vienna Initiative 2. (2013). *Working group on the European banking union and emerging Europe*. Accessed February 8, 2014, from http://ec.europa.eu/economy_finance/articles/governance/2013-05-02-vienna-2_en.htm

Wolff, G. B. (2013). *Continued financial fragmentation will put ECB on the hook*. Accessed December 22, 2013, from http://www.bruegel.org

A World Without Money Needs No Banks and No Rating

Ottmar Schneck

The USA narrowly escaped state bankruptcy in January 2013. Cyprus is on the verge of bankruptcy, and many other European states require the extension of public sector loans or debt rescheduling to sustain the confidence they enjoy in the money and capital markets. At the moment, however, faith is dwindling in the ratings that are supposed to express this confidence in the form of valid assessment of the solvency status of debtors. The USA is even instituting legal actions against Standard & Poor's, because it was apparently unable to foresee the crisis in some states in good time.

Politics is reacting in a Pavlov-reflex manner by further tightening the regulation of credit institutes and is already debating Basel IV—a long-known separation of loan and deposit businesses by banks. It is becoming clearer in the process that an ever-stricter and thus more bureaucratic and transaction-cost-generating process of regulating banks is quickly reaching its limits (Arestis 2011; Binswanger 2012). The system of money and capital markets is therefore questioned by scientists while alternatives are being sought. At present, long-known and new alternatives that may be capable of replacing the current monetary system are widely being debated in politics and science.[1]

[1] There are two different discussions in the banking world: One is to chance the whole financial system, and the other is to add complementary money currencies to the current system. We want to discuss the second approach. An overview of the system's critics can be found www.ijccr.net.

O. Schneck (✉)
Reutlingen University of Applied Sciences, ESB Business School, Alteburgstr. 150, Reutlingen 72762, Germany
e-mail: ottmar.schneck@reutlingen-university.de

T. Azarmi, W. Amann (eds.), *The Financial Crisis*,
DOI 10.1007/978-3-319-20588-5_5

1 Fiat Money in Discussion

In the process, the point of departure of this re-discovered debate in a world without (traditional) money is the criticism of the policy of monopolist cash generation by central banks without gold or commodity coverage, multiplicative loan approval by banks on the basis of their own capital instead of the limitation of credit issuance on the savings deposit of the customer, and finally, the criticism of growing disintermediation in investment banking, which renders the control of money by central instances impossible through derivative instruments. The term "Fiat money system" has thus started to appear more often in written sources and has already been consolidated in macroeconomics textbooks in Anglo-Saxon countries. "Fiat" is the Latin word for "being" or "emergence" and indicates that money in the current loan-money businesses may simply emerge from nowhere and not require the need for saving or value coverage of the money created by the central bank and issued by the banks.[2]

The debate about alternatives to a fiat money system is mostly rooted in the Austrian School.[3] This liberal school that was essentially formed by Ludwig von Mises and Freidich August von Hayek is founded on the premise of the fundamental failure of central planning systems, which means in effect that even a central bank is never in a position to detect, monitor or control changes in the demand and supply of money.[4]

2 Back to History

In the current debate, reference is repeatedly made to the year 1844, in which the Peel's Banking Act[5] was passed in the United Kingdom, named after the country's then–Prime Minister Robert Peel (1788–1850). Following numerous banking and financial crises that are definitely comparable to today's situation, there was no longer any appetite to accept that banks had granted loans in excess of their own deposits in money and gold and the savings of their customers, and that a huge amount of the so-called fiat money emerged. This multiplier effect, which was limited to 12.5 times the liability equity capital in Basel II and was subjected to a further limitation of the assignment of equity capital in banks in Basel III, was—at the time—to be virtually set to 1. Only as much money was to be loaned as was (in reverse) covered by depositors or the bank itself.

[2] The discussion of fiat money started with Silvio Gesell in 1916 and was further developed from Selgin George, cf. Selgin (1988).

[3] Faber, Berlin 1979. Gloria-Palermo: 1999.

[4] Cf. Hayek, 2012; Mises, 1924, 2005 (engl. 2013); www.hayek.de; www.mises.org

[5] Bank Charter Act, 1844, Bank of England Archive, Retrieved 2010-10-27.

Much like those engaged in the debate today, the major players at the time based their arguments on the much older facts of the Spanish schoolman and subsequent Roman legal philosophy, which refused to accept the multiplication of savings deposits in loans and thereby, the Floor Balance theory. The law, however, had a crucial weaving flaw. Loans at the time were still granted largely through the issuance of bank notes, on which the law was based. The banks therefore shifted their activities from the regulated issuance of bank notes to the certification of sight deposits, which at that time were not yet customary. The politics of the time was able to integrate sight deposits into the concept and definition of money supply only in 1870, around the time the gold standard was introduced, which permitted the right of exchange at all times for all notes and sight deposits. The gold-based currency system that was adopted by some states in Bretton Woods in 1944 was to advance this philosophy. The abolition of the gold coverage of the dollar in 1931 and the Bretton Woods system in 1971 is now history. The fact, however, that financial crises have since become frequent may be a coincidence, or it may be the result of uncovered monetary systems. How then could it have happened that since the 1970s an estimated 50 times more money is available and in circulation today than would be required for the exchange function of commodities and services in accordance with the predominant Fisher Transaction Equation? According to this equation, every central bank should generate only as much money M at a fixed circulatory velocity V as is required for transaction purposes T at current price level P ($\mathrm{M} \times \mathrm{P} = \mathrm{P} \times \mathrm{T}$). One possible reason is that precisely these central banks do not want to admit that the circulatory velocity of money has in the meantime become hardly calculable, and many payment transactions today are made through alternative Internet pay systems (see Bitcoin, PayPal, Bonus miles, Customer Cards) and are therefore no longer controllable.

The fact that the volume of transactions for production—and above all, for services in a global and inter-connected world—is hardly still calculable may be another reason for the failure of the value creation-related control of money supply. It therefore becomes compelling to ask the question whether money can still be centrally controlled in any way, or whether a liberal market approach should not rather be followed, in which case the issue can be made free-for-all to allow market participants decide for themselves which means and systems are more trustworthy for making payments. In written sources, "free banking" is used in this context as the magic phrase and would be the opposite of "central banking". Precisely, in this free banking system, "money production" would be left to the market, and it could be assumed that market participants trusted only such systems that promise, for instance, 100 % coverage through real values (gold, material assets). Confidence would also be shown in non-governmental institutions, whether or not their mere sizes (e.g. Google, eBay, payback) are known and are obligated by virtue of their reputation not to operate in real money but in real swap options (for example, bartering). It can further be assumed that market participants rather trusted regional currencies (compare Chiemgauer, Donauthaler),[6] for which issuance would be

[6] Detailed descriptions and overview of "Local Money" in: Bernard, 2002. Based on: http://www.complementarycurrency.org/ccDatabase/les_public.html

comprehensible or visible on the spot. The Free Economy School of Silvio Gesell (1892–1930), which suggests index-secured depreciative money, goes even farther than the Austrian School,[7] which basically only calls for free market economy and seeks to leave cash generation to market forces.

Given the well-known statement that everything except money rusts and is subject to wear and tear, it is concluded that the hoarding of money is prevented through "demurrage" in the sense of charges placed on shipping vessels for anchoring in harbours. A wear fee would be virtually equivalent to negative interest and would continuously devalue money in a systematic manner in such a way that money owners would have an interest in circulation and thus consumption and investment. Such depreciative money has always had its place in existing monetary systems only when the countries were hit by financial crises that threatened their basic existence. Such depreciative money (e.g. Corn Giros) already existed in ancient times, for example, in Egypt in the first century BC, and there are several examples from the Middle Ages where economic cycles were financed by money that systematically lost value year in and year out.

3 The Austrian Experience

The well-known "Miracle of Wörgl" during the Second World War has gone down in history as a testimony that depreciative money, accepted by all members of the community, led to a boom in this community in a region that otherwise was enduring a dire period of economic recession (Unterguggenberger, 1934). Had the Austrian government not stopped the experiment in 1933 at the prompting of the Austrian National Bank and banned the Wörgl Shillings, we would today have had one more experience with an alternative currency system in the form of depreciative money in the modern age.

The findings would probably have been that economic growth is not only possible through interest-based borrowing and the hope of future debt repayment but also through limited money flow and real covered notes and sight deposits, which may even lead to (real) welfare. In any case, with alternative monetary and currency systems at the heart of the debate, it can be ascertained that the classical functions of money, namely, value protection and the exchange and payment function, are losing significance. Local exchange trading systems (LETS) and time banks, regional monetary systems and bartering, and technical forms of payment such as Bitcoins[8] are already in use. However, other far-reaching models of the free banking system will require political majorities. To understand the

[7] A very good differentiation between the Austrian and the Chicago schools appears in: Skousen, Washington 2005.

[8] Aron (2011), S. 23 ff.; original website to BITCOIN: www.bitcoin.org

alternatives to the current monetary system, we will specify below the main features of the five most popular alternatives.

4 Five Alternatives for Money

4.1 LETS and Time Banks

LETS are economic cycles on a non-monetary basis. Michael Lintons, who introduced (working) time as an exchange value in Canada at the beginning of the 1980s, is considered the founding father of this alternative exchange and payment system.[9] Whoever operates within the scope of such a local exchange trading system, for instance, posts its offer of services or commodity in an index of money in a bank which hardly knows the borrower; the communalizing function of a Local Exchange Trading System should thus be highlighted. It quickly becomes obvious that this alternative system of payment functions only within a limited regional radius and for smaller services or a limited exchange of goods. The global trading of investment goods would rather hit its limits in this case. However, the emergence of the so-called care banks, in which services today can be swapped with time units (with subsequent care services in time), has made these models increasingly interesting in the sense of the value protection function of time.

4.2 Regional Currencies

As opposed to transactions with time currency, regional currencies are substitute currencies that are used equally as notes or sight deposits but only within a defined region, often as a means of payment used by market participants that are organised in associations or cooperatives. There are over 60 members recorded in the German Regiongeld e.V. parent association (Registered Association of Regional Money). Regional currencies are usually introduced or managed by non-profit organisations, often cooperatives. The German regional monetary systems (e.g. Chiemgauer, Donauthaler) are exchanged at a ratio of 1:1 to the euro, are convertible and fitted with the right to be converted into the euro at all times such that it is virtually always covered. Since Gesell's theory of depreciative money is often applied in this case, and the notes are regularly devalued by invalidation stamps, a high circulatory velocity of the money is expected to be attained. The objective of such currencies is often to strengthen the regional economy and stimulate the industry for small- and medium-scale enterprises of the region. The regional

[9] Cf. the homepage of Michael Lintons at http://www.gmlets.u-net.com or http://www.gaianeconomics.org/linton.htm

money with the strongest turnover in Germany, the Chiemgauer, thus charges a safe-deposit fee of 0.02 % per day or 8 % per annum. As with numerous regional currencies, the fees in this case are used for non-commercial purposes. At the moment, municipal–political involvement, a degree of technical organisation (notes versus cards) and acceptance in the regional economy vary strongly in the known regional currencies in Germany.[10]

4.3 Bartering Systems

Bartering systems are exchange systems that are not executed in terms of time but in a fictitious currency. There are 500 commercial barter currencies in the USA alone.[11] The system that is currently most popular in this country is the Swiss Wirtschaftsring (WIR),[12] founded in 1934, with which about 60,000 small and medium-scale companies are currently affiliated. In the meantime, the self-help organisation runs a bank that is licensed to operate as a bank and could boast a turnover in excess of 2.5 billion Swiss francs in 2011. WIR uses the Swiss franc as coverage currency and exchanges WIR at a ratio of 1:1 against the Swiss franc in a way that virtually makes it a parallel currency. Members make mutual payments through a central clearing system without any physical currency, which means there are no WIR banknotes. With WIR, credit interests are not paid, and demurrage is not calculated. Precisely at times of restrictive lending by banks in accordance with Basel II, WIR became enormously significant to small- and medium-scale enterprises, which put trust in and finance each other on a mutual basis, thus sidelining the banks. The scope, however, remains limited to the circle of the cooperative, even though the high membership number and the confidence that has in the meantime been placed in the complementary money flow speak for themselves. While the three alternatives presented so far are absolutely effective in their regions and membership structures and can already be ruled out terminologically for a national or supranational system, system-changing models will still be presented in this discourse.

4.4 Irvin Fisher's 100 % Money

In the face of the global economic crisis of the time, a group of economists from Chicago proposed in the 1930s that money be issued only with a 100 % reserve obligation. Hence, the value coverage of the money can be realised with gold,

[10] Kennedy and Lietaer (2004), Hubert (2004).

[11] An overview of bartering systems in: Oberländer, 2008.

[12] WIR-Bank, Annual Report 2012; www.wir.ch

savings deposits, or bundle of goods. This would then mean stripping the commercial banks of the option of cash generation and having them concentrate purely on the role of intermediary in lending money, i.e. intermediation between lending and deposit transactions. Theoretically, the risk of inflation or deflation would have been averted and the currency system made much more stable. Even current surveys, such as the study by Binswanger of 2012, address the implementability of the system for the global economy of the present day. It is understandable that a paradigm shift will be required in the overall economy and monetary economy (Binswanger 2012). Banks would be stripped of immense income opportunities, and economic growth on the basis of debt would no longer be possible. Recently, the deposition of covered money was also linked with CO_2 emission rights, whose value has become less in doubt.[13]

4.5 *Free Banking*

The demand for the permissibility of complementary currencies, as they have been called, goes even farther than Irving Fisher's plan up until the creation of an additional private global currency (parallel money). A free and private cash generation and the related competition would—in the view of the free banking movement—led to a good number of money types, while no such monies will have to be identified as legal tender. The institutions issuing the money would have strong incentives to pay attention to stability, and thereby the purchasing power of their money, since they may end up being displaced from the market. The term coined by von Hayek—the denationalisation of money—can be mentioned in this respect. In effect, goods would of course be priced in different currencies, and theoretically the most stable money would survive through competition under the monetary systems. The numerous game types of free banking can be seen in the different approaches of gold and commodity coverage by specific institutions up until the complete freedom to allow anyone to generate uncovered cash. The fact then that exchange rates would emerge in a market between the different complementary currencies for commodities and services or that some commodities would be swapped by their providers only against specific currencies may be considered a disadvantage. It can be assumed, however, that a strong complementary currency would eventually survive and could replace the numerous complementary currencies as a global currency. It will remain to be seen whether the blessing of currency liberalism will be left only to the covered cash generation of the private sector rather than the uncovered cash generation of the state. These considerations are not far apart from the ideas of Keynes and his Bancor plan[14] with an international clearing union that is capable of assuming the functions of central banks. The findings of an expert

[13] Douthwaite 2011; S. 432 ff.

[14] The original plan after the Second World War for a new worldwide currency in: Keynes, 1980;

commission of the United Nations, which in 2009 together with the participating President of the Chinese Central Bank Zhou Xiaochuan (2009) welcomed such a private sector global currency, show how Keynes's ideas have been reignited. Even the shopping cart-based "Terra" that Lietaer conceived in 2003 can be seen as a move in this direction.[15] Combined with the "sustainability fee" in the sense of negative interests, we end up once again with the ideas of the depreciative money of the Austrian School as already described above. Equally current are the proposals made in 2012 by Thomas Mayer of the Research Department of Deutsche Bank that the Greek state should introduce the "geuro" as a parallel currency, which would virtually mean a return to the "regional currency drachma" (Mayer 2012). The concept advanced by Douthwaite in 2011, which proposed an Irish "harp" that is available only on electronic basis, also goes in the same direction (Douthwaite 2011).

5 Summary

If the models considered are to be conclusively evaluated on the basis of monetary functions, it can be assumed in the consideration of the function of money as a medium of exchange that of all the models, the liquidity preference, i.e. the withholding and saving of money rather than putting it into circulation, will be rather low. Who would want to hoard this medium of payment when there is such a multitude of payment forms and negative interests in the model of depreciative money? On the other hand, a high circulatory velocity will then also require less monetary volume. Even in the function of money as a measure of value (unit of account), it can be assumed that the regular set-off of the accounts only in gold or shopping carts, of regional and complementary currencies, will ultimately lead to a measure of value. Finally, stock markets in the sense of foreign exchange rates would continuously reflect the values as long as the currencies are traded in a supra-regional manner. The resource-based CO_2 emission rights can serve as examples in this case.

The models will ultimately also not be useful as protection of value whereby the fundamental question may be asked whether money is an efficient means of protecting value at all, even if it emerges through the monopolist process of cash creation by a central bank. At this point, finance theory relates to the disciplines of value teachings and the question whether values such as communality, which is allegedly boosted in a regional currency, can be measured at all, and whether value protection does not ultimately end up in value creation. The readings of the business reports of the WIR Bank should absolutely be able to spur rethinking in this respect. The theory of the "ecology of money", a sustained monetary system is in this case

[15] Cf. Lietaer, Belgin, 2011. All ideas for a worldwide currency from Lietaer in: http://www.lietaer.com/

definitely still in its infancy regarding research, and it cannot be neatly described with the mere irrationality of the economic subjects from the theory of behavioural finance. In the end, no monetary system will function here without confidence (credit). Whether or not "regional or complementary" confidence in alternative monetary systems and money flows then requires the rating of international agencies will have to be debated.

References

Arestis, P. (2011). Financial liberalization and the relationship between finance and growth. In J. Philip Aron (Ed.), *Virtual money gets real. New Scientist, 2815(210)*, 23–25.

Binswanger, H. C. (2012). Finanz- und Umweltkrise sind ohne Währungs- und Geldreform nicht lösbar. In Verein Monetäre Modernisierung (Hg.), *Die Vollgeld-Reform: Wie Staatsschulden abgebaut und Finanzkrisen verhindert werden können*. Solothurn. 13–25.

Douthwaite, R. (2011). *The ecology of money*. Elsevier: New York.

Hubert, E.-M. (2004). *Tauschringe und Marktwirtschaft: Eine ökonomische Analyse lokaler Komplementärökonomien*. Berlin.

Kennedy, M., & Lietaer, A. (2004). *Regionalwährungen: Neue Wege zu nachhaltigem Wohlstand*. München.

Mayer, T. (2012). *Der Geuro: Eine Parallelwährung für Griechenland?* Research Briefing Europäische Integration: Deutsche Bank.

Selgin, G. A. (1988). *The theory of free banking: Money supply under competitive note issue*. New York.

Xiaochuan, Z. (2009). *Reform the international monetary system*. BIS Review 41, Basel, 2.

Put–Call Parity Violations Under Limited Arbitrage: A Case Study and a Simulation Tool for Detecting Financial Irregularity

Ted Azarmi and Paul Borochin

1 Introduction

Here, we consider the price pressure effects of deliberate attempts to manipulate the options market and the strategies for detecting these manipulations in the presence of limits to arbitrage. We use simulated data to examine the ability of standard statistical tests to detect the presence of price pressure resulting from attempts to manipulate the stock options market. We find limited ability of difference tests to detect anomalous price pressure in cases where limits to arbitrage are absent or the degree of price pressure is low and when the anomalous price pressure occurs for a short period relative to the overall window analyzed.

To help with pedagogical use of our method, we are providing a detailed case study of Porsche's takeover attempt of Volkswagen (VW). The case study helps students to devise tools for detecting and taking timely actions against financial misconduct. In particular, in the Porsche–VW case, limits to arbitrage were in place, meaning that VW-Gesetz (Volkswagen Law) in Germany gave the state of Niedersachsen veto power and substantial ownership rights to prevent an unfriendly takeover. The German government also actively worked through the EU commission to block takeovers by taking legal action in the courts against the VW-Gesetz. Students are asked to help detect market manipulations in the options and derivatives market using violations of Black and Scholes, this chapter's put–call parity violations, and relations between options expiring on various dates under limited arbitrage.

T. Azarmi (✉)
Heilbronn University and University of Tuebingen, Max-Planck-Str. 39, Heilbronn 74081, Germany
e-mail: ted.azarmi@hs-heilbronn.de

P. Borochin
University of Connecticut, 2100 Hillside Rd, Unit 1041, Storrs, CT, USA
e-mail: paul.borochin@business.uconn.edu

T. Azarmi, W. Amann (eds.), *The Financial Crisis*,
DOI 10.1007/978-3-319-20588-5_6

2 Literature Review

This research bridges two main threads of finance literature: price pressure in options and limits to arbitrage. We use an examination of put–call parity to identify significant departures from equilibrium prices. These departures can arise for a number of reasons, but our investigation focuses on market manipulation.

The first area of the literature that we examine extensively documents the effect of price pressure on option-implied volatilities. Price pressure exerted by market actors, as described in Bollen and Whaley (2004) and Garleanu et al. (2009), can cause significant deviations from uniform-implied volatilities across strike prices for the same option or across option types for the same strike and maturity. The classic buying pressure example in Bollen and Whaley (2004) is the implied volatility smirk in index options: out-of-the-money put option prices (and their corresponding implied volatilities) are bid up by investors who want to purchase insurance against a crash.

Xing et al. (2010) found significant predictive power in implied volatility differences between out-of-the-money put and in-the-money call options on the S&P 500 index. Cremers and Weinbaum (2010) found evidence of the former in that implied risk-neutral volatilities for contemporaneous puts and calls are not always equivalent, and the gap between the two has predictive power for stock returns. These predictive gaps in implied volatility are further examples of the price pressure theory of implied volatility deviations. A similar sort of price pressure, which we consider here, can arise from a deliberate attempt to manipulate security prices.

The second area we draw from the literature is on limits to arbitrage. Classical finance theory derives the *put–call parity* (PCP) relation by the law of one price argument. Instead, behavioral finance allows a certain degree of irrationality, a setting in which PCP may not necessarily hold. A subset of the literature limits to arbitrage and concerns specific settings in which violations of the law of one price may obtain.[1] Arbitrage strategies that seek to correct and profit from violations of the law of one price can be both risky and costly. Cremers and Weinbaum (2010) point to a substantial number of frictions that may make put/call arbitrage infeasible: early exercise premia, short-sales restrictions, timing of simultaneous trades necessary to arbitrage the PCP relation, transaction costs, lending/borrowing rate differences, margin requirements, and taxes. The existence of these limits to arbitrage may make the detection of price pressure easier by reducing arbitrageurs' ability to absorb departures from equilibrium, thereby making it easier to detect manipulation.

[1] See Barberis and Thaler (2003) and Shleifer and Vishny (1997) for a comprehensive review of limits to arbitrage.

3 Using Put–Call Parity to Identify Market Manipulation

Abnormal price pressure in the options market directly results in violations of put–call parity (PCP) defined by Stoll (1968) as

$$c + Ke^{-r(T-t)} = p + Se^{-\delta(T-t)} \tag{1}$$

where c and p are call and put prices, respectively, S is the price of the underlying asset, K is the strike price, r is the risk-free interest rate, δ is the annual dividend yield, and $(T-t)$ is the time to expiration. PCP states that a portfolio A consisting of a European call option, plus the present value of cash equal to the option strike price, must equal portfolio B. Portfolio B consists of the underlying asset's spot price, reduced by dividends, paid over the option's life, plus the corresponding European put with the same strike price and expiration date. Since both portfolios will have the same value at expiration, and therefore the same present value now, their prices must also be the same. If that is not the case, arbitrageurs could exploit this violation of the law of one price by selling the overvalued portfolio and buying the undervalued one in order to make profitable trades without risk until the PCP relationship is restored in Eq. (1). However, limits to arbitrage may prevent this from occurring.

Demand pressure in the options markets (Bollen and Whaley 2004; Garleanu et al. 2009; Cremers and Weinbaum 2010) can cause violations of put–call parity. This demand pressure can arise when a large number of small positions or a small number of large positions are opened, as would be consistent with market manipulation. Persistent violations of put–call parity can, therefore, be used as a preliminary screening tool by regulators for further analysis.

The existence of a persistent put–call parity gap means that excess demand for either the call or put option is present, relative to the other. The origins of this demand can then be traced using order flow data or potentially determined from statistical analysis of the PCP gap.[2] To do this, we first rearrange the PCP expression in Eq. (1) to the left to form the PCP "gap" below:

$$c + Ke^{-r(T-t)} - Se^{-\delta(T-t)} - p = 0 \tag{2}$$

Since we know the equilibrium value of Eq. (2) should equal zero, we can test statistically for abnormal price pressure on the call or the put by substituting market data for the parameters c, p, K, S, and δ. Specifically, we can use either the Student's t-test or the nonparametric Wilcoxon sign-rank test, depending on the justifiability

[2] This approach may be useful as a preliminary identification strategy that can then be corroborated by a financial regulator who examines matched order flow data. It is also the only option for market participants who do not have access to matched order flow data.

of the t-distribution that the parametric test assumes. For ease of exposition, we use simulated price data for c, p, K, and S and assume a nondividend paying stock.[3]

3.1 PCP Gap Simulation

We generate a 3-month time series of c, p, K, and S under a variety of environments to illustrate the feasibility of PCP gap tests to identify market manipulation. We define market manipulation as a deviation of the "implied volatility" (or IV) of the at-the-money, 1-month call from the at-the-money, 1-month put. Since IV is directly related to price, this is simply a restatement of the Bollen and Whaley (2004) price pressure theory. In equilibrium, the IV of the call and the put should be equal, and the magnitude of the difference is proportional to the amount of simulated price pressure. On average, the equilibrium IV is set to 0.45. We also assume an IID, normally distributed, 0.01 standard error for both the call and the put IVs, which proxies for the effect of noise trading.

Without losing generality, we simulate the effects of price pressure through market manipulation on the at-the-money call option[4] by increasing its implied volatility, following the Bollen and Whaley (2004) price pressure argument. On each day manipulation occurs, we vary the degree of concerted price pressure from market manipulation from 0.045 (10 % of equilibrium level) to 0.0045 (1 % of the equilibrium level). This variation can be attributed either to the degree of market manipulation (with higher price pressure corresponding to stronger manipulation) or to the presence of limits to arbitrage (with higher price pressure corresponding to higher limits to arbitrage). We also vary the persistence of the simulated manipulation over 65 trading days in the 3-month time series. We simulate different relative lengths of anomalous price pressure with manipulation occurring within our sample over 48-day (75 % of observations), 32-day (50 % of observations), 16-day (25 % of observations), 6-day (10 % of observations), and 3-day (5 % of observations) periods. We consider varying periods of price pressure to account for the fact that an outside observer may have a general sense of when potential manipulation may be occurring. However, pinning down the precise start and end points may be impossible from price data alone.

Equation (2) delivers the PCP gap for each 3-month time series generated in this way. Figure 1 shows the PCP gap for two different simulated time series: one with a high degree of observable manipulation (5 % of equilibrium IV over 50 % of total observations) and one with a low degree (1 % of equilibrium IV over 50 % of total observations), consistent with an absence of limits to arbitrage.

---

[3] This enables us to omit δ without losing generality in the analysis of differences. To generalize this approach to American options on stocks paying a discrete dividend, we would need to consider a parametrization of the early exercise premium, a consideration beyond the scope of this work.

[4] Identical results, though with reversed sign on the PCP gap, can be obtained by increasing the price pressure and IV on the at-the-money put option.

Fig. 1 Sample simulated PCP gaps by degree of manipulation

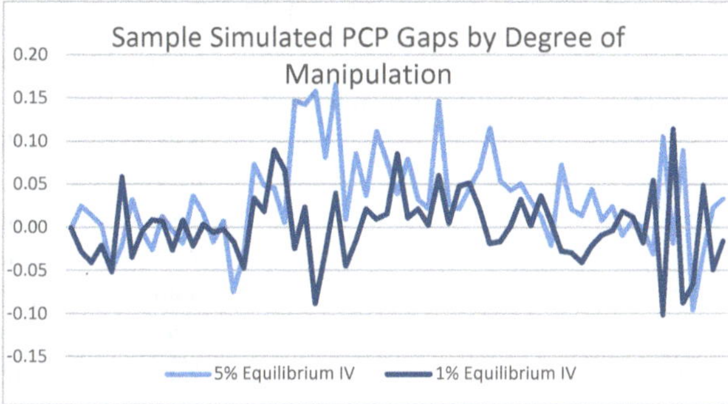

3.2 *Statistical Tests*

For each simulated time series, we evaluate a standard statistical test's ability to detect a significant PCP gap as observable evidence of market manipulation. We consider two approaches, the Student's t-test, assuming a thick-tailed symmetric distribution of the PCP gap,[5] and a Wilcoxon sign-rank test that is robust to alternative possible distributions. The t-test follows the standard procedure for a test of significant difference from zero, the null hypothesis of PCP equilibrium. The two-sample Wilcoxon sign-rank test uses a simulated PCP gap with zero manipulation and the standard 1 % noise terms in the IV processes for calls and puts. In a real-life application, a matched time series of non-manipulated calls and puts on a firm with similar equilibrium IV may be substituted. The significance of these results, across durations and magnitudes of manipulation, illustrates the ability of superficial statistical analysis to detect this manipulation. Table 1 presents the results.

In general, the Student's t-test outperforms the Wilcoxon sign-rank test at identifying departures from PCP equilibrium due to the simulated price pressure on call options: in most cases where the anomalous price pressure is identified with statistical significance, the Student's test reports a higher p-value than the sign-rank test. Furthermore, it correctly identifies significant price pressure for some situations missed by the sign-rank test, such as the 25 % relative sample duration of market manipulation and 5 % or 2.5 % equilibrium IV cases. As expected, extended periods of anomalous price pressure simulated by the 75 % relative sample duration case can be reliably identified even at the lowest level of 1 % of equilibrium IV. However, as either relative duration or strength of the anomalous price pressure decreases, the ability of a simple statistical test to pick it up also decreases. In broad terms, the simulation evidence seems to suggest that if manipulation occurs in 25 % or less of the test sample and if the magnitude of the observable manipulation is less

[5] In the presence of IID normal shocks to c and p introduced by noise traders, this may be a reasonable assumption.

Table 1 Significant departures from PCP equilibrium for a set of simulated price paths

	Market Manipulation by % Equilibrium IV			
Percentage of observations manipulated	10 %	5 %	2.5 %	1 %
75 %	**9.98** ***	**6.90** ***	**5.48** ***	**2.06** **
	6.59 ***	***4.72*** ***	***3.43*** ***	*1.53*
50 %	**6.56** ***	**4.90** ***	**2.19** ***	0.09
	5.64 ***	***3.84*** ***	*1.53*	*−0.13*
25 %	**4.90** ***	**1.72** *	**1.70** *	0.80
	3.90 ***	*0.95*	*1.04*	*0.80*
10 %	**2.47** **	1.05	−0.31	−0.96
	2.12 ***	*0.40*	*−0.24*	*−0.40*
5 %	1.15	−0.69	−0.22	−0.83
	1.27	*−0.59*	*−0.39*	*−0.80*

This table shows the test statistics from the Student's *t*-test (*t*-statistic, top of each row) and Wilcoxon sign-rank tests (*z*-statistic, bottom of each row in italics) of significant departures from PCP equilibrium for a set of simulated price paths. We simulate price paths with varying strength (weakness) of market manipulation (limits to arbitrage) to range from 10 % to 1 % and duration of price pressure period from 75 % to 5 % of the observed sample. Significant test statistics are denoted in bold, with 1 %, 5 %, and 10 % significance levels denoted by asterisks

than 5 % of equilibrium at-the-money IV,[6] the anomalous price pressure resulting from this manipulation may go undetected by simple statistical testing.

We illustrate the importance of finding evidence of alleged market manipulation of stock option prices using the case study of Porsche and Volkswagen in 2004.

4 Porsche and Volkswagen: A Case Study

In October 1992, Porsche AG was in a difficult financial situation. Porsche car sales dropped to close to 15,000 units from their mid-1980s level of close to 55,000. Correspondingly, the firm's revenue was almost cut in half during this period. Porsche then undertook a turnaround operation under the leadership of Wendelin Wiedeking, who became the new CEO in August 1993.

Mr. Wiedeking negotiated an innovative contract with the banks that provided credit to Porsche. As CEO, he took a liability equal to his entire wealth in exchange for bank loans, which were necessary to the survival of Porsche as an independent company. The loan contract stipulated that Mr. Wiedeking would receive a salary only if Porsche became profitable. In that case, his pay would be 0.9 % of Porsche's net income. In addition, close to 80 % of Porsche's executive board compensation was performance based.

[6] The observable strength of anomalous price pressure would be moderated by the ability of arbitrageurs to absorb it, i.e., the limits to arbitrage.

It is easy to mistake this contract as an innovative solution to the well-known agency problem of focusing on how to best align a manager's interest with that of the shareholders. Conventionally, compensation packages providing stock options are used to mitigate managerial agency costs. However, maximizing net income is very different from maximizing stockholders' wealth. Net income is short term, as it is based on 1 year's operations. Both underinvestment and high short-term returns that fail to adequately compensate for excess risk can be utilized to manipulate net income, while owners' wealth (measured by stock price) might be reduced or remain unaffected.

Initially, Porsche's value improved dramatically under Mr. Wiedeking's tenure. He instituted a number of changes, including:

1. Japanese-style lean production techniques, total quality control, and just-in-time inventory management implemented by two Japanese efficiency experts hired in early 1993. A complete overhaul of the company and the introduction of Toyota-inspired production methods. Mr. Wiedeking even went down the production line once with a saw and cut off the shelving that held parts, in order to make a point about lean manufacturing to his workers.
2. Employing and rewarding the best German production engineering talent.
3. Cost reductions, including discontinuing Porsche 928 and 968 model platforms to reduce complexity, maintaining only the Porsche 911 production line.
4. Customer and worker satisfaction initiatives.

As a result, Porsche sold 18,402 cars in 1993/1994 fiscal year, and the unit sales increased substantially to 32,383 in 1996/1997. Its revenue also showed a similar improvement, increasing from 1.2 million euros in 1993/1994 to 2.1 million euros in 1996/1997. Porsche moved from experiencing a substantial loss in 1993/1994 to netting a large positive gain (EBT) in 1996/1997.

The beginning of the end for Mr. Wiedeking's career came in 2009 when it was reported that Mr. Adolf Merckle, who was one of the world's richest men, committed suicide by jumping in front of a train. Reportedly, he had spent his life building up a business with some 100,000 employees and had lost it all to a short-squeeze of VW shares. It was alleged that Porsche had cornered the VW stock market by announcing that it held most of its free-floating shares. Those who had naked shorts[7] needed to purchase VW shares at extremely high prices to cover their short position. In fact, due to the resulting market price manipulation, VW briefly reached 1000 euros a share, thereby becoming the world's highest capitalized firm. Market participants clearly perceived the high price of VW to be out of line with its underlying economic value due to its relatively poor performance as an automobile manufacturer at that time.

On July 23, 2009, Mr. Wiedeking tenure at Porsche ended. He received 50 million euros in severance pay. In November 2011, he faced criminal charges over his alleged role in market manipulation as CEO of Porsche, a trial still in progress in

[7] Naked short selling was legal at the time in Germany.

2015 at the time of our study. His actions have been viewed as one of the largest trading scandals involving a nonfinancial firm. Financial trading scandals usually involve speculation in derivative contracts such as options and futures, something one does not expect to see in the automobile industry.

One may view Porsche as both an automobile manufacturing and a speculative financial trading firm under Mr. Wiedeking's tenure. For example, in 2007, Porsche's pre-tax profit of 8.57 billion euros exceeded its total car sales revenues of 7.47 billion euros. Therefore, despite lack of precise data, it is reasonable to assume that a large share of these profits did not come from its car business, but may be attributed to derivatives trading.

Derivatives trading at Porsche began early on, with dollar vs. euro currency options that the firm used as a hedge. Approximately, 40 % of Porsche's car sales were in US dollars, while all of its production costs were in euros (it manufactured only in Germany and Finland). Mr. Wiedeking had a deputy and chief strategist named Holger Härter who showed considerable talent in selecting the right mix of currency option hedges. As both men's compensation was tied to yearly net income of Porsche, it is alleged that they began speculative trading in currency options. Strictly speaking, currency speculation by an automobile firm is legal.

However, sound academic finance scholarship and practice consider financial speculation as an illegitimate method for enhancing owner wealth at manufacturing companies on two important grounds. First, those owners who wish to engage in financial speculation may do so—without imposing the risk on other owners who do not wish to trade—by using firms that specialize in that activity. Second, creditors provide debt financing to an automobile manufacturing firm at a much lower capital cost than available to a speculative derivative trading firm. Combining the two activities gives rise to a conflict of interest between creditors and a firm's management. This is an agency problem with associated agency costs.

Porsche's speculative option trading in US dollar vs. euro happened to be profitable in those early years. In fact, some estimate that more than 40 % of its operating earnings were from currency option trading, which involved high risk. Shortly thereafter, Porsche moved to trading in stock options.

In September 2005, Porsche announced that it planned to acquire more than 20 % of VW shares to become its largest shareholder. Prior to that date, Porsche held 5 % of VW shares. At the time, VW performed relatively poorly, both financially and in its operations as an automobile company. A classical takeover analysis would suggest that if a highly profitable and efficient firm, such as Porsche, acquires an inefficient company (VW), the acquirer should increase the target's efficiency and thereby create additional wealth for owners of both firms. However, that analysis is too simple to be applied in this case. Here, there were a number of complexities, which we now enumerate.

The second generation of the founding family of Porsche (the Piëch and Porsche families—practically the same individuals) had large ownership interests and board presence in both Porsche and VW. There were rumors of internal family difficulties between the Piëch family and the CEO of VW, Mr. Winterkorn, the Porsche family and Wiedeking. Therefore, the expertise and business-production knowhow at the board level of these two firms were not different enough to lead to efficiency gains from a takeover.

The two founding families held all 8.75 million shares of common stock and thereby controlled all voting rights. In addition, 8.75 million shares of preferred stocks of Porsche traded at Frankfurt and a number of smaller German exchanges. Fourteen percent of these preferred shares were also held by the Porsche and Piëch families. Eighty-six percent of preferred shares traded publicly.

Porsche did not report quarterly financial results. In fact, it was removed from the Frankfurt exchange's stock index in September 2002 due to lack of quarterly accounting statements. In 2002, Porsche was invited to list on the New York Stock Exchange. Even though academic financial research showed a significant valuation premium associated with the NYSE listing, Porsche refused to list there on the grounds that the requirement of Sarbanes-Oxley (that senior management be held personally accountable for the company's accuracy of the financial statements) was not in keeping with German law. Given that all of Porsche's voting common shares are privately held and in light of the current criminal trial of its former CEO for market manipulation, Porsche's objection to Sarbanes-Oxley can be taken as an argument for the merit of that requirement.

The second complication was that Porsche received significant income from option and derivative trading in VW shares. Porsche's takeover attempt enhanced its revenues from derivative speculation. In fact, Porsche earned approximately 800 million euros in 2005/2006, 7 billion euros in 2006/2007, and 19 billion euros in 2007/2008, mostly derived from VW option trading according to reports.

Porsche's option trading in VW included writing put options on VW shares, purchasing calls with a strike price close to the VW market share price and calls with a strike price that significantly exceeded VW's market price at the time. Porsche experienced a substantial increase in income from option and derivative trading in VW shares as a result of its takeover attempt. A financial regulator may forbid the combination of these options and a takeover attempt on the grounds that they could lead to market manipulation. However, before 2007, BaFin, the German Federal Financial Supervisory Authority, had no rules obligating Porsche to report its options position.

Also noteworthy is that in Germany, naked short selling was legal at the time of the VW short squeeze, allowing for unlimited short positions that could theoretically exceed the number of available shares. This regulatory position has reversed and naked short selling is now prohibited.

Another fact that complicated the Porsche takeover attempt was a 1960s German law. Paragraph 2 of the VW act stipulated that a block shareholder may only vote 20 % of its shares in VW, regardless of the percentage of shares owned. Paragraph 3 of the VW act required an 80 % majority for any major shareholder decisions at VW. More than 20 % of the total shares of VW were granted to the German state of Lower Saxony. One seat on the VW Board of Directors is granted permanently to Lower Saxony and another seat to the government of Germany. VW corporate decisions on relocation required a two-thirds majority vote. Therefore, in practice, a takeover of VW was possible only through an agreement with Lower Saxony and was likely to involve the German government.

In fact, the European Commission filed an action against the VW law and in October 2007, the European Court of Justice ruled that the act was illegal. Germany revised the VW act in May 2008. In the revised version of the act, there were no state-appointed members in the VW Supervisory Board. Block shareholders could vote their entire holdings and were no longer restricted to a 20 % maximum voting share. However, other aspects of the VW act were retained.

By November 2006, Porsche owned 27.4 % of VW shares and announced that it did not intend to exceed 30 % ownership. Nevertheless, Porsche increased its ownership of VW to 31 % in March 2007. According to German law, exceeding the 30 % shareholding limit required Porsche to make an offer to purchase the remaining common and preferred shares of VW. Normally in Germany, takeover offers are made at a significant premium over the market price of the shares in order to facilitate a quick takeover. But Porsche intentionally priced its offer at the minimum legally required price of 100.92 euros for common stocks and 65.54 euros for preferred shares, while the market prices for VW ordinary shares were 111.39 euros and the preferred shares were 74.54 euros.

Porsche's below-the-market offer was accepted by only 0.6 % of VW shareholders. It appeared that Porsche intended its offer to fail, which would have caused VW share prices to decline after the expiration of the offer, allowing Porsche to then buy the shares cheaper. Additional legal disclosures regarding VW share purchases by Porsche would no longer have been required. The strategy worked and a significant number of investors reduced their VW exposure, consequently decreasing the share price. Then Porsche announced its intent to gain approximately 50 % ownership in VW.

The next milestone in German takeovers was to reach the 75 % ownership limit. A majority owner with more than 75 % of the shares has "domination and profit transfer." In practice, this meant that Porsche could access VW's treasury and could utilize 8 billion euros in cash VW held. Porsche announced, however, that it had no intention to own more than 75 % of VW and restated this position between March and October 2008.

On October 26, 2008 Porsche announced it intended to reach the 75 % ownership limit and revealed that it owned 42.6 % of VW shares and that it could exercise share options for an additional 31.5 %. This meant that only 5.9 % of VW shares could be traded (as there was a 20 % non-tradable state ownership). There were more than 5.9 % naked short positions in VW. After all, there were good grounds for shorting VW shares due to falling demand for its cars and a looming recession—it was facing a tough financial situation.

Porsche's announcement triggered a short squeeze and VW share prices briefly traded at 1000 euros. Reportedly, hedge funds lost about $24 billion on their VW naked short positions, while Porsche had an unrealized gain of over $100 billion.

The financial crisis of 2008 caused Porsche's creditors to retract some of Porsche's loans and to refuse to extend it additional credit. Consequently, there was insufficient financing available for Porsche to complete its VW acquisition.

Porsche approached the Emir of Qatar as an outside investor to provide it with additional cash. However, the German government interfered and convinced Qatar to invest directly in VW. With no other available creditors, Porsche was 11.4 billion euros in debt and faced a liquidity crisis. Consequently, it consented to be taken over by VW. Following that decision and after contribution of capital from founding families, Porsche's debt was reduced to 1.5 billion euros in 2011.

Porsche had high profits every year for a period of nearly 10 years. It also paid a special dividend of 14 euros per share in 2002 and increased its regular dividend payments.

5 Conclusion

We have considered the ability of outside observers to detect market manipulation in stock options in the presence of limits to arbitrage. Our objective has been to focus on training students to detect financial manipulations. Several data sets and supporting simulation Excel sheets are prepared as supplemental material to the case study presented in this chapter. The additional material is available to students at www.azarmi.org. We also demonstrated that while statistical analysis of an observable PCP gap is sufficient to identify major manipulation in cases of high limits to arbitrage, in many other cases a more in-depth analysis of option price or order flow data is required.

In addition to teach students how to detect and take timely action against financial misconduct, we have provided a dataset of VW stock and option prices for the relevant period of our study and a spreadsheet that generates a put–call parity simulation at this case study's support board at www.azarmi.org. Our simulation tool allows students to take the stock price as given, while generating shocks to call and put implied volatilities during periods of manipulation (denoted by a dummy variable in Column B of our Excel sheet) with a severity specified in the call implied volatilities in column (J). This tool models price pressure (following Bollen and Whaley 2004) that is exerted on call option prices by buyers (or sellers) trying to manipulate the market. The model then computes Black–Scholes option prices with the (potentially) manipulated implied volatilities, which are perturbed both by daily supply/demand shocks (column Z) and the manipulation shock (column Y). This means that call implied volatilities can be different from put implied volatilities, meaning that call and put prices will violate put–call parity (column V).

Students can modify this model to simulate other situations, such as put market manipulation, and the duration and intensity of the manipulation event, so as to observe the effects on the put–call parity gap.

References

Barberis, N., & Thaler, R. H. (2003). A survey of behavioral finance. In G. Constantinides, M. Harris & R. Stultz (Eds.), *Handbook of the economics of finance* (pp. 1051–1119).

Bollen, N. P., & Whaley, R. E. (2004). Does net buying pressure affect the shape of implied volatility functions? *Journal of Finance, 59*(2), 711–753.

Cremers, M., & Weinbaum, D. (2010). Deviations from put-call parity and stock return predictability. *Journal of Financial and Quantitative Analysis, 45*(2), 335–367.

Garleanu, N., Pedersen, L. H., & Poteshman, A. M. (2009). Demand-based option pricing. *Review of Financial Studies, 22*(10), 4259–4299.

Shleifer, A., & Vishny, R. W. (1997). The limits of arbitrage. *The Journal of Finance, 52*(1), 35–55.

Stoll, H. (1968). The relationship between put and call option prices. *The Journal of Finance, 24*, 801–824.

Xing, Y., Zhang, X., & Zhao, R. (2010). What does the individual option volatility smirk tell us about future equity returns? *Journal of Financial and Quantitative Analysis, 45*, 641–662.

Enabling Holistic Finance Education in Turbulent Times

Wolfgang Amann

1 Introduction

Two examples illustrate the need for a more holistic finance education very well. One of them has recently seen investors complaining about the loss of volatility in currency fluctuations—a development that rendered speculation and profits harder to achieve. In fact, between 2008 and 2014, the Deutsche Bank Currency Volatility Index showed a volatility reduction of 72 %. Simultaneously, this complaint also evidences how split and at times diametrically opposed the interests of various stakeholders in international business can be. In turn, companies active in international trade prefer predictability and less volatility with regard to currencies for their operations. When it comes to these focused, isolated views on what investors prefer, there is a need to ensure the pre- and post-experience education of finance experts provide them with a holistic view of their impact.

This insight is further supported by a second example in the form of an anecdote. A major business school, with the highest international AACSB accreditation for its faculty, was recently approached by a large financial services organization. The latter first politely suggested, then offered stronger encouragement, that the business school drop general management and refocus on finance education, while not necessarily emphasizing ethics education. What the financial service organization thought it needed was a larger number of graduates who were finance experts—specialists, not generalists with a solid, holistic education. However, as they climb the organizational hierarchy, they would need more than just specialized skill sets. Once again, finance education would risk being too narrow.

This chapter outlines three dimensions that, if implemented, could improve not only individual career chances, the performance of financial service organizations,

W. Amann (✉)
HEC Paris in Qatar, P.O. Box 5825, Doha, Qatar
e-mail: amann.wolfgang@gmail.com

T. Azarmi, W. Amann (eds.), *The Financial Crisis*,
DOI 10.1007/978-3-319-20588-5_7

and the industry, but quite likely societies around the world. The basic goal of the chapter is not to prove ideas or provide ample statistical evidence via multivariate analysis but to stimulate critical thoughts and derive recommendations regarding the way in which finance education is delivered today. As such, this chapter aims to be constructive in its positioning and not simply to point fingers at business schools. The latter has already been done at length (cf. Amann et al. 2011). Business schools were attacked for their lack of relevance, outdated learning methodologies, extensive Anglo-Saxon focused content while simultaneously neglecting the knowledge and idiosyncracies from local cultures—to name a few examples. It did not help, for example, to see Harvard MBA graduates waving plastic sharks during graduation to mock the critics seeing them as future Wall Street sharks. The derived recommendations presented in this chapter are bolstered with several arguments and relatively easy to implement. Thus, they help business schools walk the talk of constant and never-ending improvement that they want to see in companies as they preach in their seminars.

2 Embracing the Concept of the Development Channel

The first key insight on understanding a more holistic finance education acknowledges that individuals need to perform very different tasks at various stages of their careers. Yet, many experienced faculty members use the very same slides, case studies, exercises, illustrative examples, and even jokes, no matter their audience. The explanation these faculty members provide is even worse: 'We are not paid enough for programme development'. Consequently, master's students with 3 years of work experience and top managers all too frequently enjoy the same 'show'. Such a one-size-fits-all approach is not timely any more. In fact, it never was. Different target groups have heterogeneous training needs. Each managerial level usually fulfils different tasks, entailing separate target groups, as portrayed in Fig. 1. This figure incorporates elements from several leading thinkers. The work by Charan et al. (2000) serves as a point of reference for level-specific descriptions of tasks, while Krueckeberg et al. (2011) serve as a source for the general concept of development channel and the burnout versus bore-out zone.

- Individual or personal performers should learn and practise vocational skills to get their assignments done. At times, they simply serve as loyal soldiers—complying, subordinating, implementing. Course participants need the basics, or at times the somewhat advanced 'hard skills' of finance and accounting.
- Line managers have seen their work shift from doing to getting things done through others. They help others perform effectively. Even in teams consisting of finance experts working on financial challenges and tasks, skills need to evolve. Finance skills do not represent 100 % of what is required any more. Great faculty thus also shares the limitations of finance skills.

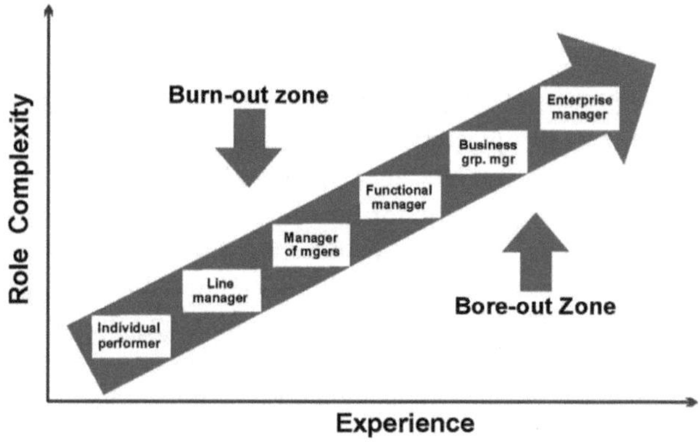

Fig. 1 The potential target audiences for executive education

- Managers of managers notice that their individual contributions are no longer part of the role. Instead, they manage others fully. They must start to form their own, substantiated opinions on key issues of higher-order relevance. Here, finance skills must include a more thorough understanding of what really drives and could significantly alter the financials. In addition, soft skills start to take centre stage. If finance skills dominate, they may well impede the team's success.
- Functional managers (in a number of organizations they may be referred to in different ways) should learn how to see a bigger picture to comprehend new fields and other units fast. They need to master delegation.
- Business or group managers deal largely with autonomy, integrate across functions, balance demands, and learn how to excel at allocating resources.
- Enterprise or real top managers develop a global perspective, manage external stakeholders, create and communicate visions, and need to excel at shifting business paradigms.
- Representatives in the bore-out zone should learn to leverage their subjectively felt experience in bigger roles.
- Representatives in the burn-out zone should learn to manage themselves and their environments so that sustainable performance becomes possible.

Specialists and individual performers need to learn the tools and vocabulary commonly used and when to move on to different skills. Yet, for their advancing careers, finance skills are increasingly marginalized. Even high-level CFOs have to manage teams, as they can no longer cope with all the workload they face. They ought to learn how to replace existing solutions and models: how to creatively destroy established logics, assumptions, and views or communicate more effectively.

3 Enhancing Complexity Skills

According to Collinson and Jay (2012), the largest 200 firms in the Global Fortune 500 list lose up to 10 % of shareholder value because of complexity, and the complexity strugglers even up to 40 %, if not more. A drastic case in point is Juergen Schrempp, the former CEO of DaimlerChrysler, who destroyed $60 billion in shareholder value, and the company lost 10 years of strategic development, ended up being less global, less technologically strong, and with a tarnished reputation due to the enormous complexity he generated by merging Daimler-Benz with the Chrysler Corporation and buying stakes in Korean and Japanese companies. Finance skills without the ability to understand and manage complexity will not suffice!

Complexity skills initially address how to better comprehend complexity. Figure 2 illustrates key drivers. Graduates of finance programmes ought to learn how their firms use diversity, for example, in clients and served markets, but also in internal HR, to their advantage. They need to see through the various ways of minimizing the negative impact of harmful complexity drivers. They embark on a learning journey of how their companies can optimize interdependency, fast flux as a proxy of the overall speed of change, and the number of directions in which change takes place, as well as ambiguity. The latter refers to the emerging phenomenon that there is less and less clarity, too much information, and increasingly fewer simple cause-and-effect relationships. Often, it is not only one complexity driver that haunts a company or an individual, which is why simplifying or complexifying in one area may not be enough. In the following figure, the call for

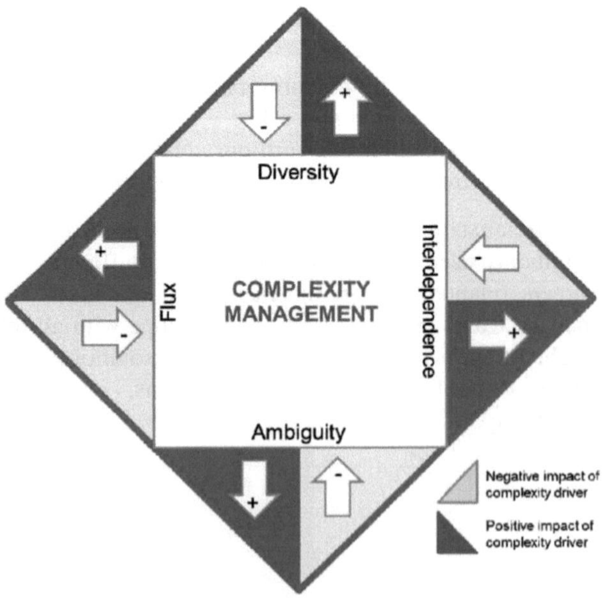

Fig. 2 Elements of a holistic complexity management as a complementing study field in finance

skills to be matched with the actual designed and implemented solutions, which in turn alter the perception of how difficult certain complexity challenges actually appear, is implicitly included.

4 Including More Learning Levels

In addition to understanding what skills may actually matter more than finance skills in certain career paths, or complement them most appropriately, as well as rendering oneself sensitive to the complexities in companies, the third gap to address in the chapter investigates the various learning levels. The latter are not equally addressed—a shortcoming that has to be worked on. Learning can generally take place on three levels.

- On the KNOWING level: The facts, models, or theories that are at the core of our profession, such as option pricing. Recent criticism pointed to the underlying flawed assumptions of understanding firms and markets as controllable machines and human beings as rational and always optimizing homo economicus beings. Also, for far too long, normal distribution curves have dominated risk analysis, while they should have been complemented by more realistic power law distributions, especially in today's turbulent times where it is more common to have a crisis than not.
- On the DOING level: The skills, capabilities, and techniques at the heart of work in finance departments or an understanding of a firm's financials, e.g. the skills needed to analyse balance sheets or profitability ratios. Recent criticism has pointed to substantial knowing–doing gaps and given the real-world statistics of how often projects and innovations fail, being able to incorporate dynamics in the planning or analysis process becomes crucial.
- On the BEING level: The values, attitudes, and beliefs forming a manager's view of the world and identity, e.g. behaviours exemplifying integrity and honesty. Recent criticism has targeted the ruthless self-enrichment, short-term profit maximization, or lack of care about people and the environment.

Finance courses often overemphasize the first level of 'knowing'. They may practise and test the 'doing' level. Yet, too often, the underlying assumptions are too clinical and sterile and insufficiently include uncertainty and complexity. Too frequently, the analysis is ex post and for a static environment. Courses usually score a perfect F on the being level. Here, course participants reflect upon what kind of finance expert or, more generally, what kind of manager, leader, and person they want to be. One could argue that this is not the core responsibility of a finance course, and interested candidates may well be referred to personal development or ethics courses. This train of thought ignores the insights that one cannot or should not give someone the tools without clarifying the responsibilities they entail. Postponing such thoughts to a later point in time does not represent a viable option either. Once confronted with a heavy workload, deadlines, and pressures to perform, such much-needed reflection time too frequently does not exist. It is only through an upfront clarification of values that future dilemmas can be avoided in the first place.

5 Integrating Humanism in Finance

This reflection opportunity is linked to the fourth insight into how to create a more holistic finance education. Why is more debate necessary about a more normative finance education? Do we not have great business schools around the world? Do we not perceive management education as something that has professionalized and matured over the years and decades? There is reason to believe that this is not the case. A recent, large-scale study in cooperation with the Association of Business Schools investigated the trends that the deans of the world's Top 1000 business schools saw since 2010. Figure 3 summarizes the responses of the study. Business school deans see three main mega-trends, and fortunately enough, ethics and CSR are part of it. So far, this is good news.

The surprising insight stems from their views that ethics and CSR will not matter at all in the next 3 years. Only one mega-trend would characterize their education efforts, and it has nothing to do with normative formation. Instead, business schools see a strong rise of online education, either commercialized or in the form of free 'massive open online courses' (MOOCs), as Fig. 4 indicates. Business schools and their leaders may not adequately see the true need of educating finance graduates on the normative level as well.

In a separate research project (An. 2014), we showed that banks performed quite differently during the financial crisis of 2007–2010. While some banks went

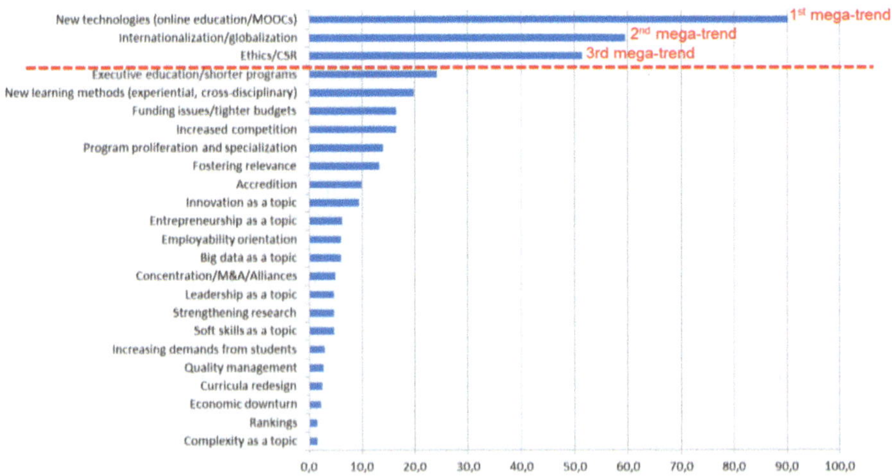

Fig. 3 Trends in management education 2010–2013

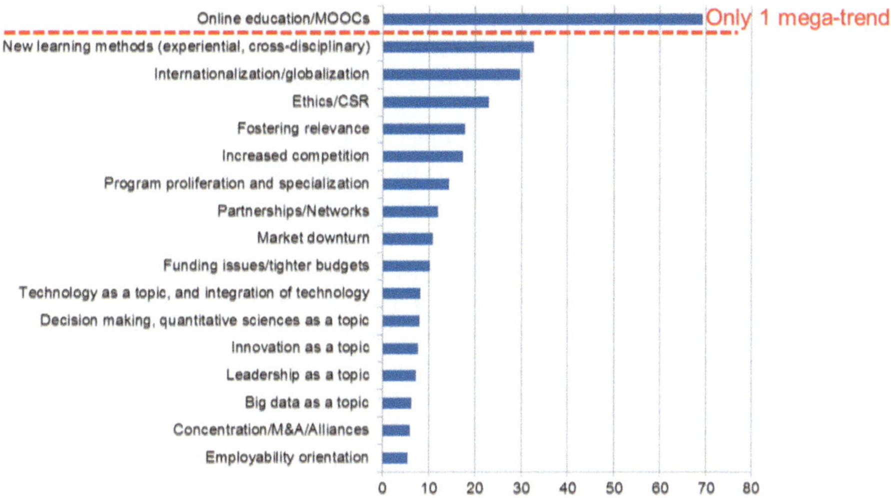

Fig. 4 Trends in management education 2014–2016

bankrupt (more than 250 organizations in the USA alone), were nationalized, or struggled for survival, others increased their market share, attracted more customers, and avoided home evictions of their clients. By looking at the healthier population of financial service firms, it was shown that these banks had stronger ties with the society around them contributing both to financial and human development. By staying close to clients and stakeholders, involving them in corporate governance mechanisms, and exercising strict risk management practices, they avoided the negative consequences that other banks experienced. As crises are likely to recur, business schools ought to 'reload' the normative element of a sound education, as an analysis of the behavioural patterns of successful banks during the financial crisis suggests that there is a clear-cut business benefit of more ethics in the financial service sector. Beyond understanding ethics as a means to a better bottom line, establishing more ethical practices as an end itself continues to be an option as well.

6 Conclusions

The chapter outlined four areas where today's finance education shows insufficiencies and thus remains far from being holistic. The first major construction site is the insensitivity to the levels at which graduates of finance courses operate. Although there may well be an objective truth about the hard skills and core models characterizing finance as a field, tasks and responsibilities shift at different hierarchy levels, and this cannot be ignored.

Secondly, in today's world, we see the rise of the 'creative destruction' paradigm. Crises happen more often than before. Initiatives often have opposite effects than the ones originally envisaged. Reality becomes harder to interpret or predict. Reality even becomes very subjective. Complexity renders financial modeling drastically more challenging. Therefore, finance education must integrate complexity to a substantially larger degree to catch up with contemporary developments.

Thirdly, finance education primarily focuses on the knowing and the doing level of learning, but hardly on the being level. More time must be devoted to the individuals in the system and to the very type of finance experts they aim to be.

The final point is linked to the fourth gap. Teaching how to use the tools in finance without a clear allocation of responsibilities falls short of what is needed in today's fast-paced world. Also, trust in companies and the financial service industry has fallen drastically after the governance scandals at the beginning of the new millennium, as well as in the aftermath of the financial crises over the past few years. Integrating more normative, ethics-oriented elements into finance education will help to restore some of the lost trust and lower the frequency and intensity of future crises.

References

Amann, W., Pirson, M., Spitzeck, H., Dierksmeier, C., & von Kimakowitz, E. (Eds.). (2011). *Business schools under fire – humanistic management education as the way forward*. Houndmills: Palgrave.

An. (2014, March 13). Currency investors mourn loss of volatility. *Financial Times*, p. 22.

Charan, R., Drotter, S., & Noel, J. (2000). *The leadership pipeline – how to build the leadership-powered company*. San Francisco: Jossey-Bass.

Collinson, S., & Jay, M. (2012). *From complexity to simplicity*. New York: Palgrave.

Krueckeberg, K., Amann, W., & Green, M. (2011). *Leadership and personal development: A state of the art toolbox for the 21st century professional*. Charlotte, NC: IAP.

Actual Problems of Finance Teaching in Ukraine in the Post-Crisis Period

Serhiy Lyeonov and Olga Liuta

The financial crisis of 2008 radically changed the goals and objectives of the financial education and professionalization of people, because at present the conditions of their employment require new forms of economic thinking and behaviour. Today, success in business is no longer determined by the ability to perform standard business processes and to manage them within the standard rules of management. In today's uncertain economic environment, it is not enough to possess the skills and abilities that students obtain under the uniform standards of education. The demand for professionals who are capable of preventing the bankruptcy of companies and ensuring their economic stability in the conditions of unbalanced economic system, harsh competition, and unpredictable changes in the environment of the companies' functioning has increased sharply. Ukraine has found itself among the countries most affected by the financial crisis. The scale of the crisis phenomena in the financial system and the national economy demonstrates the need to improve the training of bachelors and masters in the field of finance. A detailed analysis of the current practices of financiers' training at Ukrainian universities has allowed a definition of the following areas that need to be changed in line with the challenges of economic development in the post-crisis period: the revision of the modern economic theory, the increase of the analytical and practical components of training, and the introduction of disciplines related to behavioural finance.

S. Lyeonov (✉) • O. Liuta
Ukrainian Academy of Banking of the National Bank of Ukraine, 57, Petropavlivska str., Sumy 40000, Ukraine
e-mail: leonov@uabs.edu.ua

T. Azarmi, W. Amann (eds.), *The Financial Crisis*,
DOI 10.1007/978-3-319-20588-5_8

1 Revision of Economic Theory

The training of skilled finance professionals capable of competently assessing economic processes is impossible without a thorough training in economic theory. Therefore, one of the important areas of financial education reform in Ukraine under the conditions of a transition economy is a critical review of modern economic theory, the main purpose of which is a deep understanding of the economic theory in the context of real-world events. In our opinion, it is necessary to rethink fundamental theories of the modern economics such as "neo-liberalism" and "neo-Keynesianism". As the experience gained during the financial crisis demonstrates, the basic tenets of the progressive forward development of a market economy are not justified.

It is believed that the foundation of neoclassical theory is the teachings of Adam Smith. Which ideas of Adam Smith's scientific heritage did the neoclassical economic theory inherit in the post-Soviet period?

Currently, in the process of teaching the "History of Economics and Economic Thought", emphasis is placed on the following provisions of the neoclassical theory: the decisive role of the natural market forces, the principle of the "invisible hand of the market", the idea of individualism based on private property, and the creation of the free market capitalist model of the economy.

However, Ukraine's experience during the financial crisis and the significant negative events that have taken place in the country's economy are grounds for a critical analysis of these postulates. It turned out that neoclassical theory was unable to make predictions even for short historical periods. The global economic crisis has clearly shown the failure of the neoliberal model of global development both in the world and in the countries of the former Soviet Union. Considering the basic provisions of the neoclassical economic theory, it is difficult to accept the omnipotence of spontaneous forces, because today a variety of institutions, especially the state, play an important role in the economy.

Characterizing the principle of the "invisible hand", we can agree with Professor V. Kozyryev, who convincingly argues that Adam Smith did not mean the hand of the market but the hand of the one who is invisible, that is the invisible hand of the divine (Kozyrev and Smith 2012).

The third postulate about the idea of individualism based on private property, according to which each individual seeks to maximize his or her individual utility, is losing its relevance now, as it is an undeniable fact that the individual well-being of each employee depends on the efficient operation of the whole enterprise. The welfare of the company's employees depends on the efficiency of the higher economic structures and the macroeconomic situation in the country.

These views are supported by the works of the Harvard University professor and a Nobel Prize Laureate in Economics A. Sen, who states: "Smith is often called the father of modern economics. It is acknowledged that he made a major contribution to its development as a scientific discipline". Not all the arguments of Adam Smith's supporters reflect the true meaning of his ideas. Many of them present

Smith only as a guru of the market economy—a person of one idea that promotes the self-sufficiency and perfection of the market. Smith showed the conditions under which markets may require restrictions, corrections, and additions from other social institutions to prevent instability and inequality and to eliminate poverty. One of the most important aspects of Smith's theory is his assertion that it is impossible to explain poverty without considering the problem of inequality. Smith showed that poverty entails inequality. Smith described the detrimental effect of those he called speculators. Today, in light of the crisis in the financial world, such analysis is of tremendous value. Smith did not consider the market mechanism an absolute ideal (Sen and Smith 2011).

The quotation above suggests that Adam Smith made assertions that should be accepted, comprehended, and taught to students: the fact that the most reliable source of wealth is not the market with individualism, but effective work, especially in the sphere of material production.

2 The Deepening of Analytical Component of the Financial Education

An important role in the process of modernization of finance education belongs to the deepening of analytical professional training in various types of analysis and expansion of disciplines related to the assessment and analysis of risks from financial operations. It is caused by the fact that the quality of analytical functions performed by finance employees has a significant impact on the timely detection of adverse development tendencies and their consequences and the effectiveness of measures designed to mitigate possible financial and economic problems.

In the current economic situation in Ukraine, the urgent challenge for higher education is the training of specialists capable of performing skilled analytical work. To date, there has been a discrepancy between the knowledge that students receive and the demands put forward by the labour market. This concerns the ability to use modern technologies to carry out the financial, investment, operational, strategic, portfolio, and other types of analysis, to understand the cause–effect relationship between different economic phenomena and processes, and to predict changes of the economic situation in the current period and in the future. The quality of education of finance professionals is largely determined by the level of the modern analytical instruments that they possess.

The depth of knowledge of the basic theoretical principles of analysis and the skills to apply them in practice depend on the status of analytical disciplines defined by their belonging to the groups of normative disciplines or optional disciplines with the appropriate forms of final knowledge control and differences in the amount of allocated credits. The study of the latest trends in the educational training programs in the field of finance and credit indicates a gradual disappearance of analytical disciplines as independent subjects of general economic, professional, and practical training (Boyarko 2010). On the basis of an analysis of the composition and structure of disciplines of general economic training, it is worth noting that out of the 43 credits allocated to the study of these disciplines there is not a single analytical discipline. This leads to an underestimation of the role of analytic disciplines in the educational process and, consequently, the overall reduction in the level of theoretical and practical training in the field of finance.

At the same time, it should be noted that there is an increase in the number of analytical disciplines among the subjects of specialized professional training. For example, the disciplines of professional and practical training that students study during their 7–8 semesters at the Ukrainian Academy of Banking of the National Bank of Ukraine are divided into two groups: state finances and financial intermediation. The total amount of credits for the specialization in state finance is 43 credits, while the subjects with analytical components are allocated only 10 credits. Students of financial intermediation study analytical disciplines in the amount of 17 credits among the total of 43 credits. In addition, analytical disciplines included in the curricula are often devoted to the study of theoretical aspects of analysis without emphasis on the use of appropriate techniques and identification of opportunities for their further improvement and adaptation to certain circumstances. Studying the content of disciplines dedicated to analysis, it is necessary to note that the overwhelming majority of them are focussed on the implementation of retrospective analysis. However, in the conditions of unstable economic environment there is a growing need in the ability of specialists to carry out a prospective analysis and to establish connections between the economic events of today and their implications in the future. Insufficient attention is given to the teaching of the financial analysis methods based on Western standards. Evidently, this situation does not contribute to the students' ability to correctly analyse the current situation and predict its changes under the influence of internal and external factors.

In this regard, during the creation of curricula for bachelors and masters in the finance and credit specialization, we consider it necessary to increase the analytical component (especially for specializations focused on further analytical activity in the areas of investment and finance) in order to help improve the competence of the future employees in the relevant fields.

We believe that in order for the students to successfully master analytical skills in the learning process, it is necessary to apply the latest methods and techniques that could combine theoretical and practical aspects of students' training and strengthening the practical orientation of students.

3 Improvement of the Practical Component of Bachelors' Training in the Specialization "Finance and Credit"

There is a contradiction between financial education focussed on the paradigm of "knowledge" and the modern business, which requires practice-oriented professionals. The ability to apply the knowledge that increases the competitiveness of business is especially important for successful activities on the market.

In-depth practical training is very important for bachelors in the field of economics and entrepreneurship. The solution of this task depends on the organization of educational process that can be achieved through classroom instructions, workshops, and practical training of students. Each of these stages of the learning process has its own characteristics and possibilities for practical training.

Exploring the ways to improve classroom lessons, it is worth introducing virtual computer-simulation games, based on the principle of imitation modelling, into the teaching of financial disciplines. Their application opens up new possibilities of using business games in the process of teaching the strategic management of enterprises in the changing market environment. It is necessary to use those interactive models of management of financial and economic activity, the realization of which requires the knowledge of financial management, financial planning, financial analysis, marketing, and other economic disciplines (Varfolomeev 2010).

In our opinion, strategic business games are relevant because, based on the simulation models they have created, they generate professional knowledge and expertise in the management and forecasting of companies' activities in competitive market conditions.

The purpose of imitation modelling is the development of practical skills among the finance students, which will make them well-versed in the multidimensional complex of management of companies' activities making strategic decisions in different economic situations.

Virtual games can simulate various manufacturing and market situation enabling finance students to gain skills in the making of adequate management solutions.

The complexity and flexibility of strategic games is determined by the complexity of a simulation model on which they are based. Simulation computer models of economic systems can reproduce the processes occurring within the system and the factors of external financial environment that directly or indirectly affect their dynamics.

Thus, the use of different versions of virtual economic models that can be presented in an interactive computer strategic game makes it possible to conduct efficient trainings and for finance students to form the practical skills of competent strategic management of companies.

Practical training is an important component of the students' curricula that is focussed on the deepening and consolidation of theoretical knowledge of the basic, professionally oriented subjects received at the university. It is also focussed on the acquisition of the necessary practical skills and helps students to become proficient in modern techniques and methods and capable of using them in their future profession. According to the curriculum of the bachelor's level education in the finance and credit specialization, practical training consists of three credits and is conducted in the eighth semester. During practical training, the foundations of professional experience, practical skills, and professional qualities of future specialists are laid. However, in the process of organization of practical training, including the choice of places for practical attachments, students should be sent to those enterprises that achieved positive financial results under the conditions of the financial crisis, have not lost their competitive position on the market, and have ensured their solvency and liquidity. We believe that a necessary component of practical training should be the analysis of techniques and methods of a company's financial management and management measures that were used by the company's administration to maintain stability in a difficult economic situation.

4 Behavioural Finance

In the current economic situation, financiers must possess theoretical and practical skills not only in the field of conventional finance but also in the field of behavioural finance. The global financial crisis is the motivation that makes many entrepreneurs, investors, and other market participants rethink their concepts and beliefs. Gradually, finances cease to be a purely technical discipline, and experts in the field of psychology increasingly come forward to assist financiers. Behavioural finance questions the assumption of the rational behaviour of market participants and tries to identify in the behaviour of individuals the systematic deviations from the rational model of decision-making and to create new financial theories that would consider this deviation.

The majority of economic theories are based on laws suggesting that a person always chooses the most efficient options, that is, acts like a precise mechanism. The classical political economy is built on this assumption, in particular, the teachings of William Petty, Pierre Boisguillebert, Adam Smith, David Ricardo, and many other representatives of this scientific trend (Vashchenko 2006).

Numerous studies of foreign scientists confirm that, acting under conditions of uncertainty and risk, people are prone to different illusions, emotions, false perception of information, and other "irrational" factors.

The development of stock markets and the emergence of numerous market instruments have led to a number of financial theories and models designed to equip potential investors with the necessary tools for developing effective investment strategies.

At the same time, numerous studies conducted in recent decades, as well as the analysis of the financial crisis in 2007–2008, suggest that the movement of market prices and market behaviour cannot be described by classical financial theories and models with sufficient credibility. The reason is that the behaviour of investors on the market is not rational; in other words, it does not meet the assumptions underlying these theories.

The most significant discoveries in this area belong to West European and American scientists. A large number of researchers—experts in financial science, faced with the impossibility of explaining many phenomena on the financial markets by means of classical theories—have begun to study the relationship between psychology and the market behaviour of investors.

The main achievement of behavioural finance is the realization of the fact that in finance, as in all other spheres of their activities, people make decisions and act under the influence of the prevailing stereotypes, illusions, perceptions, preconceptions, emotions, and errors in the analysis of information (Coyle 2012).

The inability to explain human behaviour in terms of classical theory increasingly leads to the search of a relationship between economic science and psychology. Therefore, in order to achieve success in the business, marketing, investment, and financial environment, it is insufficient to use only such orthodox models as standard approaches to the balance of supply and demand as well as macroeconomic theories.

The leading companies and professionals are taking into account the psychological characteristics of irrational behaviour of both individuals and entire societies. It appears that absolutely all people are prone to irrational behaviour, regardless of their intellectual level, training, and sphere of activity or professional experience (Vashchenko 2006). Thus, the study of psychological aspects within the framework of economic behaviour can significantly improve the effectiveness of activities and strategies in different branches of the economy.

In teaching economic and financial subjects, the Ukrainian universities do not place emphasis on the disciplines that are at the junction of psychology and finance. Among the humanities disciplines, the subject of psychology is lacking and among the disciplines of professional and practical training—subjects dealing with investors' behaviour on the market. Consequently, confronted with the real situation on the market, experts try to explain and predict its effects only on the basis of the knowledge of the classical finance theory, which they received during their training. Experience shows that this practice is wrong and leads to a failure to assess such events on the market adequately.

The study of various market situations with a large number of examples proving the irrational nature of human activity, including in the financial and investment sector, has led to the understanding of the need to introduce a new discipline for the training of students in the finances and credit specialization: behavioural finance. The study of behavioural finance will enable students to gain knowledge, which takes into account the irrational nature of the behaviour of investors and financiers on the market in conditions of uncertainty and risks in making decisions pertaining to finance and investment.

The financial crisis revealed serious problems in the teaching of finance at Ukraine's economic educational institutions. One of the main reasons for that is that the content of financial courses is lagging behind the developments in the theory of finance. Thus, traditional approaches have proved to be ineffective for the training of qualified financial specialists. The variety of economic phenomena and processes, the specific problems that need to be addressed, and informal and personalized nature of business operations necessitate changes in the approaches to the organization of financial education.

References

Boyarko, I. M. (2010). *The National Bank of Ukraine*. C. 47–50.

Coyle, D. (2012). *Teaching economy after crisis*. http://www.res.org.uk/view/article7Apr13Features.html

Kozyrev, V. M., & Smith, A. (2012). The role of finance in the development of economic science. *Herald RIAT, 2–3*(5–6), 48–58.

Sen, A., & Smith, A. (2011). *Problems of economics, 11*, 25–27, 29–31.

Varfolomeev, A. M. (2010). *Simulation models of financial and economic activity of the enterprise – the basis of preparation of competitive specialist financial-credit profile*. The National Bank of Ukraine. C. 53–56.

Vashchenko, T. V. (2006). *Behavioral finance – a new direction in financial management: History and development*. http://www.dis.ru/library/fm/archive/2006/1/4068.html

Executive Compensation and Risk Taking: The Impact of Systemic Crises

Alon Raviv and Elif Sisli-Ciamarra

It is widely accepted that managerial compensation packages contributed to the excessive risk-taking practices that led to the onset of the Great Recession (2007–2009). We argue that the relationship between managerial compensation and risk taking is procyclical. A given level of performance incentives may result in significantly lower firm risk when economy is in a systemic crisis because managers face an increased employment risk during economic downturns. Students of finance who will become policy makers or who will sit on compensation committees would benefit from realizing that in order to implement a given level of firm risk, managerial compensation packages may need to be adjusted according to the state of the economy.

1 Introduction

Executive pay practices have been identified as one of the main reasons behind excessive risk taking that led to the 2007–2009 financial crisis (e.g., Bebchuk et al. 2009; Cheng et al. 2010). Financial Stability Forum (April 2, 2009) stated "perverse incentives amplified the excessive risk taking that severely threatened the global financial system." G20 Pittsburg Summit (September 24–25, 2009) emphasized that "excessive compensation in the financial sector has both reflected and encouraged excessive risk." Guidance on Sound Incentive Compensation Policies

---

A. Raviv (✉)
Bar-Ilan University, 320, Building 504, Jerusalem 5290002, Israel
e-mail: Alon.Raviv@biu.ac.il

E. Sisli-Ciamarra
Brandeis University, 415 South Street, Waltham, MA 02453, USA
e-mail: esisli@brandeis.edu

T. Azarmi, W. Amann (eds.), *The Financial Crisis*,
DOI 10.1007/978-3-319-20588-5_9

(June 21, 2012) stated that "banking organizations too often rewarded employees for increasing the organization's revenue or short-term profit without adequate recognition of the risks the employees' activities posed to the organization."

With such a strong call from both academic and policy making circles, a major response to the crisis has been to regulate executive compensation in order to discourage risk taking. For example, the Dodd–Frank Act enacted in the USA has required additional disclosure about certain compensation matters. In particular, Section 953 (a) of the Act requires firms to disclose "information that shows the relationship between executive compensation actually paid and the financial performance of the issuer." Also, the European Union adopted a provisional deal that limits the amount of bankers' bonuses to the amount of fixed remuneration, where the cap could be increased to 2:1 with the backing of a supermajority of shareholders.

While this regulation is still pending and under debate among policy makers, practitioners, and academic researchers, we argue in this chapter that there may not be a robust relationship between managerial pay-for-performance incentives and firm risk. In particular, we take a stand that the macroeconomic environment has a significant impact on how managers respond to the performance incentives. We argue that a manager with exactly the same level of pay-for-performance incentives would optimally target a lower risk level when the economy is in a recession than when the economy is not in a recession. Our discussions in this chapter are based on the theoretical work by Raviv and Sisli-Ciamarra (2013).

In this chapter, we summarize the theoretical model developed by Raviv and Sisli-Ciamarra (2013) and its calibration under different economic states. This model is a standard option based valuation of executive compensation. However, the novelty in the model is a component that we label "loss due to systemic crisis," which measures the loss in the value of an executive's expected wealth from employment if the firm becomes insolvent during a bad state of the economy. The additional loss occurs because an executive's alternative employment opportunities are expected to be less during a systemic crisis. This theoretical assumption is supported by empirical work that shows being displaced in recessions may lead to higher income losses compared to being displaced during non-recession periods. We show that there is a possibility for a given compensation package implementing different levels of firm risk during economy-wide recessions. Most importantly, we show that the positive relationship between equity-based compensation and risk taking that has been shown in earlier literature may disappear during systemic financial crises.

These findings contribute to the small but growing literature on the impact of different economic states on risk-taking behavior. For example, Kempf et al. (2009) show that mutual fund managers decrease risk during years marked by negative stock market returns when "employment risk" dominates "compensation incentives." Schoar and Washington (2011) shows that managers who start their careers in recessions have more conservative management styles throughout their tenures as CEOs. Similarly, Malmendier and Nagel (2011) report that individuals who have experienced low stock market returns throughout their lives so far report lower willingness to take financial risks. DeYoung et al. (2013) show that banks facing stronger (weaker) economic conditions choose more (less) risky business policies.

The rest of the chapter is organized as follows: Sect. 2 presents the theoretical model and its predictions. Section 3 concludes with some policy implications and some general advice on how students of finance could benefit if we adjust our teaching in the classroom in light of the evidence provided in this research.

2 Executive Compensation, Performance Incentives, and Risk Taking: Theoretical Framework

Performance incentives are provided to executives mainly by stocks and stock options. Since the value of stock and stock options would increase with the firm value, such stock-based compensation is expected to induce managers to take financial actions that increase the stock value. However, the opponents of stock-based pay blame the convex payoff structure generated by stock options for providing excessive risk-taking incentives. The managers are compensated for increases in stock prices, because the value of option holdings would increase when the price of the company's stock increases. However, they would not be punished for large decreases in firm value. If the stock price declines significantly, the executive would pay no penalty relative to the case when the stock drops modestly. In this section, we summarize the option-based valuation of executive compensation (Raviv and Sisli-Ciamarra 2013) and calculate the optimal level of risk from the point of view of the executive whose objective function is to maximize the value of her compensation.

2.1 Equity-Based Compensation and Firm Risk

We first consider a manager who is compensated by a base salary and stock-based compensation. For simplicity we assume a myopic model, where the executive receives a payoff at the end of the period denoted by T. Let us also assume that this manager also has accumulated stocks and stock options during his tenure in the company. Let α denote the percentage of the firm's assets that belong to the manager as a result of her holdings of stock and stock options. At the end of the period T, the value of the manager's wealth that is tied to her employment and that is sensitive to the underlying asset risk can be expressed as:

$$\text{EquityWealth}_T = \alpha \max\left(\frac{\text{FirmValue}_T - \text{Strike}}{\text{Strike}}, 0\right) \tag{1}$$

This equation states that as the firm value increases beyond the strike value, the manager's wealth from his stock and stock options will increase by α percent. Therefore, α quantifies the sensitivity of the compensation to an increase in the value of the firm's assets above the strike price and is a measure of pay-for-performance sensitivity. The value of the equity wealth today can be replicated by a European Call Option, which can be priced using the standard Merton (1974) assumptions and model:

$$\text{EquityWealth}_0 = \alpha \frac{1}{\text{Strike}} \text{Call}(\text{Firm Value}, \text{Strike}) \tag{2}$$

Let V denote the firm value, H denote the strike price, σ denote asset volatility (i.e., firm risk), and $N()$ denote the cumulative normal density. The pricing equation for the European call can be expressed under the standard assumptions for risk-neutral contingent-claim valuation as follows:

$$\text{Call}(V,H) = VN(d(V,H)) - H^* e^{-rT} N\left(d(V,H) - \sigma\sqrt{T}\right) \tag{3}$$

where the function $d(I,J)$ is defined as:

$$d(I,J) = \frac{\ln(I/J) + (r + \sigma^2/2)T}{\sigma\sqrt{T}}$$

The executive's optimization problem is to choose the level of asset risk that would maximize the value of her compensation. We solve this optimization problem numerically using the baseline parameters listed in Appendix. The baseline parameters are chosen according to the empirical literature and are discussed in detail in Raviv and Sisli-Ciamarra (2013). According to this analysis, if equity-based compensation is the only component that is sensitive to asset risk, then executive compensation strictly increases with firm risk (Fig. 1). Therefore, the executive whose objective is to maximize the value of personal compensation will optimally target the maximum asset risk. This result is consistent with the conclusions of Jensen and Meckling (1976) and Galai and Masulis (1976).

2.2 *Incorporating the Effect of Firm-Specific Financial Distress on Executive Compensation*

The analysis in the above section suggests that it is optimal for an executive to increase firm risk as much as possible in order to maximize the value of her firm-related wealth if she is compensated by firm stock. In this section, we extend the analysis to incorporate the recent literature on inside debt (Sundaram and Yermack 2007) and argue that the probability that the firm may experience financial distress

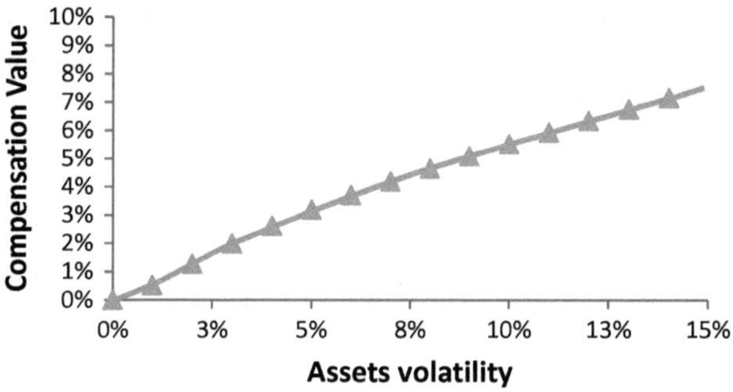

Fig. 1 The value of executive compensation for different levels of asset risk and different levels of equity-based compensation. This figure plots the value of executive compensation for different levels of asset risk and equity-based compensation. The sensitivity of executive compensation to a 1 % increase of asset value above the strike price (α) is set to 2. There is no other component of compensation that is sensitive to form risk (i.e., $\beta = \gamma = 0$). All other parameters are set at their base case values as summarized in the Appendix Table.

would change the optimal choice of a manager. In Sundaram and Yermack (2007), inside debt refers to uninsured pension benefits that a manager would lose in the event of bankruptcy. We further generalize this notion and define "Loss due to firm-specific insolvency" as any managerial benefit that has a positive sensitivity to a decrease in the value of a financial institution's assets below the face value of firm's debt. Accordingly, loss due to firm-specific insolvency would also include more intangible assets as reputation costs and loss of future employment opportunities. The payoff by the end of the period T due to this component can be described as follows:

$$\text{LossDueToFirmSpecificInsolvency}_T = \beta \max\left(\frac{\text{Face Value Of Debt-Firm Value}_T}{\text{Face Value Of Debt}}, 0\right) \quad (4)$$

According to this equation, the loss due to firm-specific insolvency has a positive sensitivity to a decrease in the value of the firm's assets below the face value of its debt. The parameter β represents the percentage of firm's debt the manager holds and also measures the change in the executive wage wealth for a given percentage change in the firm's assets value below the face value of deposits. The current value of this component can be replicated by a European Put Option, which can be described as follows:

$$\text{LossDueToFirmSpecificInsolvency}_0 = \beta \frac{1}{\text{FaceValueOfDebt}} \text{Put}(\text{FirmValue}, \text{FaceValueOfDebt}) \quad (5)$$

As before, let V, H, σ, and $N()$ denote the firm value, strike price, asset volatility, and the cumulative normal density, respectively. The pricing equation for the European put can be expressed as follows:

$$\mathrm{Put}(V,F) = Fe^{-rT}N\left(\sigma\sqrt{T} - d(V,F)\right) - SN(-d(V,F)) \tag{6}$$

When we incorporate the loss due to firm-specific distress, the executive's wealth that is sensitive to firm risk (asset volatility) becomes:

$$\mathrm{Executive's\ Wealth} = \alpha\frac{1}{H}\mathrm{Call}(V,H) - \beta\frac{1}{F}\mathrm{Put}(V,F) \tag{7}$$

This framework is similar to Sundaram and Yermack (2007), but allows the strike price of the call option on a firm's assets to exceed the face value of the firm's debt (i.e., $H > F$) as in Landskroner and Raviv (2009). Next, we solve numerically the executive's optimization problem, which is to choose the level of asset risk that would maximize the value of her compensation. In Fig. 2a, we fix α at 2. β is fixed either at 0 (absence of sensitivity to firm-specific distress) or at 1 (a relatively low value for sensitivity to firm-specific distress, $\beta < \alpha$). The rest of the parameters are at their baseline values as listed in Appendix. It can be observed from the graph that when the sensitivity of compensation to a decrease in the firm's value below its face value of debt (F) is relatively low compared to the sensitivity of executive compensation to an increase in the firm's value above the strike price (H), i.e., when $\beta < \alpha$, the value of executive wealth is a strictly increasing function of asset risk. Under such conditions, the executive would optimally target the highest possible asset risk in order to maximize compensation. This result is identical to Sundaram and Yermack (2007).

In Fig. 2b, we analyze the case where the sensitivity of compensation to a decrease in the firm's value below its face value of debt (F) is relatively high compared to the sensitivity of executive compensation to an increase in the firm's value above the strike price (H), i.e., $\beta > \alpha$. We fix α at 2 and β at 3. Under this scenario, the value of executive compensation is a convex function of asset risk with a global maximum. The optimal choice of the executive is to choose an asset risk of 5.51 % in order to maximize her wealth. Furthermore, as shown by Raviv and Sisli-Ciamarra (2013), the optimal asset risk would decrease as the sensitivity of executive's wealth to firm insolvency (β) increases.

The main conclusion from the analysis in this section is that when a manager considers the negative effect of firm-specific financial distress on her wealth, she may not find it optimal to take the maximum level of risk.

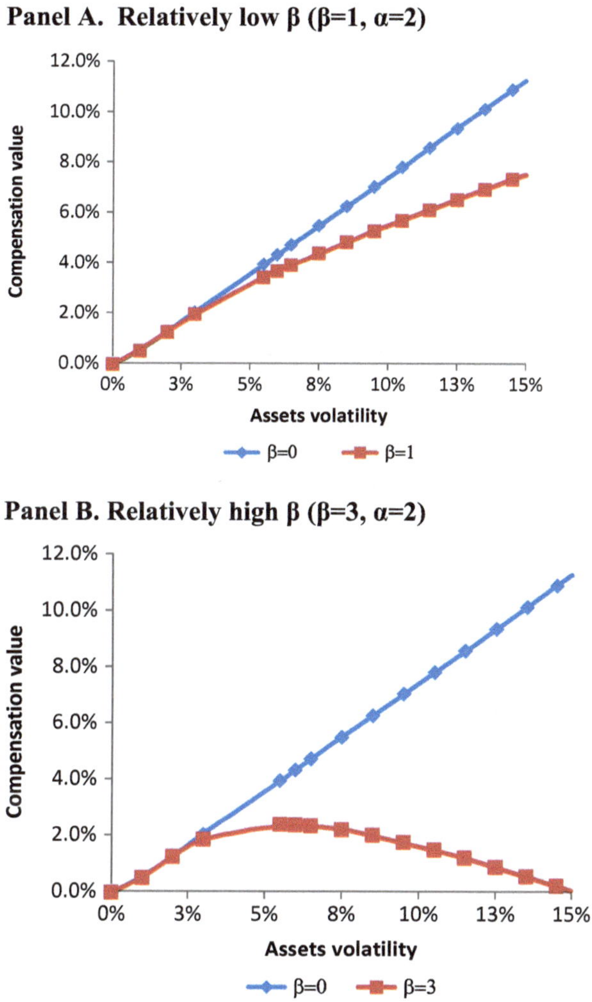

Fig. 2 The value of executive compensation for different levels of asset risk and different losses due to firm-specific insolvency. This figure presents the value of executive compensation for different levels of asset risk and loss due to firm-specific insolvency. The sensitivity of executive compensation to a 1 % increase of asset value above the strike price (α) is set to 2. The sensitivity of compensation to a 1 % decrease in asset value below the value of liabilities (β) varies between 0 and 3. γ is set to 0. All other parameters are set at their base case values as summarized in the Appendix Table. Panel (**a**): Relatively low β ($\beta = 1$, $\alpha = 2$). Panel (**b**): Relatively high β ($\beta = 3$, $\alpha = 2$)

2.3 Incorporating the Effect Systemic Crisis on Executive Compensation

In this section, we argue that if a firm faces financial distress during a time of economy-wide crisis, there will be an additional loss for the executive. The additional loss during a crisis arises because an executive's alternative employment opportunities would be more limited during bad economic times. Even if the executive finds a new job during a systemic crisis, she is likely to receive lower compensation. The recent empirical literature in labor economics provides ample evidence that being displaced in recessions may lead to more significant losses compared to being displaced during non-recession periods for high level executives. A detailed review of this literature can be found at Davis and von Wachter (2011) and Raviv and Sisli-Ciamarra (2013).

When we model the effect of systemic crisis on the value of executive compensation, we assume that there is an index that tracks the state of the economy. We also assume that there is a threshold value for this index below which the economy faces a systemic crisis. The following equation summarizes the loss that the executive would incur if the firm she is managing faces financial distress at a time of economy-wide crisis at time T:

$$\begin{aligned}&\text{LossDueToCrisis}_T\\&=\gamma\max\left(\frac{\text{FaceValueOfDebt}-\text{FirmValue}}{\text{FaceValueOfDebt}},0\right)1_{\{\text{Index}\leq\text{CrisisThreshold}\}}\end{aligned} \tag{8}$$

If the index is below the crisis threshold, the economy is in a systemic crisis. In this case, the loss in executive compensation if the firm faces financial distress is the sum of the loss due to firm-specific distress and the loss due to systemic crisis. However, if the firm is in financial distress and the economic index is above the threshold, where the economy is not in a systemic crisis, then the loss in executive compensation is limited to the loss due to firm-specific distress. The parameter γ measures the sensitivity of executive wealth to the joint event of a decrease in asset value below the face value of debt and a decrease of the economic index below the threshold of systemic crisis. At time 0, the value of this loss can be replicated with a Two-Asset-Correlation Put (TACPut) option:

$$\begin{aligned}&\text{LossDueToCrisis}_0\\&=\gamma\frac{1}{\text{Face Value}}\text{TACPut}(\text{Firm Value},\text{FaceValue},\text{Index},\text{Threshold})\,1_{\{\text{Index}\leq\text{CrisisThreshold}\}}\end{aligned} \tag{9}$$

As before, let V, F, and σ denote the firm value, face value of debt, and asset volatility, respectively. In addition, let I denote the economic index and K denote the crisis threshold. The pricing equation for the Two-Asset-Correlation put can be expressed as follows:

$$\begin{aligned}\text{TACPut}(V,F,S,K)=&\,Fe^{-rT}M(y_2,y_1,\rho)\\&-SM\left(y_2+\sigma_V\sqrt{T},y_1+\rho\sigma_V\sqrt{T},\rho\right)\end{aligned} \tag{10}$$

Where

$$y_1=\frac{\ln(S/K)+\left(r-\sigma_S^2/2\right)T}{\sigma_S\sqrt{T}},$$

$$y_2 = \frac{\ln(V/F) + \left(r - \sigma_V^2/2\right)T}{\sigma_V\sqrt{T}},$$

M(.) is the bivariate normal distribution of two stochastic variables with a given correlation of ρ executive's wealth that is tied to her compensation can be expressed as the sum of the three components that are sensitive to firm risk:

$$\text{Executive's Wealth} = \alpha 1/H\text{Call}(V,H) - \beta 1/F\text{Put}(V,F) \\ - \gamma\text{TACPut}(V,F,S,K)\ 1_{\{S\leq K\}} \tag{11}$$

We next solve numerically the executive's optimization problem, where the decision variable is the level of asset risk that maximizes the value of her compensation. We fix α and β at their baseline values of 2 and 1, respectively, and γ is equal to 2. The rest of the parameters are also at their baseline values as listed in Appendix. In Fig. 3, we plot the value of executive compensation for different levels of asset risk and three different states of the economy. First, we plot the value of executive compensation when *S/K* is 1.3, in which case the index is 30 % above the crisis threshold. Under this scenario, the value of compensation strictly increases with asset risk and the executive's optimal choice would be to target the maximum amount of asset volatility. This result is intuitive—when the economy is far from systematic crisis, the expected value of loss due to systemic crisis is close to zero.

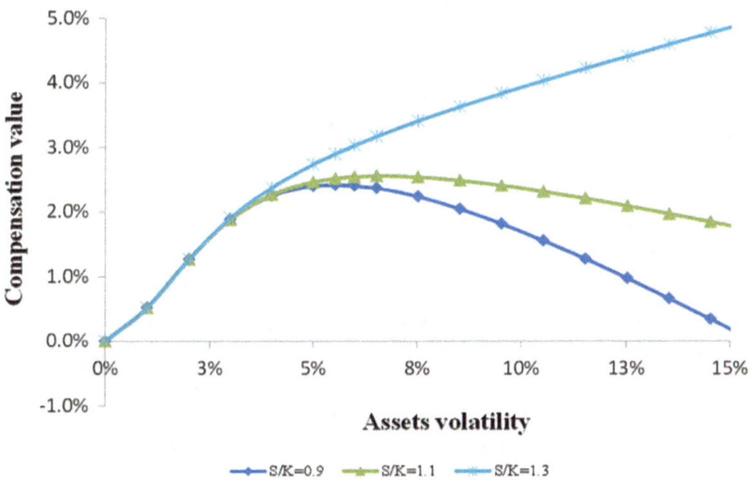

Fig. 3 Value of executive compensation for different levels of asset risk and different states of the economy. This figure presents the value of executive compensation for different levels of asset risk and states of the economy. Economic index levels vary between 30 % above and 10 % below the threshold. All other parameters are set at their base case values as summarized in the Appendix Table

Next, we plot the value of executive compensation when *S/K* is 0.9, in which case the index is 10 % below the crisis threshold; therefore, the economy is in a systemic crisis. Under this condition, the component of loss due to systemic crisis influences the risk-taking decision of the executive. The executive may optimally choose not to target the maximum possible level of asset risk, but may target an intermediate level of asset risk of 5.53 %, even for cases in which equity-based compensation dominates the executive pay package (i.e., $\alpha > \beta$). In the intermediate case, where *S/K* is equal to 1.1, the effect of the loss due to systemic crisis is moderate and the value of compensation has its maximum at a level of assets risk equal to 6.65 %.

To summarize, the above analysis shows that loss in executive compensation due to a systemic crisis might have a significant impact on the relationship between executive compensation and risk taking. We show that during good states of the economy, an executive may optimally target the maximum possible level of asset risk. However, when the economy is in a systemic crisis, the same executive with exactly the same pay package may find it optimal to choose a lower and intermediate level of asset risk.

3 Conclusion and Some General Advice on Teaching Finance

We have argued in this chapter that a given compensation package may lead to different risk-taking behavior by managers depending on the macroeconomic environment. Our analyses mainly summarize the main points in our original research article (Raviv and Sisli-Ciamarra 2013). To our knowledge, we provide the first evidence for the procyclicality of how risk taking responds to managerial risk-taking incentives provided by stock-based compensation.

How could the insights provided by our research contribute to finance education? The onset of the financial crisis of 2007–2009 has altered the public's view of executive compensation. The general view after the crisis is that managerial incentives result in excessive risk taking. In our research, we show the importance of the interaction of managerial incentives with the macroeconomic environment in shaping financial outcomes. Students of finance who will become policy makers or will sit on compensation committees would benefit from realizing that if a regulator wants to limit risk taking by suggesting limits on the structure of compensation, then these limits may need to depend on the state of the economy. For example, in order to achieve similar asset risk in economic recessions as in normal times, the regulations on the proportion of equity-based compensation may need to be relaxed during recessions.

The findings in this chapter also remind students that relationships between financial (and economic) variables are not always stable. Therefore, teaching and discussion of theoretical and empirical models, along with policy prescriptions, should be mindful of the time-varying nature of financial relationships. Changing macro-conditions and their effects on the relationship between executive compensation and firm risk is a manifestation of this general principle.

Acknowledgement We thank Iftekhar Hassan, the Editor of the Journal of Financial Stability for his valuable comments. We are also indebted for useful comments and suggestion to Jens Hilscher, Antoni Vaello Sebastià, Catherine Mann, David Yermack, Dan Zhang, the Editor and referees, as well as seminar participants at Brandeis University, Williams College, the 2011 FMA Annual Meeting in Denver, 2012 EFA Annual Meeting in Boston, the Ackerman Conference on corporate governance in Bar Ilan University, and the conference on Teaching Finance at Turbulent Times at Heilbronn University. Alon Raviv thanks the Raymond Ackerman Family Chair in Israeli Corporate Governance for its support.

Appendix: Baseline Values for the Model Parameters

Parameter	Notation	Base value
Leverage ratio	LR	0.95
Face value of debt	F	100
Firm value	V	102.15
Time to maturity	T	1
Economic index volatility	σ_S	20 %
Risk-free rate	r	3 %
Economic index value	S	90–110
Crisis threshold	K	100
Sensitivity of compensation to a 1 % increase of asset value above the strike price	α	2
Sensitivity of compensation to a 1 % decrease in asset value below the value of debt	β	1
Sensitivity of compensation to the joint event of a decrease in asset value below the value of liabilities in a financial crisis	γ	2
Correlation between returns of the firm's assets and the economic index	ρ	0.8
The strike price of equity-based compensation	H	105.57

References

Bebchuk, L. A., Cohen, A., & Spamann, H. (2009). *The wages of failure: Executive compensation at Bear Stearns and Lehman 2000–2008*. Harvard Law and Economics Discussion Paper No. 657.

Cheng, I., Hong, H. G., & Scheinkman, J. A. (2010). *Yesterday's heroes: Compensation and risk at financial firms*. ECGI – Finance Working Paper No. 285.

Davis, S. J., & von Wachter, T. (2011). *Recessions and the costs of job loss* (pp. 1–72). Fall: Brookings Papers on Economic Activity.

DeYoung, R., Peng, E. Y., & Yan, M. (2013). Executive compensation and business policy choices at US commercial banks. *Journal of Financial and Quantitative Analysis, 48*(1), 165–196.

Financial Stability Forum. (2009). *FSF principles for sound compensation practices*. Accessed January 4, 2014, from http://www.financialstabilityboard.org/publications/r_0904b.pdf

G20 Pittsburg Summit. (2009). Accessed January 4, 2014, from http://www.g20ys.org/upload/files/Pittsburgh_0.pdf

Galai, D., & Masulis, R. (1976). The option pricing model and the risk factor of stock. *Journal of Financial Economics, 3*, 631–644.

Jensen, M. C., & Meckling, W. H. (1976). Rights and production functions: An application to labor-managed firms and codetermination. *Journal of Business, 52*, 469–506.

Kempf, A., Ruenzi, S., & Thiele, T. (2009). Employment risk, compensation incentives, and managerial risk taking: Evidence from the mutual fund industry. *Journal of Financial Economics, 92*, 92–108.

Landskroner, Y., & Raviv, A. (2009). *The 2007–2009 financial crisis and executive compensation: Analysis and a proposal for a novel structure*. NYU Working Paper, No. FIN-09-003.

Malmendier, U., & Nagel, S. (2011). Depression babies: Do macroeconomic experiences affect risk-taking? *Quarterly Journal of Economics, 126*, 373–416.

Merton, R. C. (1974). On the pricing of corporate debt: The risk structure of interest rates. *Journal of Finance, 29*, 449–470.

Raviv, A., & Sisli-Ciamarra, E. (2013). Executive compensation, risk taking and the state of the economy. *Journal of Financial Stability, 9*(1), 55–68.

Schoar, A., & Washington, E. (2011). *Shaped by booms and busts: How the economy impacts CEO careers and management styles*. NBER Working Papers 17590, National Bureau of Economic Research.

Sundaram, R., & Yermack, D. (2007). Pay me later: Inside debt and its role in managerial compensation. *Journal of Finance, 62*, 1551–1588.

Measuring the Success of Executive Education: Comprehensively Depicting Holistic Finance Education

Wolfgang Amann

1 Introduction

The financial crisis starting in 2007 has not only hit banks of countries hard, it affected business schools in executive education providers equally. Few companies invested in executive education initiatives. As a consequence, executive education markets consolidated, which is exemplified by the recent Hult and Ashridge merger in 2014 (cf. Bradshaw 2014).

Across the board, executive education providers are currently tempted to enhance their customer orientation and to commit themselves to uncompromising customer satisfaction. This would be a natural reaction. However, this chapter argues in favor of a more holistic change in mindsets amongst business school leaders in executive education providers. In fact, corporate clients and individual course participants might not actually know the very areas from which they would benefit most. Consequently, real needs might well remain unaddressed. This explicitly refers to ethical content in executive education seminars, as well as enhancement of complexity skills in order to deal with independent issues. This chapter argues in favor of not only being reasonably customer driven but also to drive customers more effectively, which represents a different approach. In business academia as well as practice, this approach is more and more frequently referred to as emphasizing not the "P" (which stands for performance), but the "D" or dignity paradigm. The many ways companies and individuals enhance human dignity through their cultures, processes, and structures occupy a center stage position. This chapter underlines the responsibilities executive education providers have when it comes to driving their customers towards more holistic solutions—if this is required.

W. Amann (✉)
HEC Paris in Qatar, P.O. Box 5825, Doha, Qatar
e-mail: amann.wolfgang@gmail.com

T. Azarmi, W. Amann (eds.), *The Financial Crisis*,
DOI 10.1007/978-3-319-20588-5_10

The contribution of this chapter is thus found in an enhancement of the Kirckpatrick (1976) model, which has not been compensated for by Philips's (2011) extension. This past distillation of shortcomings, which has not lowered the model's popularity, includes the model's inability to address the summative question (Was training really effective?) and the formative question (How should training be modified to boost effectiveness?), as Bates (2004) argues. Neither the summative nor the formative question really dealt with or solved the normative question (What is really the normative responsibility of the executive education provider?).

2 The Case of Trading Inc.

Trading Inc.[1] was a European market leader in its business sector and generated double-digit billions of Euros in annual sales. In its segment, it supplied a full range of products to companies throughout Europe. To all of these, Trading Inc. applied the same business model: a multichannel approach based on online and catalogue-based selling.

Given thin profit margins in the industry, national adaptations in marketing, sales, and distribution were minimized to ensure standardization and low costs. The industry saw substantial consolidation with basically only two pan-European players surviving besides a few local firms in each of the European markets it served. Trading Inc. had several CEOs and major restructuring efforts before, during, and after the big financial crisis but achieved very modest results.

Trading Inc. started to restructure its executive education efforts, outsourcing as much as possible, including photocopying and delivery of binders with printouts that an external service provider brought to the seminar room and put on the tables. In respect of key topics, Trading Inc. only gave one executive education provider, TIMSE,[2] a full mandate to train its white-collar staff across Europe.

2.1 *The New Training Request for Finance Experts*

In November 2013, Trading Inc. asked its key executive education provider TIMSE to design and implement a European training initiative for 180 finance experts. Trading Inc. was not happy with their performance at that time. There were irregularities and inefficiencies, too high a turnover of staff, interpersonal issues,

[1] The name of the company has been disguised. The presented dilemma and observed pattern, however, remain unchanged. It depicts a classic dilemma in designing, directing, and selling executive education seminar, which is also reported in Amann et al. (2016).

[2] The name has also been disguised.

and a perceived inadequate level of finance skills due to the recruitment of lower-cost staff members. Finance experts were supposed to attend a next-generation finance program, in which they would learn a new centrally coordinated way of organizing and operating finance that would be standardized across Europe. They were the lowest of basically three hierarchical levels and reported to finance managers, who in turn reported to regional or national finance directors.

From previously commissioned programs, TIMSE and its director Mr. C knew that Trading Inc. was focused on numbers and the financial bottomline. TIMSE realized that in the future it would have to prove to the board and other senior leaders of Trading Inc. that the executive education program had provided expected returns on the approved investment. TIMSE thus decided to analyze the situation thoroughly to enable a strictly tailored finance program for the subsequent roll-out across Europe. After all, training 180 program participants in several linked modules would provide a significant amount of income for TIMSE.

The analysis phase of executive education explored established finance practices, skill sets, and behaviors. TIMSE knew that their training of finance experts would open up further opportunities to either train them in other topics later on or would lead to organizational development consultancy opportunities once trusted relationships with the finance directors emerged. Established contacts were substantially more attractive than acquiring new ones. In this regard, executive education did not differ from other industries.

In order to determine the program details, Mr. C decided to interview key program participants and their superiors. All the program participants were surveyed quantitatively regarding their perceived training needs and the context in which they needed to excel. They rated challenges, skills, and future potentials to tap based on five-point Likert scales.

2.2 Results of the Initial Analysis

After speaking to finance directors, managers, and experts, as well as scrutinizing the survey results, Mr. C realized that the problems with Trading Inc.'s finance teams were bigger than expected. These finance experts suffered from a variety of parallel issues.

First of all, it was revealed that they had little knowledge of what the company strategy, mission, vision, and values were. Since there were frequent turnovers in the CEO and the top management, ideas and winning recipes came and went, leading to confusion.

Secondly, there was a big gap between what the finance experts felt was needed and what the top management felt.

Thirdly, there was a lack of resources to fulfill the assigned jobs and responsibilities, which had also been evident in the previously ignored training. These previous sessions had been infrequent, half-hearted, and often cancelled at the

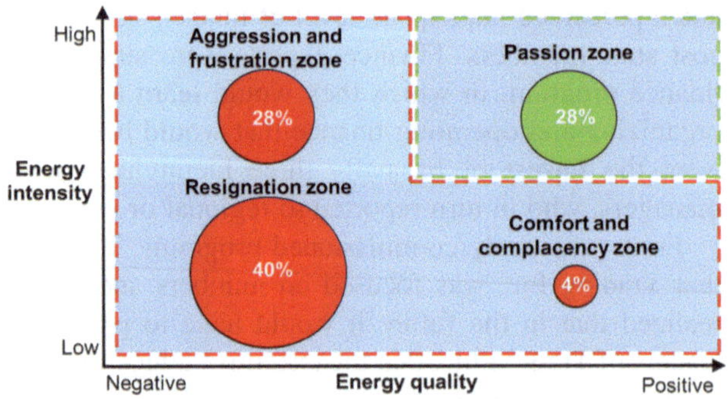

Fig. 1 Distribution of finance staff members across energy groups

last minute to avoid staff losing opportunities due to attending training. The skills required were confirmed to be insufficient.

Fourthly, the performance pressure was increasing all the time. Nothing was ever good enough, but there was no form of performance coaching. The finance experts did not have time to breathe or to recover from periods of peak workloads. New initiatives were added all the time, while none of the older ones had been abandoned. Priorities were frequently changed depending on what the finance managers and directors thought would be trendy that week or month. In turn, the upper management was perceived to be refusing to provide help and lacked appreciation of what had been achieved. Those finance experts who could no longer stand it, left as swiftly as possible.

Fifthly, the general dynamism (see Bruch and Vogel 2010) with which the staff members in finance tackled matters was a tremendous cause for concern. Figure 1 summarizes the distribution of the staff members across the four essential groups depicted in it. Among finance experts, hardly anyone was passionate about what they did, but higher up in the finance organization there was true passion.

TIMSE's designated program director, Mr. C, understood why there was friction in the finance organization, their innovativeness was less than expected, and why most people shied away from further initiatives and change. A substantial share of 40 % of these finance experts experienced resignation. Nevertheless, Trading Inc. was probably not the only large company with attrition resignation challenges. Yet, when it came to enhancing performance, there were major impediments to change.

2.3 TIMSE's Reaction

On the basis of the interviews and results of the quantitative surveys Mr. C had conducted, he concluded that Trading Inc. did indeed need finance training for the finance experts, but there was something else. With a focus merely on the latest finance skills and without at least some corresponding change within the European finance organization, it was unlikely that finance experts would be reenergized and thus leave the resignation zone. Representatives of this group needed a different kind of leadership. The same held true for all those employees suffering from too much aggression and frustration, as well as for those in the comfort zone. Merely offering and implementing finance technique training would not fix the root causes of the disappointing finance performance across Europe.

Mr. C thus decided to offer a holistic executive education program, which would include but not be exclusively centered on the latest finance techniques only for the finance executives, in addition to a transformational leadership program for finance managers and directors, which would set the stage for a high-performance finance organization.

Transformational leadership development programs enhance performance training participants by presenting positive, inspiring role models, higher levels of caring for all individuals equally, promoting a working atmosphere in stark contrast to the existing one, ensuring more trust, as a necessary condition to move, and moving people to the "passion zone" work level as shown in Fig. 1.

Mr. C clearly observed that human dignity was not really well protected in Trading Inc.'s finance departments and needed improvement. The individuals did not really matter. They were treated as human resources, and their output had to be maximized. Mr. C could present studies and experiences from other clients where such transformational leadership programs had actually led to the desired outcomes for Trading Inc.'s finance directors.

2.4 The Litmus Test for TIMSE

To Mr. C's surprise, the finance directors of Trading Inc. voted against the program proposal, requesting nothing but a focused finance program. They thought highly of their work, assumed that the lower levels would always complain anyway, and referred to the times when they themselves were at that level, working long and intense hours. They ignored the statistics and the idea that they would have to receive executive education. If at all, the finance experts had to first demonstrate a different attitude and better performance to deserve their better supervision.

This boiled down to a litmus test for Mr. C. Would he be willing—in the aftermath of the financial crisis—to forgo sales and profits, as no program that made sense could be delivered, or would he cave in and merely be customer-oriented? The latter meant that he would contribute to the perpetuating of nonhumanistic working conditions and to the overarching problem at Trading Inc.'s finance department not being resolved.

Mr. C took a decision that many other business schools and executive education institutions would have ignored: Based on his analysis and needs assessment, which he discussed with Trading Inc. Executives, he recommended that the company clearly communicate that only a comprehensive leadership and organization transformation program in addition to the finance skills training made sense. TIMSE's doors would always be open to Trading Inc. if they were interested in fundamentally revamping their finance department.

Nine months later, during a regular customer relationship call, he learned that another supplier had sold Training Inc. a simplistic finance program, which time showed did not improve anything on the ground. The staff turnover at Trading Inc. continued to be high in the finance department.

3 The Need for a New Success Measurement System

The abovementioned case and litmus test led to the question: *Do business enterprises know how to assess organizational needs and evaluate program results that lead to business success and sustainability?* The best-established ways to date has been the Kirckpatrick–Philips way (Philips 2011), which scrutinizes the five impact layers of executive education:

1. Rigorous and consistent assessment of level of satisfaction of program participants, measured with the well-known Likert scale (or smiley-face surveys) at the end of each program.
2. Effective methods to assess program outcome and participants' learning, which is measured by the assessment of performance improvement and improvement in organizational climate.
3. Impact, which refers to the degree to which the participants actually apply the program content and lessons in their jobs.
4. Systematic assessment of business outcome and results, which are measured as the impact that the implementation of the training programs has on the business.
5. ROI of the training beyond the partly qualitative and partly quantitative results mentioned under (4).

This chapter argues in favor of a sixth leader emphasizing how executive education providers in finance normatively drive customers and course participants. This relates primarily to the nonfinancial, more humanism-related aspects of normative management, since the ROI is already considered in the measurement framework. Responsibly developing clients beyond their original specifications could refer to improved working conditions, receiving appreciation, experiencing inspiration, and more realistic resource endowments to actually achieve goals. While the ROI is a clearly established figure, humanism in business is a broader variable, which might not be easy and should not necessarily be ex ante predefined for all situations. It is an ideal vector construct: the more, the better, not an ideal point.

Humanism in business is contingent upon what it can mean in a specific situation. This chapter thus argues in favor of an extension of the Kirckpatrick–Philips model by adding a sixth question and detailing the preceding ones as shown in Table 1.

Table 1 Key questions for executive education's success

Level	Key questions
Level 1	Did the learners enjoy the training?
Level 2	Did knowledge transfer occur?
Level 3	Did learners' behavior change as a result of the training and with regard to the original specifications in the RFP?
Level 4	Did the training have a measurable impact on performance improvement as understood in the original specifications?
Level 5	Did the training-generated investment provide a positive return on investment?
Level 6	Did the executive education provider holistically develop the client beyond the narrow specifications? In particular, did humanistic assumptions, values, and practices improve beyond the mere functionalist purpose of the training?

4 Conclusion

Finance education provides a plethora of knowledge nuggets, skills, and tools to corporations and individual seminar participants. However, as this chapter outlines, they need to be linked to a clearly allocated responsibility on how to use them. Once markets see more and more liberalization around the globe; governments see their role as watchdogs become weaker and weaker. It is therefore the responsibility of executive education providers to not only be customer driven, but also drive the ethical, normative development of the clients. The litmus test can easily be formulated as it was done in this chapter. Can executive education providers give up sales and profits in order to do the right things and do their jobs right? Or are they merely complying with whatever clients desire. If this is the case, these executive education providers might well contribute to the next crisis and show zero learning over time.

References

Amann, W., Khan, S., & Tripathi, S. (2016). Driven by customers or driving customers: What really should matter in executive education. In M. Lepeley, E. Kimakowitz, & R. Bardy (Eds.), *Human centered management in executive education*. London, UK: Palgrave MacMillan.

Bates, R. (2004). A critical analysis of evaluation practice: The Kirkpatrick model and the principle of beneficence. *Evaluation and Program Planning, 27*, 341–347.

Bradshaw, D. (2014). *Ashridge and Hult International announce plans to merge*. Accessed July 4, 2014, from http://www.ft.com/intl/cms/s/2/c12b55b2-0368-11e4-817f-00144feab7de.html%23axzz3O3bSEwv4

Bruch, H., & Vogel, B. (2010). *Fully charged*. Watertown, MA: Harvard Business Press.

Kirckpatrick, D. (1976). Evaluation of training. In R. L. Craig (Ed.), *Training and development handbook: A guide to human resource development* (pp. 317–319). New York: McGraw Hill.

Philips, J. (2011). *Return on Investment*. London: Routledge.

Conclusion: Emerging Insights on Teaching Finance in Turbulent Times

Wolfgang Amann

This book issued a call for innovations when it comes to teaching and carrying out research in business schools in the aftermath of the financial crisis. The latter more accurately describes a series of interlinked crises starting with the subprime crisis, transitioning to a banking crisis in which more than 400 US banks failed or entered receivership.[1] Next came the related economic crisis, in which some 39 % of households in the USA were suffering from unemployment, negative equity, or arrears in their house payments.[2] The crises were not contained there. Subsequently, the fiscal and debt crisis in many countries unfolded, aggravating the situation in many debt-prone, noncompetitive economies. The crises had long left the US real estate and banking sector, spreading to other regions and economic sectors. The magnitude of this set of crises also raised the question of responsibilities of business schools. As outlined in this book, changes needed to happen in several regards.

Firstly, teaching assignments will have to integrate a normative element much more than was the case before. It is irresponsible towards the course participants to merely teach them the tools to speculate uppon risk levels and major investment decisions, without a concurrent clarification of the responsibilities that lie within. In line with this thought, teaching knowledge and skills on the knowing-and-doing level simply will no longer suffice in the future. A third layer of learning is outlined in this book and is referred to as the being level. Course participants must be encouraged more than ever before to critically reflect about what kind of financial

[1] Cf. http://thelawdictionary.org/article/how-many-banks-have-gone-bankrupt-since-the-current-credit-crisis-began/ accessed on April 21, 2015.

[2] Cf. Hurd, M. and S. Rohwedder (2010). Effects of the Financial Crisis and Great Recession on American Households. NBER Working Paper No. 16407.

W. Amann (✉)
HEC Paris in Qatar, P.O. Box 5825, Doha, Qatar
e-mail: amann.wolfgang@gmail.com

T. Azarmi, W. Amann (eds.), *The Financial Crisis*,
DOI 10.1007/978-3-319-20588-5_11

expert, manager, and leader they would like to be. Learning has to become much more comprehensive. Presenting and discussing the results of a business school deans' survey, it seems that over the past 3 years schools have accepted these enlarged responsibilities. When it comes to the upcoming years, however, precisely these responsibilities seem to disappear from the radar of business school deans, and they emphasize these responsibilities less than in the past. This is a trend that must be reversed if business schools want to prevent becoming silent partners in crime.

Secondly, this has repercussions for how programs in business schools ought to be structured and how we should teach. It won't suffice to merely add a sustainability or ethics elective in the middle or toward the end of the program. Normative management considerations have to be integrated throughout the entire program—at the beginning, in each module, as well as at the end. Course participants have to be exposed to and become familiar with the complexities of taking ethically and financially sound decisions with ease and without getting overwhelmed by the complexity of the required analysis. From the teaching methodology point of view, emerging best practice framework consists of four phases of high-impact learning. In the initial phase, we need to clarify why dealing with ethical considerations becomes ever more important, and why a realistic view on the finance function and financial skills matters. In the subsequent investigation phase, we need to shed light on the interdependencies that financial decisions inevitably show, how the real sector and the financial sector are connected, and how downsizing decisions affect both the financial bottom line and a social bottom line. In the third phase of active experimentation, we need to allow course participants to experiment with the consequences of their financial decisions. In the ensuing reflection phase, we need to devote substantial time to reflecting on the impact of financial decisions with a sound, modern understanding of normative management and ethics. To sum up, merely focusing on functionalist knowledge and skills in finance won't suffice anymore in the future. The standards have evolved.

Thirdly, although it comes to the core content of finance knowledge and skills, there are major changes that have already been implemented or still need to be carried out. Banking regulation, the creation of a banking union, risk policies, equity requirements, and supervision are just a small selection of directions in which change has already materialized. Business schools must adopt state-of-the-art content to reflect the recent changes. These changes also relate to very basic probability curves, such as the normal distribution curve, which describes events more drastically deviating from the norm. As the financial crisis has proved, normal distribution curves and the corresponding logic that extreme events are less likely have largely become outdated.

Fourthly, in order to sustain change, we need to alter, as outlined in this book, the very relationship between companies in business schools on the one hand and the very way we measure success of educational efforts on the other hand. If business schools merely see themselves as providing a service to the market and to their customers, they risk not meeting their responsibilities. They need to drive the development of their course participants, as they partly serve as character gyms. This boils down to viewing the course participants differently. They are at least as much products of the schools as they are the customers. If need be, schools need to drive the knowledge of development against the expectations of the course participants and the corporate learning partners. Mere customer orientation is not enough.

Fifthly, the two core activities of teaching and research in business schools cannot be separated. As the teaching site evolves, it needs fresh content from the research site of the value chain in academia. Integrating normative thinking into finance research is absolutely critical and necessary. An optimization of investment decisions on pure financial terms represents an outdated understanding of the responsibilities, if holistic trains of thoughts continue to be ignored. Focusing on new research topics, such as a banking union, will not suffice either. Next to becoming more integrated, research has to increase its degree of innovation. A world without money, a possibility raised by one of the chapters included in this volume, serves as a case in point.

As the repercussions of the financial crisis can still be felt, it is far from being over in many countries and economies, and our focus is on developing both the teaching and the research activities in business schools further. If we, the authors and editors of this book, have shed light on this need and rendered you, the reader, sensitive to this necessity, then we need to see innovation and have reached our goal.

MIX
Papier aus verantwortungsvollen Quellen
Paper from responsible sources
FSC® C105338

If you have any concerns about our products,
you can contact us on
ProductSafety@springernature.com

In case Publisher is established outside the EU,
the EU authorized representative is:
Springer Nature Customer Service Center GmbH
Europaplatz 3, 69115 Heidelberg, Germany

Printed by Libri Plureos GmbH
in Hamburg, Germany